THE POLITICS OF PUNK

THE POLITICS OF PUNK

PROTEST AND REVOLT FROM THE STREETS

David Ensminger

ROWMAN & LITTLEFIELD
Lanham • Boulder • New York • London

Published by Rowman & Littlefield
A wholly owned subsidiary of The Rowman & Littlefield Publishing Group, Inc.
4501 Forbes Boulevard, Suite 200, Lanham, Maryland 20706
www.rowman.com

Unit A, Whitacre Mews, 26-34 Stannary Street, London SE11 4AB

British Library Cataloguing in Publication Information Available

Library of Congress Cataloging-in-Publication Data

Names: Ensminger, David, author.
Title: The politics of punk : protest and revolt from the streets / David Ensminger.
Description: Lanham : Rowman & Littlefield, [2016] | ?2016 | Includes bibliographical references and index.
Identifiers: LCCN 2016002706 (print) | LCCN 2016005219 (ebook) | ISBN 9781442254442 (hardcover : alk. paper) | ISBN 9781442254459 (electronic)
Subjects: LCSH: Punk rock music—Political aspects. | Punk rock music—Social aspects. | Punk culture.
Classification: LCC ML3918.R63 E56 2016 (print) | LCC ML3918.R63 (ebook) | DDC 781.66—dc23
LC record available at http://lccn.loc.gov/2016002706

∞™ The paper used in this publication meets the minimum requirements of American National Standard for Information Sciences Permanence of Paper for Printed Library Materials, ANSI/NISO Z39.48-1992.

Printed in the United States of America

To Julie Ensminger
Endless Love, Spiritual Compass, and Ductile Backbone

Prof. Daniel Wojcik
Mentor and Inspiration

And my brother Michael and sister Laura
For pointing the way

CONTENTS

Introduction: Punk: Zombiefication or Renewal? ix

1 This Land Is Punk Land 1
2 Know Your Enemy 43
3 Zones of Influence: Washington, D.C., and San Francisco 89
4 Shot from Both Sides: M.D.C. 129
5 Litpunk Furor: The Wit of Jennifer Blowdryer 147
6 Slam Dance in the No Time Zone: Punk as Repertoire for Liminality 155
7 Through the Lurid Looking Glass 165

Works Cited 207
Index 219
About the Author 227

INTRODUCTION

Punk: Zombiefication or Renewal?

One night in early June 2015, with most of this manuscript complete minus some nuts and bolts of grammar and flow, I scribbled introductory words as the streetlamp next door shined gauzy yellow through the hush-hush bathroom where I huddled with pen in hand as my wife slept fitfully prior to an early-morning start to her job. Unable to silence the buzz in my brain, I recalled the speech delivered by Joan Jett during her induction in the Rock and Roll Hall of Fame in spring 2015. "Rock 'n' roll is . . . the language of a subculture," Jett adamantly surmised, "of integrity, rebellion, frustration, alienation," and "the glue that set several generations free of unnatural societal and self-suppression. Rock 'n' roll is political . . . a meaningful way to express dissent, upset the status quo, stir up revolution, and fight for human rights."

As a former young kid who cranked her singles loud-as-bombs on a portable plastic record player in my shag-carpeted bedroom, I agree with her wholeheartedly. This book is testament to such untrammeled passion. I seek to map out the allure and algorithm of punk's allegiances, to trace its capacity to engage civic debates, to show how it essentially tries to tear down the boxes thrown around the human condition. Punk remains a moving metaphor, a grain that splits what was once considered the stable concrete of monoculture as it grows in sudden spurts and fissures. Yet this book is not meant to deodorize the messiness of punk or to make-believe that it succors all woes. For me, punk is an extended, feisty poem about the politics of the heart played out in blitzkrieg beats; hence, I try to decode the ever-evolving spirit and praxis of the people burrowed deep in its territory.

For years, armchair-addled academia barely examined the genre and community. Rare early observers like Dave Laing and Dick Hebdige tried to strike the right balance in describing the savage pop and sheer annihilation-time diatribes of a rebel music brimming with intuitive, heartfelt, and bracing ethos as well as unhinged musical craft. Occasionally, other researchers from different disciplines joined the fray during the next decade, including professor Jack Levin of Northeastern University and professor Philip Lamy of Brandeis, who penned a 1984 sociological conference paper titled "Punk and Middle Class Values: A Content Analysis," later printed in *Youth and Society* in 1985, which proved punk literature contained no more violence than *Reader's Digest*. This interpretation counterbalanced the assertion by Harold Levine and Steven Stumpf, written just a year earlier, that punk remained a nexus of hyper-disturbing tropes—"death, violence, perversion, loathsomeness, chaos" (1983, 430). For Levin and Lamy, punks were simply "attention-getters with their loud music, outlandish fashions and theatrical stage stunts" ("Punks Not So Violent, Study Says" 1984). Though their objective approach to evaluating punk's perceived violence seems refreshing, they still seemed to create a decontextualized look at punk political rhetoric and lifestyles.

Now the subject of punk studies is spiraling. It has evolved into the very embodiment of a critical discourse that remains open to a million slippery interpretations by academics and participants, each vision no more than an impermanent tattoo, easily replaced or swept aside, edited and retracted. As such, punk has become a contested space of separate truths, a democratic history in action, that often allows punks to control their own narratives.

In a positive step, an entire journal of peer-reviewed essays edited by punk academics called *Punk and Post-Punk* explores punk's diverse range of possibilities: subjects have included the space-time nexus of scenes in Manchester and Russia, punk's rampant use of logos, as well as discussions of do-it-yourself designers affixing gig flyers as imperfect forms of insurgent street art in cities overrun with posters and other media. By 2015, punk seems like a perfect postmodern storm to many academics, for it evokes the ripe intersection of bricolage, pastiche, feminism, queer and post-colonial theory, detournement, Situationism, and disintermediation (cutting out the "middleman" championed by do-it-yourselfers). Most now agree that punk soaked up, appropriated, and hijacked style, manners, and content from Futurism, Constructivism, Dada, Surrealism, and Beatniks to Warholian popsters, Yippie antiestablishment agitators, and guerrilla media makers.

For punk insiders, one cannot help but to wax poetic about its original appeal. Since the mid-1970s, punk often attacked pious left-leaners just as much as it attempted to skewer conservative moral agendas and backcountry right-wingers. Really Red sang, "Middle-class liberals all make me sick. . . . The KKK can kiss my ass" on their tune "Too Political?" while decrying the Revolutionary Communist Party as "a big pile of shit" in a *Maximum RocknRoll* interview (Scott 1983). In turn, the Circle Jerks yelled, "Resist 'em Communism / resist 'em Fascism" on their tune "Forced Labour." Though such politics seemed rife within the DNA of punk, others like Matt Wobensmith of queer-oriented *Outpunk* declared in *Interbang* fanzine, "The vast majority of punk is devoid of politics" (Brucato n.d.). Either way, punk remains infused with contempt, and it exudes an irate, fatalistic, and lacerating tone. The bile exuded from Sex Pistols and Feederz onward to Krum Bums, Paint It Black, Fucked Up, and beyond is practically an operator's manual, since bands mimic a riveting, weaponized sense of language repurposed by each generation, oscillating between rage and redemption. Each fragmented, defoliated, drunken, and savage vocal and charred guitar chord becomes a counterpoint to the surface of quivering pop song ornamentation.

A letter to *Rolling Stone* in 1980 underscored the bifurcation: after seeing Public Image Limited on the *Tomorrow* show, an acrid reader's letter to the editor decried the "sniveling wretches and the musical wasteland they inhabit. It's enough to make one nostalgic for disco" (Bilbrey 1980, 7). To survive, punk had to maintain its perennially gritty, blunt trappings, especially as some gave up the ghost and entered the FM airwaves. For every Replacements, Husker Du, Jawbreaker, and Jawbox, there came a Los Crudos, Capitalist Casualties, and Tragedy, which did not openly welcome unfettered Big Brother capitalism, an entity understood as "rapacious record execs, managers and lawyers" driving "450 SLs" and meeting to discuss "how to rip off the rubes while pocketing large sums of cash" described by a fan of the Rubber City

Rebels, Chi Pig, Pere Ubu, and Dead Boys (Lewis 1980, 7). In contrast, "do it yourself" (DIY) became the nonalignment zone, a place to ground the punk economy to small-scale mail order and human touch. DIY remains a survivor's honor code woven into the web of DNA that created the first homegrown singles like the Buzzcocks' "Spiral Scratch."

As a subculture, punk lurked around the perimeters of dominant culture, which masquerades as natural and common sense, as Dick Hebdige forewarned, until it broke through such fabricated reality and disrupted, as in the case of "Holidays in the Sun" by the Sex Pistols, the system of representation enforced by "manners, commodities, and routines," creating a challenge to official ideology (Marcus, May 1980, 28). That was punk's serial threat, sometimes lucid, sometimes not: it frazzled, fissured, and usurped official culture, exposing uncertainty, opposition, and gaps, digging its way into the future by grasping the notion of politics with a lowercase *p*. As Clash bass player Paul Simonon recounted, "When somebody says, 'You can't do that,' we think you should stand up and ask why, and not go, 'Well, all right'" (Henke 1980, 38). No wonder that songs like "Stand Up" by Pennywise and "Stand Up" by Minor Threat still resonate. They are the marquee messages of punk.

Still, punk rock's hard-bark, hardscrabble, and stubborn perseverance has surprised even veterans bored by "terminally lame, stunted-in-1981" bands (Eddy 1986, 24), as well as the seemingly defunct dross and chaff of angry youngsters grinding away at self-justified grimness, one-sided rage, pre-sequenced themes, or maniacally delivered tantrums never quite defused. Instead of mocking trends, punk tends to venerate certain styles, like the bleak topics and machine-gun speed of Discharge or the pop-culture pileup, teenage awkwardness, and even tender woe of tuneful Ramones. It became an everlasting rummage sale of barely winking sameness—different bands and titles, updated yearly from Malaysia to Columbia, restoring the same old underpinnings. Yet to complicate matters, "In Southeast Asian Islamic contexts . . . extreme music becomes a fluid hybrid," says Marco Ferrarese, a PhD researcher, travel writer, and musician for the Nerds Rock Inferno (Italy) and WEOT SKAM (Malaysia).

> In Malaysia, a multi-ethnic, plural society, such hybridity seems to be even more complex. It is related to following, embodying and performing diverse examples of global extreme music performance. A performance which *prescribes* particular authentic behaviors that local agents are compelled to replicate, and at times, even exaggerate to sanction their authenticity. Adhering to the global "code" of extreme music can result in changing one's behaviors, albeit in transitory, liminal spaces . . . based on different ethnic groups, punk and metal do not necessarily become ways to challenge authorities, but templates of pure leisure that some—particularly the Malay majority—embed with the limitations prescribed by their authority-defined society. The examples provided by Malay Neo-Nazi skinheads, or Malay anti-zionist metalheads and punks are some of the most outstanding. (Ferrarese 2015)

Teen punks remain hell-bent on trying to make heart-stopping paranoia and sneering moans each time anew. Or as Layla Gibbons, longtime writer for *Maximum Rocknroll* posited in her column in November 2006, punk was not just a ghost of a cultural movement, not a postcard from London from subcultural tourists, not an idea flogged to death, not "a fixed reality" or "snapshot of youth frozen in time." It was not just a series of obscure reference points, not the good old days kept in formaldehyde, not a genre for "salivating record nerds," "lame nostalgia," and "crass reunion tours," not the "ultimate rip-off." It was more, something remade, still full of "kicks and freedom and community," something "brave and dumb" and "ridiculous and embarrassing," driven home by bands like Mika Miko (with songs like "Turkey Sandwich") that melded early Kleenex with early Black Flag (Gibbons 2006). Punk was ever fluid, not mere static strife.

Shuddering on black thoughts of contagious nihilism or an unfettered sense of prolonged hope, punk bangs the drum. For unwashed decades, it felt feral and illegal, seeping through porous ragtag clothes and cigarette-scented albums, creating a portal in everyday culture through which cocky kids and their artful guidance systems could scramble and strike society weaned on soft twilight lullabies, the Hoover factory of vacuous hits. At first, punk in Cleveland, San Francisco, Manhattan, East London, and Manchester used a bedraggled, battered, postwar, and industrialized geography as a literary terrain—a maker of memes—and as an incubator for ideas that rivaled the rebellion of modern classics. "Their observations, comments and feelings become part of that romantic form with all its acknowledgments to rock's history," wrote Penny Valentine in *Creem* ("Sandinista Now!" 40). Soon, such music pierced the seal-skinned darkness like jagged berserk lightning interfering with the bucolic crooning soundtrack of capitalism, which mostly pretended race riots and Vietnam never existed. At times, cultivated and calculating tycoons couldn't even see the wreckage of punk zooming in, trying to dismember their systems. Just watch *X: The Unheard Music* documentary to see corporate befuddlement.

This book is not an attempt to collectivize the entire conscience of punk in a definitive form; for instance, it does not shed light on the WTO protests, cascading contemporary queer politics, or recount the recent Occupy movement, all of which have punk antecedents and attracted elder punks like Patti Smith, who donated a tent to house the OWS People's Library in Zuccotti Park in New York. Such outcroppings deserve their own books. Instead, this navigates punk consciousness and conscience, draws upon the scenes and issues that held sway, and depicts the large struggle against a manufactured normative culture that sweeps aside notions of dissent. It also tries to unveil the heartbeat behind the rhetoric and poses, as well as the wily intuition and barbed intelligence at play in the music.

In doing so, I dedicated this to my siblings, who delivered punk to me and stood their ground as others fell away; to innumerable fans, rockers, and partners that provided resources and inspiration; to my wife, who has been my beautiful, knowledge-bearing better half for twenty years and my adroit partner in all things; and to professor Daniel Wojcik, who helped to give me the courage, sensibility, and skills to tell the story, which now unfolds sometimes highly personal, sometimes nonlinear and circular, sometimes theory rich, but always searching for the truths.

To that end, I explore the slogans and sentiments, actions and praxis, as well as visions and frame of mind that gave birth to the howl. This is what I give to you.

Special thanks to Greg McWhorter, Jack Johnston, plus Randy Smith (Rebel Time Records), for their support and archival knowledge and to the editors and publishers who have printed portions of the following material in various forms, including *Maximum Rocknroll*, PM

Press, *Artcore*, *Houston Press*, *Magyar Taraj*, *Trust*, *Popmatters*, *Left of the Dial*, Rowman & Littlefield, University Press of Mississippi, *Liminalities*, and *Razorcake*.

1

THIS LAND IS PUNK LAND

To speak of punk politics as offering a singular, cogent perspective is problematic at best, given that punk contained a wide political spectrum sweeping left to right. Seth Tobocman, a founding editor of *World War III Illustrated*, member of Autonomedia ("an autonomous zone for arts radicals in both old and new media"), and political artist, first saw the likes of Patti Smith and Talking Heads at CBGB for $3 a gig during the mid- and late 1970s. He admitted that a later generation of punks involved in 1990s shows at ABC No Rio in New York City would likely have been "horrified" by the right-wing views about women and food espoused by John Holstrom, founding editor of *Punk*, the early groundbreaking illustrated periodical of the genre (Myers 2000). Meanwhile, Jeff Bale, cofounder and longtime columnist for *Maximum Rocknroll* (*MRR*) and future editor of *Hit List*, widely attacked punk media's "simpleminded rhetoric" and "pseudo-Marxist" pieces that reeked of "ignorance, fanaticism, and outright stupidity" (1993); furthermore, in 2012, on the thirtieth anniversary of *MRR*, he attested to a "contrarian, individualistic" perspective "bitterly opposed to sectarian political 'lines'" (2012).

I floated amid the left-liberal sectarian divide. I joined the Young Socialist Alliance at Drake University in Des Moines in 1989; documented the AIDS movement in rust-belt Rockford, Illinois, in the early 1990s; and became a college campus activist in New Mexico examining sports and school policies as well as the Contract with America espoused by Richard Armey and Newt Gingrich. I also wrote parole boards and set up benefit concerts; penned editorials against invasions and racism; was ticketed by police in Houston, Texas, for handing out Food Not Bombs fare; stopped eating meat in 1988 and married a meat eater; and spoke to the CBS morning news about my campaign for Jerry Brown in 1992. Basically, I adhere to no party line and consider punk as existing beyond a singular code.

Punk is a mode of being—an engine of sorts—a means to catalyze and propel so that people can find and multiply their own paths, however crooked, conflicting, and meandering they might be. As Bale argued in a *Hit List* editorial in 2000, "true rebels . . . are always inclined, personality-wise, to go against the grain" and "refuse to conform to existing social, political, and cultural norms in the particular environment within which he or she happens to be operating" Hence, that rebellion is "contextual and situational" (7). Tupelo, Mississippi, he argues, is not the same as San Francisco, California; therefore, resistance is nuanced, driven by local factors, though as media converges and cities and towns conform to the contours of twenty-first-century modern capital flow—chain stores supplanting mom-and-pop store democracy—these differences may become less distinct.

I tend to see punk as a folk subculture of like-minded fans, musicians, writers, photographers, and others glued to loose-knit customs, traditions, and lore. As Tony Parsons described the movement in 1976, punk was fueled by amphetamines, "high energy, gut-level dole queue rock'n'roll, fast flash, vicious music played by kids for kids" driven by a set of inner-city, psychologically ghetto-tough, and post–World War II gritty geographies that spelled out a sense of rebellion that felt real as factory steam gushing from a brick monolith. Most of this was an illusion of sorts, since much of the punk contingent could be tied to university origins, including members of the Clash, Buzzcocks, and Malcolm McLaren, a media contortionist-cum-Svengali. "He's as middle class as they come," former Sex Pistols bass player Glenn Matlock reminded *Zigzag* (Anger and Thrills 1978), who lived awash in Englishness. He dolled up the band in "a Dickensian street-urchin look" for publicity pics (Zuberi 2001, 50) and imagined Steve Jones, guitarist of the Sex Pistols, as a street tough who "could hardly read or write . . . an extraordinary Dickensian creature" (Martin 2000, 48). Furthermore, Marcus Gray suggests, "The Dickensian aspects of punk and of the archetypal punk character . . . owe much" to the "true-life experience" of Clash manager Bernie Rhodes, whose family had suffered from Russia's civil war upheaval, living in dour housing in the bombed-out East End of London (2010, 41). Punk seemed to revisit and reinvent the tropes and personas of a whole other era of deprivation and wiliness.

In fact, some argue the Pistols shared more in common with dissenting pamphleteers and "the English music hall tradition" capable of theatrics outside the "legitimate theater" than as acrid and blasphemous "menaces to society" (Adams 2008, 470). Hence, the "arsenal of symbols" threatening the status quo were just that: threats interwoven with historic precedent and steeped in rhetoric, pose, attitude, and couture fashion found at locales like Sex (Worley 2014, 7–8). That arsenal often contained swastikas on the likes of Siouxsie Sioux and the Dead Boys, as well as the hammer and sickle used by bands or promoters of the Dils, Rich Kids, and New York Dolls. In the year zero, "Either punk stood for the inversion of values, by extolling that which was still most (taboo); or punk stood for the negation of all values (even the swastika no longer carried historical or ideological significance)" (Ward 1996, 161).

Critics seem to underestimate the sociopolitical consciousness of the Dead Boys, but tunes like "Sonic Reducer" and "3rd Generation Nation" seem steeped in keen observations and powerful commentary about the state of the world. "That's funny," guitarist Cheetah Chrome admits, "because Stiv wrote one and Dave the other, and you never met two more different people! I never did feel we made a powerful statement unless the statement was, 'The whole world is going to hell, and we're the spearhead of the movement!' I always tried to get more political stuff into things, used to say we played 'dick' songs: they were all about sex and partying. 'Ain't Nothing to Do' I always considered a political song. 'Not Anymore' was a definite social statement.

"I used to rag on Stiv because, of course, as soon as he gets in the Lords of the New Church, it was *all* political!" Chrome continues. "When I started out, the music business was a very dirty game, and we were very naïve boys from Cleveland that wanted to be rock'n'roll stars. And while the people we met were the first people we were exposed to in the business, we were far from the first batch of naïve kids from the Midwest they'd met. . . . We signed some very cruel documents that were standard in the industry at the time, and to this day I am trying to extricate myself from a couple of them. It's nice to be in a position now where I can offer a band a contract that isn't basically a printed minefield—that comes from the perspective of an artist, not a greedy bean counter" (Ensminger "CBGB," 2014).

To critics, punk was flammable material never meant to last, a metaphor for tumult, duress, contagion, and riotous behavior. Punk was the poison cloud that should have blown away, but it recognized no borders, disheartening to many, like the normals. Yet, punk refused to go gently into the night. It amounted to an ecosystem of constant effort, of boiling sympathies, of pithy pretensions. Punk is always the gale, always the sounding rod, renewed with spit and spite, as if child's play turned deadly serious, ready to be molded for millions who can play the part without blinking.

REVOLT AND RENEWAL WITHIN ROCK 'N' ROLL

> We are tired of being prisoners, we are tired of being slaves. The choice is yours.—HR, Bad Brains, live in San Francisco, *Rat Music for Rat People*

> I've got a right / to be poor and radical.—Sacred Order

Throughout the mid-1970s, punk was construed as a loose term referring to primitive, raw, and amateur music, fashion, and art that erupted amid bloated and manufactured mid-1970s rock 'n' roll, a rather tepid culture no longer mirroring or embodying the cultural upheavals of the 1960s. Bands like Jefferson Airplane, the MC5, and Creedence Clearwater Revival, as well as performers like Phil Ochs and Nina Simone, were each in part dedicated to a spirit of resistance often informed by civil rights, the antiwar movement, and the sexual revolution and had long given way to apolitical "stadium" rock 'n' roll bands. The era emerging into disco, broadly speaking, seemed to reek with self-contentment and sentimentality, not a sense of vitriolic revolt and a bold stance to reclaim rock 'n' roll's rebellious fiber.

Hence, as bands like the Clash developed their songbook, they broke from the perceived escapist excess underscoring Led Zeppelin, Queen, Deep Purple, or others of the heavy-metal ilk, whose fantasy-based landscape, including swords and sorcery, had little appeal to singer and guitarist Joe Strummer, whose own amateur guitar style compared to "thrashing . . . [like] a Veg-o-matic" (Henke 1980, 38) and fueled the intensity. If rock 'n' roll had become no more than operatic "Bohemian Rhapsodies," punk from Slaughter and the Dogs to Eater appeared to amount to a guttersnipe response and return to a 1950s short sharp form, including robust seven-inch singles often barely two minutes in length, the preferred soundtrack to the revisionist music revolution.

This back-to-basics approach, though, quickly gave way to unbridled experimentation and expanded musical palettes. The Clash, a barometer of this shift in style and content, chronicled class-conscious biography ("Career Opportunities," "Guns of Brixton"); new journalism–style reportorial urges ("London's Burning," "This Is England"), anthemic poetics that bridged William Blake and George Orwell ("Spanish Bombs," "London Calling"); and ever-shifting, multicultural, and hybrid music forms ("Police and Thieves," "The Magnificent 7," "The Leader," "Sean Flynn") that incorporated a slew of inspiration from reggae and rockabilly to funk and even movie soundtrack–style ambience borrowed from the likes of *Apocalypse Now*. A line from the film, actor Robert Duvall's famous scorched yell, "Charlie Don't Surf," referring to the Viet Cong holding a beachfront featuring imposing and resplendent wave action perfect for a surfboard, became the lyrical fodder for the Clash tune of the same name.

The politics-as-fashion of the band seemed applied with equal fervor, too. Early on, as "roots rock rebels," they were "urban guerrillas"—purveyors of "terrorist chic" sporting Doc Martens (akin to combat boots) and distressed Brigate Rosse (Italian Red Brigade terrorists) tee shirts, a seemingly controversial endorsement. "If you look at the Clash and you look at him, maybe it wasn't about agreeing with the Red Brigade," suggests Mauro Codeluppi, longtime singer for Italian hardcore punk pioneers Raw Power, who stem from formerly communist-thronged Reggio Emilia. "I am not even sure he knew about the Red Brigade. It might have been he fancied the tee shirt and thought the name was cool. But I'd like to think he knew what it was and he wore it because he shared their ideas, or at least some of the ideas of the Red Brigade. They lost the sympathy of the normal people. If you were like one of them or the circle around them, maybe you agreed with everything they did. At a certain point when [Red Brigade] started, people really liked them because they were against the government. At the time, it was really bad, but in the end they made mistakes" (Ensminger 2015).

"It would be too easy to dismiss the Clash as hollow opportunists," Mark Anderson of the activist network Positive Force wrote in the *Washington Times*. "Yes, they made compromises. No, their actions didn't always live up to their idealistic rhetoric. But while they were imperfect in their embodiment of their ideals, they were never insincere. They were human, but they were not hypocrites. On a good day, the Clash reinvested rock music with meaning beyond mere commerce" (2003). The band made a profound impact, he confesses, for they spurred his "embrace of campus activism," which later transformed into his long-lasting efforts to steer punk musicians toward social justice outreach in Washington, D.C., since 1985. The message: continue the mantle of the Clash's fluid idealism and uncompromising craft, remain wary of their tilts toward "rock messianism," and reject their "crass" compromises, too. For Anderson, D.C. bands ranging from Fugazi to Rain Like the Sound of Trains seemed to represent a new, self-reflexive punk wedge completely aware of blunders and conundrums embodied within "romantic punk" rebellion.

Echoing that romantic strain and heavy flirtation with galvanizing radicalism, the Clash named their fourth album *Sandinista* (Columbia, 1980) in homage to insurgent Marxists in Nicaragua and years earlier famously posed in front of a military installation in Northern Ireland. In 1979, The Undertones booked the Clash to play an open-air festival in Derry with the Damned; however, the Clash singer Joe Strummer received a warning letter from the Red Hand Commandos (Ulster loyalist paramilitary), which threatened to shoot him on the spot due to the singer's support for the Troops Out movement in the national publication *New Musical Express* (Bailie n.d.). Members of later bands like Chumbawamba visited Northern Ireland, including pubs and parks, in 1988 as part of a Troops Out delegation intended to open the eyes to the British public about the conditions of ongoing British occupation and "security measures," including rampant violence, harassment, systematically weakened councils, decaying housing, and rampant unemployment, a lethal combination. Amid the rancor and grit of the Divis Flats, where some of the most deleterious conditions in all of Western Europe existed, some hope prevailed, including "organized workshops, a play scheme (for children), and a social center," organized and promoted by and for the community (Spence 1988). To highlight its concern, Chumbawamba released a leaflet in November 1987 titled "Enniskillen and the War in Ireland," reprinted in *Maximum Rocknroll*, which deplored recent bomb attacks as "the IRA at its worst; blundering, ineffective, and careless" yet also strongly condemned the "media/state onslaught" that served only the "purpose [of] the British government," which brutally wanted to contain the problem and perpetuate colonialism (Spence 1988).

Even members of the Clash's own "blank generation" felt they were "full of shit," declares Paul Weller of the Jam, also a member of the Campaign for Nuclear Disarmament (CND) (the Jam played a number of gigs in support of the CND, including Finsbury Park and Hammersmith Palais). "All their songs got that real hardened image, the urban guerrilla touch and all that bollocks, it's stupid," especially during the time of the Falkland Island invasion by the British (Mirkz 1982). The Jam eschewed the entanglement of party politics and aligned itself with everyday people: leader Paul Weller, in a diary written for *Flexipop* in 1981, avowed, "There are still hundreds, probably thousands, of ordinary, decent people . . . who don't want to know about wars of fascism or power . . . who want to get on with their loves and treat others decently and receive the same back. . . . That's why I hate today's power politics, because they have no respect for life, not a single grain" (30).

To help such folks, the band played a Right to Work gig in Liverpool, then called the "Bermuda Triangle of British capitalism" in a report by the Merseyside Socialist Research Group, and raised £1,500. Leaflets by the Right to Work campaign read "Stop the Murder of Merseyside," while banners held aloft during a Manchester-to-Liverpool nighttime march read "Enough Is Enough!" At a Brighton demonstration at the Conservative Party Conference, marchers were clad in bright yellow vests hand-scrawled with pithy phrases like "I'd rather be a Muppet than a Tory!" and band names like PiL and Sex Pistols. Photographer Homer Sykes caught such scenes on film. Obviously, the Jam sided with the victims of severe economic turbulence and those trying to agitate for them, as well. Such events helped foment albums depicting the volatile era within a few years' time, including the steadfastly populist punk of *Two Million Voices* by Angelic Upstarts in 1981, which one fanzine rightly declared amounted to "a crusade against unemployment" that combined "the raw rage of street rebellion with the positive anger of organized protestors like the Right to Work Marchers and the urchins who swelled the ranks of the People's March for Jobs" (Bushell, "Angelic Upstarts," 1981) The album also lamented the closure of the Consett steelworks, which followed on the heels of such earlier tunes as "King Coal" and newspaper accounts of the brutish Soviet incursion into Afghanistan.

Earlier like-minded marches occurred as well, including in 1978, right before the Brighton Rock against Racism event with Tom Robinson. This attracted the likes of Colin Revolting, who joined the "march from Bethnal Green Hospital occupied by staff against cuts, heading towards the TUC conference in Brighton, calling on the trade unions to save jobs, stop cuts and fight unemployment. The march is like the 1930s hunger march of the unemployed from Jarrow, this time the lead banner reads 'Anger on the March.' The whole procession follows the band Misty. Later that night, RAR provide bands and people sleep huddled in circus marquees" (Revolting 2014). In such spaces, punk merged with pop and reggae, becoming a nucleus of politics on the move.

For Strummer, who admitted he was just a lousy guitarist, the Clash made "music that [somehow had] an extra dimension of meaning . . . we raised some issues that needed debating, probably altered a lot of people's thinking about a few subjects," he attested live on air to Britain Channel 4 in 1988 (Night Network 1988). He desired for the songs to "be a part of the whole world . . . part of everybody living a life." This is contiguous with earlier messages delivered onstage, including the sun-baked U.S. Festival near Route 66 funded by Apple founder Steve Wozniak in 1983. Strummer began the Clash set by admonishing the San Bernardino, California, crowd, "If there's going to be anything in the future, it's going to be from all parts of everything, not just from one . . . way down the middle of the road" ("The Clash" 1983). This sentiment inaugurated the Clash's headline position on the New Wave bill featuring Men at Work, Stray Cats, English Beat, INXS, and more. After finishing a raucous version of "Know Your Rights," Strummer taunted the crowd by mocking normative rock 'n' roll banter (just as he subverted traditional environmental slogans like "save the whales" to "save us / not the whales" in "Radio Clash"), uttering, "Try this on for size, 'Well hi everybody, ain't it groovy' . . . ain't you sick of hearing that for the last hundred and fifty years?" ("The Clash" 1983). More importantly, after realizing that tickets cost $25 for the event rather than the agreed-upon $17, the Clash forced the hand of Steve Wozniak, who then promised to donate $100,000 to send impoverished Latino youth in East L.A. to summer camps. Strummer sealed the deal by complaining to the entire crowd about the microchip generation's "You-make-you-buy-you-die mentality" (Wadlow 2014). In May of the previous year in Asbury Park, New Jersey, before unleashing "Spanish Bombs," Strummer chided, "This is not a Bruce Springsteen number, this is supposed to be poetry." ("The Clash Live 1982" 1982). In each scenario, by acknowledging a specific sense of place and upending traditional stage lingo in which a band usually slavishly thanks an adoring crowd, he pointedly took aim at rock 'n' roll's outdated gestures. By utilizing wit and parody, he forced audiences to give up their passive, gullible roles. Punk bands often used such effects.

At a Devo gig in Cincinnati, Ohio, in 1978, Boojie Boy (a caricature of an infant played by Mark Mothersbaugh) yelled out, "Now, Cincinnati, we love you! We *know* . . . where your heads are at" tells a writer, and "the grateful rubes . . . cheer even this sarcastic blessing, overjoyed that Devo have condescended to sneer at their own humdrum Cincinnati lives" (Riegel 1979, 64). Yet I argue that such antics do not enforce the dichotomy between audience and performer (which would maintain a band's position of power), for collusion likely takes place; that is, *both performers and fans* understand Devo's sarcasm, so "the detachment and idolatry" associated with stadium rock, noted by writers like David Cuatt, is actually deflated and erased (Cuatt 1984). By resisting cliché onstage banter and "groovy" self-mythologizing, acts like Devo and the Clash skewered inherited rock 'n' roll norms; however, their sheer physicality admittedly seemed in line with vintage rock 'n' roll performativity. Still, the idea of punk was to push against the grain, not merely to blindly submit to a series of conditioned responses in which audience and performers congregate and aggregate empty phrases and hollow gestures. The intended effect is more akin to parody and catharsis: bands use wit to catalyze an audience's self-examination of their roles and to create a space in which both parties are privy to those intentions. The sneering jibes do not constitute an inside joke by the band meant to belittle common fans—they are an inside joke between the audience and the band, who exist in a potent and interconnected relationship of equals. This leads to a mutual purgation of emotions like anger, bitterness, anxiety, and bellicosity.

In effect, audiences become active, volatile, and performative agents who participate fully and actively deconstruct a band's cultural meanings. The audiences sense an alienation or estrangement effect when bands hijack and subvert norms. "I don't want to give them their money's worth. . . . I want to challenge them," Ian MacKaye of Fugazi, famous for stopping shows when violence unfolded, told *No Idea* fanzine. "As long as they don't feel like they just came out and went, 'Oh, yeah, some band played. Yeah, it was really fun.' I like to think more is going on. . . . I don't have an interest in being an entertainer like that" (Cometbus 1989). Any shred of violence in front of the band—even "a grain of stupidity on the dance floor"—could make MacKaye feel "worthless" and "useless" if Fugazi merely became a backdrop to a select few "being total moron[s], fuckin' stupid, ritualized bastard[s]." The old modes of interplay between band and performance, shredded since the Sex Pistols taunted and torpedoed old clichés of rock'n'roll behavior, were null and void. Of course, not all fans understood this, but many who read band liner notes, lyrics, and interviews did, for such texts catalogued a band's ideologies, values, attitudes, goals, and intentions.

Yet performance rituals inherited by each subsequent generation and often enacted by simulating an imagined past can seem, to the likes of MacKaye, no more rebellious than youth listening to their parents' records. He felt the original ideas driving hardcore punk's youthful ethos had become a closed circuit—"tedious and boring"—in which even the physicality of rote slam dancing seemed as moribund as doing the Twist. Fugazi, and others of its ilk, was not interested in dispersing its "product" via live gigs, the old treadmill of musical enterprising; they were interested in catalyzing inchoate, one-off experiences.

Maskell argues that hardcore performances by the likes of Bad Brains propelled a "violent kinesthetic imagination, whereby both the band and their audience use their bodies as a way of performing history and contemporizing its effects." Such a band and audience "use their bodies in a violent and purposeful way to react to and take control of the current social and political situation . . . a violence in reaction to authority . . . violence as their own authority . . . a war against political and cultural conservatism" (Maskell 2009, 414–15). Yet Fugazi realized that such kinetic altercations and atavism belonged to a time and place; hence, reenacting it blindly meant engendering male-dominant gig spaces every bit as invalid and threatening as the violent apparatuses of local authorities. Such crowd violence eventually felt like the product of bankrupt imaginations disentangled from history. Pogoing begat slamming begat moshing begat fight clubs. As hardcore became a mass phenomenon via MTV videos (Cro-Mags, Gang Green, Bad Brains, Bl'ast), instead of stoking dynamism rife with audience-performer power sharing, the music steadfastly became mere aural wallpaper stimulating muddled melees. Onstage at venues teeming with thousands, like the Olympic in Los Angeles, bands at times appeared akin to battered puppets trying to complete songs as the masses roiled. But 1970s punk fostered a different promise.

In the case of Gang of Four, Greil Marcus proposed that the band was actually deconstructing the very nature of false consciousness "in rebellion against itself." In fact, the songs are not aimed at the audience, unleashing blues or rock 'n' roll tropes with their celebrations, regrets, demands, and imparted knowledge. Instead, "the voice is talking to itself," which produces the feeling of discontinuity and dislocation permeating a listener's mind: "at home you feel like a tourist; sex becomes a contract; history becomes a trick . . . the 'real world'—consumer society, the class system, the romantic myths one was raised on—is organized to divert you seeing it for what it is. . . . You see yourself a collaborator in the process of mystification, a beneficiary as well as victim" (Marcus July 1980, 43). The listener, far from feeling a sense of catharsis, or any ritual purge at all, is instead knee-deep in "anger, confusion, irony short-circuited by desperation, mockery, self-parody," and more, as if totally engaged, sparring with the whole symbol system and routines that keep the lid on the frail and often failing constructions of "nature" and "reality" (43). Or, as Andy Gill riposted to fellow member Hugo Burnham, "I don't think people can be entertained [by us] *without* understanding what is going on, without understanding the ideas that are there," including themes like the "paradoxes of leisure as oppression, identity as product, home as factory, sex as politics, history as ruling-class private joke" (Marcus July 1980, 43, 41).

Listening to Strummer, one begins to understand that rock 'n' roll is not an escapist medium pandering to the lowest common consumerist denominator but a way to consciously engage the world, whether local lore and inherited musical pastimes or the superstructure of economics and policies woven into daily life. As record reviewer Richard Riegel admitted, "The Clash have given me just enough lyrical rope to make me *think* (their stated aim . . .)," including the London drug scene, the fissuring English socioeconomic structure, "intellectual independence," and possible literary archetypes reminiscent of Charles Dickens found on *Give 'Em Enough Rope* (1978, 52). Visuals often bolstered this, including the Clash's projections on stage during the eighteen-gig stretch of shows at Bonds in New York City. These agitprop aids blared newspaper headlines as the band rolled through mostly *Sandinista*-era songs—"Pictures of riots . . . that day's *Daily News*, Parliament and Times Square were more of a lesson than a light show, an example of the Clash's continuing commitment to the world around them" (Blocher 1981, 26).

"Our perspective on art is that it is a lot of just selling or surface, and selling or old ideas, but at the same time, we live in a post-modern society where people tend to make up the meanings themselves in a lot of ways," said Dennis Lyxzén, singer for the (International) Noise Conspiracy (INC) and Refused, to me in *Left of the Dial* No. 2. "Take for example when you play shows. There's going to be a lot of people that are really excited about us being a political rock band. . . . Then there's people who like us because we're a rock band and play good music and think that politics don't matter, or is just bullshit. Or there are a lot of people like my friends who say everything you say and are doing is amazing, but your music kind of sucks. I think that what people extract from it is so tricky to define, especially when you come to a place where no one speaks English and you can't really sit down and talk about the tradition of avant-garde art in Europe. People would just be like, what are you talking about?" (Ensminger 2014).

Lyxzén understands that music is framed and underscored by an audience's cultural conditions. "It's really tricky, so what we tried is play music and inspire people. Though I think that music and art are very much in the line of bourgeois self-realization, I still think that it's important to express yourself, and I think that music is still a good way to express yourself if you do it honestly and sort of really incorporate something that you want to accomplish with it. So, in that sense we still play music. People ask us all the time, why do you still play music? Well, I love to play music. Though we can all sit down and get into deep discussions about the meaning of an artist, at the end of the day I still love to buy records and play, which I think is with the post-modern condition of living with contradictions all the time. That's something we have to struggle with on a daily basis."

In many ways, in the case of INC, the music and product became a compendium of embedded philosophies meant to spur ideas and actions against monoculture. "I think that if you could list un-American activities, we have participated in quite a few," laughs Lyxzén. "There is a reason why the world looks like it does, and one of the reasons is that there has never been room in America for people that think differently. . . . And there's always been hegemony of thinking. . . . We try and step back from the idea that we have all the solutions to your problems, like here's the party program that will save you. I think that the first initial stages allow people to look at what we have and sort of pick out what they find is interesting. We can also be contradictory and use a lot of stuff that doesn't make sense out of context. But for people, if they look at our records, they'll see quotes from communists, socialists, anarchists, Dadaists, everything. We just try and give a guide to the history of resistance, almost a small introduction to radical political ideas. It's up to people to find out what suits them, or to say, that's a great idea, or that's a crock of shit. We try and lay it all out on the table and see if there's anything you like."

Like Millions of Dead Cops and the Dicks, Lyxzén's band never intended to be doctrinaire or absolutist. "We're not dogmatic. We don't really have a set of ideas. Well, we all in the band have a set of ideas. . . . We try and present all these different ideas. I think that is a good start, because any time you start pointing a finger and saying, this is what we should do, then you're already in danger of becoming really boring. But then the other thing we do is when we play live. When you get our records and when you read the manifestos, there's definitely a kind of nerdy thing to it. . . . There's something like, here's a bunch of guys and girls from Sweden who read Michel Foucault, and that's not very amusing in itself. . . . There's definitely a nerdy element to it, like we read books a lot, and you should try and read. Coming from the rock point of view of sex, drugs, and rock 'n' roll, that's kind of uncool actually. We know that element exists, but if you mix that with music that we try to make very sexy, danceable, and enjoyable, especially when we play live . . . instead of being Crass, or something like that, with boring political finger pointing, we want that feeling of looking in the 1970s and the black power movement and the bands that played the sexiest, funkiest music.

"But any time you sell yourself to capitalism, which we do all the time, and any time you sell your art to capitalism there's always that chance of . . . selling the [idea]. We had that song 'For Sale' . . . that deals with the fact that everything is for sale," Lyxzén continues. "The Clash said it when they were doing all the shows at the end of their career, like here we are, just selling the revolution. In today's society, there's no real way of escaping the monetary system, no matter how hardcore and DIY you are. You still work within a capitalist framework and kind of sell your ideas. In a way, Fugazi is selling the political idea to even a further extent than we are, 'cause their whole marketing point is, we don't have a marketing point."

"Not to dis Fugazi—I think they are amazing—but when you look at it that way, that's a very powerful sales point, that they don't sell tee shirts and that they are not a commodity, so buy the record. There's always that risk of selling and corrupting the ideas, but then again I don't think that anything is that holy, and I don't think that ideas should not be able to be twisted, altered, and used for different purposes," Lyxzén argues. "If you are a punk rock puritan, and your goal is keeping punk rock from being exploited from big business, then of course I can see you being pissed off by bands that you see selling out or bands signed to major labels. But I'm not a puritan in that sense, and I really don't care. I think that the political ideas we have far supersede any youth culture or subculture."

Fugazi's situation intrigued writer and critic John Goshert to examine not only the philosophy embraced by the band but by extension their label Dischord as well, especially in regard to maintaining sovereignty over their production and distribution. Even while the band often denied interviews to major media outlets, this dismissal actually gained them notoriety and spurred coverage by such press outlets as *Pulse*, an official organ of Tower Records, and *Alternative Press*. "Such national recognition," he argues, "would appear necessarily to undermine, while paradoxically promoting the semblance of the localist practices of punk music and politics" (Goshert 2000, 95). The idea of an authentic outsider resistance to media norms itself became a selling point because a band cannot exercise total control of media or sculpt outcomes based on their own preferences. The media machine, with its omnipresent smattering of "slogans and bumper-sticker ideology," still exerts power and influence, a catch-22 for any band, for "with or without permission their anti-industry stance was opened up to flattening" (95). This in effect catalyzed a band like Fugazi to grow beyond its initial intimacies with the post-hardcore scene, both in terms of its public image and its physical gig spaces, which increased in size exponentially.

These few examples of punk being interwoven and engaged with sociopolitical issues and events are not uncommon. Punk consistently and persistently served as a kind of fiery or inflamed newspeak—the news of the world—for it occurred along the tangible front lines of a cultural epoch, initially including the waning Cold War unfolding in real time. Plus, punk foretold, and continues to witness, the information- and service-employee society replacing the industrial age. Hence, punk has always embodied much more than mere wayward leisure activities for disenchanted dropouts, for its "no rules" hodgepodge praxis bends and fissures the rules of stardom, musical craft, and fan culture traditions. As Angela McRobbie purports, "The classic subculture," such as punk, provides "members with a sense of oppositional sociality, an unambiguous pleasure in style, a disruptive public identity, and a set of collective fantasies" (1990, 66). The punk-inspired lifestyles and practices quickly became globalized by cheap fanzines and various music products—chiefly singles or cassettes, the economy of scale in most regions—that sprouted myriad, ever-expanding communities from Brazil to Japan and Australia, a patchwork of polygenesis that keeps punk in the present tense.

PUNK'S BULLSHIT DETECTOR

To be truly punk in the 1970s, one might assume in hindsight, one had to evoke more than mere taut and stripped-down musical traits and a taboo lifestyle replete with bondage pants, splattered paint clothes, jagged unkempt hair, and quasi-leftist tirades in order to subvert dominant culture at large. Potent first-generation punks, including the prescient women in Penetration, the Avengers, Slits, Siouxsie and the Banshees, and X-Ray Spex, engaged a full spectrum of issues, including late capitalism commodity fetishes; feminism; antiwar struggles; left- and right-wing ideologies; Fordism and trade unionism; and the still-feverish New Left, Hispanic, and black militant movements, perhaps most singularly evoked by such festivals as Rock against Racism, which included punk bands as well as reggae (Misty in Roots, Steel Pulse) and blues and jazz artists (Carol Grimes).

Soon thereafter, as hardcore emerged as a distinct genre and subcommunity, participants melded the older concerns with emerging issues, such as volunteerism for queer activism (People with AIDs Coalition and Act-Up), women's rights (Grassroots Women's Legal Defense Fund, as well as support for resource and crisis centers, shelters, and hotlines), animal rights (Student Action Corp. for Animals, Hunt Saboteurs Association, the Federal Association of the Liberators of the Animals, and the Animal Liberation Front), hunger (Food Not Bombs, the Institute of Food and Development Policy), environmentalism (Earth First, Earth Save, Big Mountain Legal Defense Fund, Cascadia Forest Defense, Collins Bay Action Group, Red Cloud Thunder, Greenpeace), alternative education (Ottawa Free School, Contra Costa High School, Hansel and Gretel Co-op Preschool), poverty and justice (Oxfam); and global antifascist/antiracist efforts (John Brown Anti-Klan Network, Anti-Fascist Action, Beat.Em.Down/Anti Fascist Rock Action Worldwide, and Good Night White Pride). If punk rock had not engaged such discourses, it might have remained merely a spectacle—turbulent in tone, riotous in small-scale venues, but otherwise barely scrambling the smooth monotony of culture at large. Instead, punk became an uncensored conduit of causes embodied by the likes of participants like Chriss Crass, a contributor to *HeartattaCk*, who advocated on behalf of "counter-hegemonic values of solidarity, economic democracy with an inherent critique of capitalism, self-determination," as well as "feminist principles of an egalitarian society" in his column "Building Movement, Building Power." Also, the piece explores troubling links between the rhetoric of radical environmentalists and the values of right-wing ideologues by highlighting the Sierra Club; anti-immigrant groups like Negative Population Growth; progressives like Committee on Women, Population, and the Environment; the subject of eugenics; and much more, all within the newsprint of a hardcore punk fanzine (Crass 2006).

According to Ken Lester, one-time manager of D.O.A., the alternative music scene with its concomitant fanzine and bootleg or home-recorded cassette dissemination became the "last substantial barrier to total corporate control over popular culture," forever at odds with "established authorities" (Lester 1990, 12). Punk, in essence, *became the media* years before Jello Biafra of the Dead Kennedys urged his brethren to do so on the album *Become the Media* (2000, Alternative Tentacles). Punk did so in part because major media appeared suspect, hostile, or misguided. "The printed word, when it's typed up and looking nice, people think it's the truth," Ian MacKaye of Fugazi and Minor Threat told *Option*, "but most of the time it's incredibly slanted—it's just written by misinformed writers, or it's just not telling the whole story" (Kim 1991, 80). That antipathy toward the "voice of authority" style master narratives of mainstream press coverage crystallized in songs like "Don't Believe What You Read" by the Boomtown Rats and "Meet the Press" by Circle Jerks is readily evident throughout punk's continuum.

The roots of punk's tumultuous uprising do matter. Malcolm McLaren has argued that punk's antecedents were not the taut garage rock nuggets of the 1960s or the polemics sprouted by the MC5, as many writers like Greg Shaw have envisioned, but instead the "irresponsible, low-class urchins, no-gooders" of the early blues circuit, devil-may-care men from whose music the punks "culled the feelings, the angst . . . and related it to their own politics of boredom in western society, the consumer paradise" (Flanagan, Young, and Alden 1995, 46). Hence, from this perspective, punk's vehemence was not honed by ideology—*Little Red Books* and discussions of the Situationist International—but by genuine pathos, grief, and feral outsiderness tethered to late capitalism's bored, recalcitrant, and dissatisfied youth.

The politics of punk are themselves rather unstable, mostly divorced from rigid sectarian strife and entrenched schools of thought. When pressed by a writer to explain the politics of Gang of Four, Hugo Burnham maintains, "A lot of people think 'political' is solely on the level of government-type politics. We are political in that the things we talk about, discuss, argue, and sing . . . about are the politics of your daily life: the individual attitudes you've been taught or trained, wrong or right" (Young 1981, 32). In this framework, politics is all-encompassing, germane to all situations, though it does not take shape as necessarily rigidly Marxist, for even Burnham felt he didn't "understand enough of the philosophy" to be doctrinaire (Young 1981, 32).

Punk acted like a bullshit detector disturbing the status quo and scattering outdated so-called truths on all sides of the political spectrum as well as attacking the marketplace's value system. The concept of calibrating pop music to be no more than an innocuous commodity fell apart especially poignantly under the deluge of Crass's "Nagasaki Nightmare" (Crass Records, 1980)—a single replete with fold-out liner notes examining the twin threats of atomic energy and nuclear war. The Clash weighed in on such issues as well. "Stop the World," the B-side to their coveted single "The Call Up" released during the fall of 1980, was considered a "surrealistically nightmarish vision of nuclear holocaust—a vision made horrifying given the unstable conditions of the world today" by a reviewer at *Upbeat* (R. Ellis 1981). The same issue declared that XTC songs "Living through Another Cuba" and "Generals and Majors" explored "the increasing militancy over the world that threatens to bring about our total annihilation as the human race" (Ellingsworth 1981). Hence, whether so-called radical fringe, mainstream punk, new music, or new wave, each melded such anxiety concerning the military-industrial-scientific complex deeply into the crucible of their lyrics.

The rhetoric positioning of such bands was plain: they represented the voice of blatant rationality, civilized peace, and untrammeled desire to stop the machinations of less-noble men and their Machiavellian, Cold War–encumbered pursuits that seemed less like the policies of realpolitik and more guided by sheer ideological furor, including stripping back social systems. "Many social services are getting cut away while their increasing so-called 'defense' spending so we'll have Trident and MX missiles zipping all over the planet one day," bemoaned Hugo Burnham of Gang of Four (Gibson and Springer 1981). Ronald Reagan was to blame as much as Margaret Thatcher, who presided over a right-wing government and "massive unemployment." Reagan's tough stance with the Iron Curtain appeared to a brazen attempt to heat up the Cold War and propel people's anxiety, which fits neatly with the major media master narrative: "The media is telling people they need a strong leader to make us a stronger country," Burnham forewarned, drawing a parallel to the mid-1930s: "It sounds like what the Germans were saying when they elected Hitler" (Gibson and Springer 1981).

The flexible and ductile approaches of punkers have confounded writers trying to monitor philosophies and practices. When Alice Nutter of Chumbawamba (a veteran activist band at times derided as too soft, mainstream, and corporate, who angered Class War and bands like Oi Polloi after signing to EMI in Britain and Universal in America) told fanzines, "We realize that some people are going to be unhappy with our choices . . . but it's not our job to placate people with false distinctions between 'good' and 'bad' bosses" (Wolk "Band for Sale" 1997). Writer Joel Schalit of *Punk Planet* felt Nutter was actually dissuading people "from thinking rock music could save the world" (1998). Yet the band donated $70,000, the fee paid by General Motors for the use of their tune "Pass It Along," to CorpWatch and IndyMedia, "corporate jammers" that mounted "an aggressive information and environmental campaign" against GM due to the company's unwillingness to modify production techniques as well as their support of global warming debunkers (Rowan 2002). In addition, the band turned down similar offers by Nike and General Electric to purchase song rights. They played plentiful benefits for Friends of the Earth; Prisoners Solidaritas; El Salvador Human Rights Committee; Oxfam; Artists for Animals; Swansea, Cheltenham, Scunny, Leeds, Cumberland, and Exeter Hunt Saboteurs; Hall Lane Community Centre; Middlesborough Rape Crisis; Anarchist Black Cross Prisoners; Greenpeace; squatters; and more. An Anti-Fascist Action benefit gig documented on their album *Showbusiness!* raised approximately £1,500 for the organization in 1994. While playing the *David Letterman Show*, they inserted the chant "Free Mumia Abu-Jamal" into their hit tune "Tubthumping," which, after much consternation, was aired. Hence, contrary to Schalit's cynicism toward the band's ethos, the band understood the possibilities, and inherent limits, of impacting the behavior and outcomes of multinational corporations.

Such praxis reveals much. Punk's early wave, which Chumbawamba founders like Danbert Nobacon witnessed as a member of the Crass-affiliated band Chimp Eats Banana (featured on *Bullshit Detector* #2, Crass Records, 1982), was not just a cursory stage of Western musical blowback against the pomp, spectacle, and saga of stadium rock like Foreigner, Toto, Styx, and Kansas. Those acts seemed to produce massive, inert, and passive audiences that sang along to albums chock-full of nimble artistic mastery and cutting-edge production techniques and values. "They fleeced you," argues Mick Jones, "there wasn't any thinking involved—it wasn't challenging in any way" (Flanagan, Young, and Alden 1995, 46). Punk, as suggested by fanzines' bravura aplenty—from the cornerstone 1970s-era *Sniffin' Glue*, *Up Yours!*, and *Final Solution* to the hardcore 1980s era and beyond of *Discord*, *Noise*, *Acts of Defiance*, *HeartattaCk*, and *Ripper*—was a glancing, fierce kick to obtuse systems, such as traditional media and music values as well as middle-class "creature comforts" that seemed out of step as the years of discontent began to boil on both sides of the Atlantic, steeped in governmental morass.

Whereas British civilians might have begrudged high unemployment and inflation and the fetid air of a stifling, record-temperature-setting summer in 1976, Americans grew weary of the oil shortage, post-Vietnam stagnation, unfulfilled civil rights, and increased mechanization of such industries as auto manufacturing (discussed by Joe Strummer with *Creem* writers in 1980), which left people questioning the American dream. In fact, punk might not have first gestated in the Warholian underground of New York City or the King Row boutiques of London but perhaps earlier in the soon-to-be-gutted zones of Detroit and Cleveland, where bands from Iggy and the Stooges and the MC5 to Rocket from the Tomb, Pere Ubu, Pagans, and the Electric Eels held sway in the nights following workaday routines. Those bands, though MC5 exists as a prime exception, did not necessarily embody or symbolize political ferment and discontent. They did, though, produce incisive, spurious, and cataclysmic music and catalyzed punk to come, but few people would sloganize their lyrics on tee shirts for rallies against nuclear weapons, although such songs as "Thirty Seconds over Tokyo," relating to World War II firebombing campaigns ("Flew off early in the haze of dawn / In a metal dragon locked in time"), actually were apropos to ongoing struggles against the increasingly consolidated American military-industrial complex's apocalyptic possibilities.

Soon, however, the next waves of bands like Crass and Dead Kennedys would cement the staunch sense of punk's political potency even as the Ramones and Dictators, soon followed by the Dickies and Fear, pursued more farcical, tongue-in-cheek, and ribald lyrical forms. Still, as Dunn argues, "Punk always provides valuable resources for political engagement" and "constitutes an intervention that is always political . . . that noise can represent a powerful disruption in the authorizing codes of the established social order" (2008, 207). Whereas some bands' lyrical aims and whims may not seem informed by political ideology on the literal, rhetoric-wielding surface, the musical subtext remains subversive, especially in regard to notions of commodity, suggests Stacy Thompson: "Punks never wholly escape or transcend the economic conditions in which they are mired [or] fully eschew commodification or small-scale capitalism . . . in their attempts to resist . . . they fail in commercial terms . . . a sort of punk success after all. And in their continual effort and failure to establish a zone free from commodification, punks attest to a continuing cultural desire for something else" (2004, 151, 156). So desire always seemed to speak louder than commodity exchange, and the failure to sell—a victory in terms of artists' sheer substance—meant failure seemed like a ploy to authenticate a punk vision.

Punk often feels like a trajectory of disenchantment, disturbance, and atomized desire, but its honed antithetical power may reside both in personas and actions. The singers of Bad Religion (Greg Graffin) and Big Boys (Randy "Biscuit" Turner), both former choir singers, became the voices of generational metadissent that disarticulate culturally dominant institutions. To provide political insight, Graffin favors a complex lyrical mechanism of wordplay and media observation, seemingly rooted in his own scientific background as an academic lecturer as well as his deep affinity for the literary configurations and musings of Darby Crash (singer for the Germs), a style likely favored by his father, an English professor at the University of Wisconsin (Spitz and Mullen 2001, 231). In contrast, Turner's more Dionysian-shaped dissent actively drew from traditions of alternative theater, gay camp, and 1970s countercultural elements that converged the spheres of African American musical finesse (including soul, funk, and go-go), do-it-yourself strategies (illustrated by the Big Boys' dictum "Now go start your own band"), and antiracist/antihomophobia stances.

"There weren't all these cookie-cutter punk and hardcore bands and genre-fied styles to copy," posits Jello Biafra, whose label has released recordings featuring dissident academic Noam Chomsky, as did Bad Religion ("New World Order") and Chumbawamba (*For Anarchy and a Free Humanity*). "It was a visceral reaction against all the stupid stuff going on both politically in the 1970s and especially musically, where the radio was pushing soft rock and adult rock, and we didn't want to be adults. Or they pushed *Triumph of the Will*–style arena rock for the kids who wanted something heavy. People in different places wanted more, and they put their stamp on it. You couldn't keep them off the stage anymore. So a lot of the bands had distinct sounds and personalities. Big Boys were a good example" (Biafra).

In fall 2013, Bad Religion released *Christmas Songs*, an album's worth of punk interpretations of traditional carols, and donated 20 percent of their proceeds to SNAP (Survivors Network of those Abused by Priests); in 2007, they played a gig supporting "Heal the Bay," an environmental network; they placed "Let Them Eat War" on the *Rock against Bush, Vol. 2* compilation in 2004; they were the opening act of a Rage against the Machine gig benefiting the legal efforts to release imprisoned black journalist Mumia Abu-Jamal (considered a political prisoner by many punks and whose efforts to free himself were championed by bands like Anti-Flag and This Machine Kills) in 1999; and they played a gig during the mid-1980s to raise funds for Keith Morris of the Circle Jerks after he suffered an injury. Hence, their efforts were wide ranging, not simply clustered along a single issue.

Meanwhile, the Big Boys contributed to political causes by playing multiple benefits for El Salvador, including raising money for the Revolutionary Democratic Front; playing a Fair Housing benefit ("Against Legalized Discrimination," reads the flyer); and raising money for local incarcerated musician Buxf of the politically charged band the Dicks ("Free Buxf!" screams the hand-scrawled flyer); plus, Biscuit, as a solo poet, raised funds for art spaces, such as the Big State Theatre. During one Big Boys gig with D.O.A., singer Joey "Shithead" Keithley remembers, "Liberty Lunch in Austin, I think, [was] a classic open-air Texas club, and Randy from the Big Boys called out this guy who had been handing out white power bullshit pamphlets. A small riot ensued" (2011). Biscuit often wore costumes more akin to performance art than hardcore gear, such as pink tutus, wedding dresses, and even a mutant Christmas tree. Even though one of the Big Boys' rousing songs might have been "Fun Fun Fun," an overemphasis on such sentiments of apolitical joy belies their commitment to both local and international social justice, even in a city in which a flyer for *Xiphoid Process* zine underscores a sense of intense localism, "Who Cares about El Salvador? Find out what's happening in your state and city!" Big Boys might have been local heroes, but their antennas reached further afield.

The same may be said for bands like X, close friends of the Big Boys, whose "Los Angeles" and "The Have Nots" were compressed, detail-thronged narratives of alienation in the lurid western city described by

John Leland as a "decadent-chic society" reeking with "urban claustrophobia" and self-annihilating bouts of "violent sex, heroin, and social climbing" (1984, 24). The band's worldview, however, did not stop at the perimeters of the murky, ensnaring, and noir-induced metropolis. They readily acknowledged a broader, more tumultuous world. "When media bombards you all the time, you have to learn the stuff," admits Exene Cervenka. "You can't help know the ins and outs of what happened in Beirut or El Salvador or Grenada" (Leland 1984, 26). Punk bands became agile conduits for such information, like M.D.C.'s "Multi-Death Corporation" single. "Opening up the poster and seeing the information on El Salvador and the Contras and Sandinistas, . . . we're like 'What is going on here?'" tells Joe "Peps" Galarza of Aztlan Underground and the Iconoclast. "We weren't in total war in the barrios, or civil war . . . but we were still dealing with low-intensity warfare that was happening in our neighborhoods" and in Black Mesa, Arizona, known as Big Mountain, where the local indigenous population was trying to fend off coal companies, which inspired a 1992 benefit compilation with bands like Slaughterchrist, NSC, HTN, and Hair Farm (Alvarado and Taylor 2014). That same year, Profane Existence compiled a benefit LP, *In the Spirit of Total Resistance*, with Jonestown, Los Crudos, Huasipungo, and more to benefit the Mohawk Nation of Kanesatake. Such bands deftly connected the dots between traumatized communities across the country and globe.

The Minutemen evoked the Central American conundrum abstractly in instrumentals like "Song for El Salvador" and more concretely in the anti-imperialist folk rock–inspired "No! No! No! To Draft and War" (with the refrain "U.S. out of El Salvador"), even though critic Chris Morris described their politics as "allusive rather than didactic" (1984). D. Boon handed out stickers to crowds during one American tour that read "Get Out / USA Out of Central America," which nearly caused a ruckus with jocks at Tulane College, and he propped up a sign on stage advocating the same message: "U.S. out of Central America." At a stop in St. Louis in 1985, Boon engaged writer Joe Williams of *Jet Lag* about the nuanced geopolitics unfolding in the era, "conced[ing] that just like punk, the Sandinista movement has been corrupted. The recent suspension of civil liberties and the relocation of the Miskito Indian tribe have been mistakes," which the regime was trying to rectify. One main issue was the "conflict . . . between a Euro-Hispanic and an Indian world view," argued Boon, who said he was part Native American himself. "The revolution restored the Indians to power and sent the rich European landowners scurrying to Florida." One homemade shirt worn by Boon during the era had "People's Victory in El Salvador" and "Fight Using Your Balls" scrawled on the breast of the button-up shirt. For the last full-length album before he died, *3-Way Tie (For Last)*, the band explored themes of assassination and invasion ("Political Nightmare," written by Kira Roessler), the personal and national horrors of war in Vietnam ("The Price of Paradise"), U.S. support of the bombing campaign against Nicaraguan revolutionaries and of a fascist regime in Guatemala ("The Big Stick"), questionable aspects of "blind and pure" patriotism and valor ("Courage"), and lost morality stemming from war in far-flung corners of the globe ("Just Another Soldier"). The band played benefit gigs for movements like CAPA (the Coalition against Police Abuse), and more. Even such a small song sample of the band's music and philosophy speaks to the band's ethos of stirring and supporting true democracy at home: a fervid and fecund republic both catalyzes and engages voices of dissent. This connects them to outspoken icons ranging from Thomas Paine and Henry David Thoreau to Woody Guthrie, Paul Robeson, and Phil Ochs.

"Me and D. Boon were on the same page about Central America in the 1980s, though I didn't belong to Committee in Solidarity with the People of El Salvador. I'm not sure if he was an actual member. I only went to one meeting he brought me to," recalls Mike Watt. "I don't remember D. Boon really supporting the Sandinistas, but he was not into U.S. intervention in the whole area. That incident at Tulane really happened, but you know what was funny was that the 'stickers' were actually ones you had to lick (more econo), so I don't see why them jocks got their panties so bunched up. I mean if you wanted to put that much effort into putting on a sticker, then shouldn't you be allowed to? Kind of funny" (2014).

D. Boon's sense of holistic politics extended to health and well-being, as well. He had a penchant for naturalistic remedies and supplements, like bee pollen, protein powder, and papaya pills, as Williams discovered. Thirty years later, some of that trip still resonates with Watt: "I remember for sure both the St. Louis Arch, and underneath it there with the Native American exhibit. Me and D. Boon were profoundly interested in this 'potlatch' thing we learned about there, how there were folks from European backgrounds that were interested with helping the Native people here by trying to help with some unity so they could defend themselves. I do remember the Arch (looking down on East St. Louis from up high, whoa! much different than the Missouri side!). D. Boon liked spirulina also, liked it big time. He liked things natural, yes. He got me to eat pert near only broccoli during the last part of 1985 touring, like from September 'til the accident. I quit after that happened. It was quite a blow, you can imagine. D. Boon was very concerned about my health. D. Boon really cared about things, beautiful man" (2014).

Just as the Minutemen devised a punk musical hybrid, False Prophets conjured the fluid genre-amalgam (punk, hip-hop, and South American ethnic folk) "Banana Split Republic" to explore the devastation or war, dislocation, and even genocide of such conflicts, including Salvadorans fleeing to violent Honduras. Plus, U.S. foreign policy contradictions were addressed by bands like Econochrist, a band whose members Jon Sumrall canvassed for Sane/Freeze and Ben Sizemore canvassed for CalPIRG (a public interest research group), who sardonically pointed out to *No Answers* fanzine, "I love the way in Nicaragua the rebels there are 'freedom fighters,' but in El Salvador they're 'insurrectionists' (McClard, "Interview," 1989). In the summer of 1986, *Maximum Rocknroll* contributor and publisher of *Creep* fanzine Mickey Creep experienced a bit of both countries; El Salvador felt like domineering police state, whereas Nicaragua, despite its difficulties in governance, felt multicultural and hopeful, a place where Americans could interact openly with both Sandinista Youth and Miskito Indians, traditional Catholics and liberation theologists without enduring threats or intimidation by representatives of the Marxist system.

As mentioned, X treaded carefully and consciously, never offering preachy, pugnacious, and one-dimensional disaffection. Instead, the band chose more poignant paths that dissected the "blank generation's" chilling loss of faith in institutions (politics, industry, and family), as revealed in "New World" and in the cutting, ironic, and subversive wordplay of "I Must Not Think Bad Thoughts." X penned fiercely literate songs with barbed insight about feral youth lurking in the shadows of decrepit Hollywood, and the band's cutthroat melodies and rockabilly-tinged music contrasted the gnarly noise of their contemporaries, which often were more addicted to aggression than poetry.

Disillusion still seems to imbue X singer and bass player John Doe. "How I feel about politics right now is like armed insurrection. It's so fucked up. I'm feeling a really dark presence in America's politics right now. And it's not just Obama: it's the fact that he represented something, and it's obviously not coming true. And it's the powers that be. . . . I'm not a conspiracy theorist, but I don't know. Yes, I think that people have got to be involved, but it's getting harder and harder to see where you can have an effect, and how many things are out of your control, and how incredibly backward and conservative this country is—it's like, oh my god, really? Like the motherfucker Ted Cruz.

"And it's not just him. Ron Paul is a kook too, but I sorta agree with libertarianism because government is so ass backwards, there is no reason for them to save any money," Doe continues. "You got to spend all the money, unless you want less money. It's really hard to know where to put your political money and power, or lack of power" (Doe 2013). As his partner in the band, Exene Cervenka told me in 2015, "It was all very political and revolutionary. A friend said to me recently, 'punk rockers would be considered potential domestic terrorists these days by the current regime.' We had freedom, and I would rather have freedom than wealth and fame. Really, we had it all."

Music offered by bands like X might not have appealed to the broad swath of radio listeners, but it did find singular currency in the underground, indie, and college markets, where a loss of faith was persuasive. "People have lost faith in their leadership to change the ultimate outcome of things" wrote one disgruntled music fan in a 1984 *Trouser Press* letter to the editor. "So, most of them withdraw into a falsely protective shell, listen to 'Let's Dance' (David Bowie), and try to ignore the horrid truth of holocaust, death, and destruction" (Fury 1984). In fact, as if these sentiments were a premonition, the Boston underground band Mission of Burma released its live album, *The Horrible Truth about Burma*, a country in which military atrocities during and after the prolonged, devastating civil war have occurred since Myanmar's independence from British rule and subsequent decades-long rule by a relentless, forceful military oligarchy.

That stinging loss of faith reverberated throughout 1984, the year Reagan was reelected and Los Angeles hosted the Olympics, even as punks bands like U.K. Subs, 7 Seconds, T.S.O.L., M.D.C., and Dead Kennedys drew throngs to the Olympic Auditorium, which was built for the 1932 Olympics. The Dead Kennedys introduced their set with Jello Biafra declaring, "And now a word from the official terrorists of the 1984 Olympics," then proceeding to unleash acrid tunes like "Police Truck," "Take This Job and Shove It," "Chemical Warfare," and "MTV Get off the Air." Meanwhile, T.S.O.L. opened its set by saying its song "American Zone" was about "the fine line between war and peace" as members of the crowd stormed the stage in slam-dance rituals, producing mammoth sweat and atavism ("Dead Kennedys" 2011). Meanwhile, amateur underground artists emblazoned punk gig flyers with images of Ronald Reagan—the actor turned Republican governor of California and president of the United States—as an easy target of punk mistrust and disdain. One No Business As Usual (an activist group supported by punks) flyer from April 1987 declared him "Wanted for International Terrorism" for killing 60,000 people in El Salvador, 10,000 in Nicaragua, and 400,000 in Iran and Iraq. By inserting a fake mug shot as the sole graphic, the designer potently visualized the vitriol felt by thousands of youth.

Punk's politics remain multifaceted, situational, and polymorphous. Phillipov recognized complexities at work in the grain of punk behavior and texts: "punk . . . is often highly political in so far as it is deeply bound to questions of resistance, social location and commodification. However, it is necessary to develop a vocabulary for talking about punk that can theorize its moments of political engagement without flattening . . . the music into a predetermined framework of radicalism. . . . Music isn't just about the politics of resistance" (2006, 392). She resists such tunnel vision, declaring music is much more than a platform of ideology. Moreover, she claims "punk scholars have tended to assume that the genre's politics are definitionally progressive and emancipatory" and argues both Jude Davies and Dave Laing "see punk as an essentially progressive movement articulating egalitarian, community-based, broadly leftist politics" and only differ in terms of how punk "manifests" such radicalism (2006, 386). This sensibility remains normalized. In 1996, James Ward declared, "The overall predisposition of punk . . . was (and is) vaguely, if not specifically, left" (161). As of 2012, Rob Fatal argued punk rock narratives celebrate "Marxist-rich values of the punk anti-hierarchy" (164). The truth of punk's stimulative effect on self-empowerment and political conscience, however, is rather more nuanced.

For instance, the framework of punk's roots and radicalism often evoked by writers is rather arbitrary and deterministic in most cases. John Savage believes Situationism decidedly impacted punk's sense of cultural dissent. To evidence this causal chain and influence, the book *Punk: An Aesthetic* produced by Rizzoli in 2012 features works collected and commented on by Savage, and juxtaposes ephemera from the period of late-1960s student revolt in France alongside early punk visual culture. Others, though, question or dismiss that inherent link, especially participants like Captain Sensible of the Damned, a close-the-ground first-wave participant that dismissed Savage's *England's Dreaming* as "a ripe load of shit" in an interview published in *Left of the Dial* (Ensminger 2002). Still, scholars—myself included—often choose their version of punk—both its music catalog and history—selectively in order to fit ready-made templates: punk is antithetical because it seems to rebel against *all the right* (not to pun) inherent norms, but that rebellion morphs.

HARNESSING THE MAINSTREAMING OF PUNK: NEW GOALS, NEW VILLAINS

The role of NOFX, led by icon Fat Mike, offers an interesting map of punk conscience. Its early-to-mid-period musical offerings like "Six Pack Girls," "Cops and Donuts," and "White Bread" might be considered low-culture "snotcore" tirades, no more than brash, bratty, juvenile, politically incorrect, serially sardonic, and furiously paced suburban odes/codes to teenage life. In 1991, Mike, who penned his thesis for San Francisco State University on the subject of pornography, avowed that he was a "pro-sexuality . . . irreverent . . . reactionist" who didn't mind a ratings system on records—especially 2 Live Crew. He described angry feminists in Germany throwing full bottles of beer at the band during its first European tour due to songs like "On the Rag," even after the band decided not to play the song (Soares and Morf 1991).

Their newer material, still festering with fiery and accessible pop-punk style, attempts a different reportorial angle. Tunes like "We Called It America" (in which they recall the middle-class, liberal-leaning, pre–stagnant economy America), "Freedumb" ("Is freedom of expression just a load of shit? Just another farce?" they ponder), the synthesizer-dolloped "Franco Un-American" (cataloging a youth's progression from apathy and ignorance to blindly following Michael Moore and Noam Chomsky), and "USA-Holes" (which describes a media-saturated, knee-jerk, go-to-war America) tap the band's perennial wit to provoke concern about dominant and subcultural practices, geopolitics, civil rights, and America's so-called exceptionalism, which led to the War on Terror; in turn, NOFX assembled its own guerrilla media assault, the album *War on Errorism*, which seems cinched to punk's original provocateurs as it is to *South Park*–style caricatures and ribald comedy. The band's pointed sense of sardonic jest, perhaps an homage to Jonathan Swift, does not denigrate the band's overall humanitarian aims, such as playing gigs benefiting the family of Tony Sly (deceased singer of No Use for a Name) in 2012, UCP Wheels for Humanity (mobility for children) in 2009, and other efforts, including a Fat Mike–signed bass auctioned on behalf of medically debilitated China White guitarist Frank Ruffino in spring 2013. In late 2011, Fat Mike, a vocal supporter of small community banks, joined NOFX guitarist Eric Melvin to play their 1994 tune "Perfect Government" in the Occupy L.A. encampment.

In these cases, the punk community acts more or less as a mutual aid society. Over decades, punk has spawned benefit gigs for members of Crucifix (On Broadway, 1980s, San Francisco); Burn Center (Austin, 1980s, "victim of terrorist redneck," reads the flyer); Sick Of It All (Pyramid, NYC); Thoughts of Ionesco, for parking tickets (I.O., Detroit); avant-garde Austrian filmmaker Kurt Kren, who became homeless in Texas (Studio One, Houston); Gerry Hannah of the Canadian band Subhumans and the Direct Action radical political unit, whose imprisoned members were known as the Vancouver Five (numerous benefit gigs, including Bristol Peace Centre in 1984); Mike Atta, guitarist of the Middle Class who was coping with cancer treatment (Echoplex, Los Angeles, 2013); Government Issue, whose singer John Stabb underwent extensive facial reconstruction after an assault (Washington, D.C., 2007); and many others. Riot Fest, a perennial Chicago-based all-star punk event featuring reunited vintage punk and hardcore bands, donated a portion of its proceeds in 2007 to Stabb as well as to Government Issue bass player J. Robbins, whose son continues to cope with spinal muscular atrophy. These events evidence just a small sampling of punk's peer-to-peer humanitarian efforts.

Such paternalism, one could argue, is part of the normal form of punk practices that is easy to trace throughout the subculture's history. As Mike Watt, who played the Atta benefit, conferred to me in late 2013, "I still do benefit gigs, do them all the time! [including 2013 benefit gigs for "Gimme Gimme Gimme Record Fair and Food Drive" at Space 15 Twenty and "Weight of the Sound: Benefit for the Redwood P.A." at the Redwood Bar and Grill as well as a 2015 gig for "Rock against MS" at The Whisky a Go-Go] . . . I just think it's good for the soul and karma. I never hardly turn them down unless I can't do them cuz of not being available . . . this goes back to my Minutemen days. I've done tons of benefits and will continue to do so." Watt's efforts, as well those previously mentioned, embody a persistence that forms a continuum to the earliest days of punk's blossoming. In fact, as he once told writer Chris Morris, "A band can give you confidence—the Dils and the Clash gave me confidence" (1984). Such a confidence in the ability to make an impact remains resilient in Watt.

In 2004, Fat Mike produced the effort *Rock against Bush, Vol. I* and *II*, utilized in tandem with his now-defunct Punk Voter website, which made his own efforts distinctly political and not merely fodder for irony-laden listening pleasure during an election cycle that pitted George Bush against John Kerry. The effort seemed to mirror the work of JAMPAC (Joint Artists and Music Promotions Political Action Committee), founded by Krist Novoselic of Nirvana in the early 1990s, as well as Rock for Choice. As a political action group, it functioned from 1991 until 2001, spearheaded by the band L7 (which previously played benefits for AIDS efforts, antiwar mobilization, and KXLU radio) and the Fund for the Feminist Majority. They corralled bands from Nirvana, Sister Double Happiness, and Hole to Fugazi, Joan Jett, Mudhoney, the Fluid, Fishbone, No Doubt, Pearl Jam, Primus, Corrosion of Conformity, and the Lunachicks to play benefit gigs focused on grassroots voter registration and abortion rights awareness. This crowdsourcing for punk philanthropic efforts has also worked well for such labels as Sub City, which has raised $2 million for fifty nonprofit charities (like Driving for Donors, Youth America Hotline, and Living the Dream Foundation) by coordinating successful Plea for Peace/Take Action! Tours with bands like Matchbook Romance, Hot Water Music, Alkaline Trio, and

Silverstein (the 2010 tour raised $60,000); partnered with mainstream clothing companies like Hot Topic; and released multiple compilation albums (typically donating 5 percent of retail price), as well as harnessing proceeds from individual bands, including Fifteen, the Weakerthans, and Against All Authority. Such efforts are detailed on the label's website.

On an individual level of commitment, Anti-Flag, which has openly supported Greenpeace, PETA, *Democracy Now!* and Amnesty International, used its major-label effort *The Bright Lights of America* (RCA Records) to supply listeners with band-related graphic-art stencils—perhaps in a nod to Crass record typography—but also offered postcards declaring support for Geneva Conventions tenets regarding torture and additional concerns, declaring adequate "food, shelter, and health care" a part of basic human rights, which could be mailed to the United Nations. They also released a twelve-song EP in 2007 benefiting the Center for Victims after the bass player lost his sister under violent circumstances. Some punks likely felt chagrined by the former indie band (New Red Archives, Go-Kart, and A-F Records) signing to a major label, yet the platform undoubtedly enlarged their audience.

As Justin Sane explained to me, "The reality is that our adversaries have access to a massive and all-encompassing media and PR machine, and if Anti-Flag can access that machine, can use the machinery of our adversaries to plant a few new thoughts in the psyche of the American people, then I think we would be foolish to pass up the opportunity. The reality is that our contract with RCA gives us 100 percent *complete* control over everything we write, record, release . . . everything we do! If we weren't given complete control by RCA, then we wouldn't have done the deal because there is no point to being in a band like Anti-Flag if you can't write about and address the issues that are important to you. With RCA we have a tremendous opportunity to write songs like 'The Press Corpse' and have many people hear it who have never heard of the Downing Street Memo or the other issues the song addresses" (Sane 2006). The phrase *complete control* mirrors the same language used in a Clash song title, "Complete Control," which related to the band's struggles with CBS Records. As Clash biographer Marcus Gray infers, "complete control was a total c-o-n" (2010, 251). Still, according to Sane, fans regularly told the band that they decided not to join the military, even after flirting with such a career path, because of the band's message-laden music: "It's very powerful to hear such testimony from kids because I never imagined that anyone would really hear my band, never mind thank us for saving their life!" (Sane 2006). Thus, the RCA deal might have expanded those outreach opportunities and helped turn the popular tide against the war, even if corporate infrastructure and networks delivered the agitprop.

Yet Kevin Dunn, who quotes Fat Mike in the article "Nevermind the Bollocks: The Punk Rock Politics of Global Communications," posits that punk politics are essentially brokered at the local level: "The DIY ethos and anarchist sympathies within punk provide for the articulation of a politics that are local and contingent; micro-responses rather than meta-theory" (2008, 205). Yet anarchist tendencies, such as those espoused by the band Propagandhi, in which the ideal government is considered "the kind that doesn't exist and therefore allows the decentralization of power and opportunity for people to control their own lives and communities" (Jes'ca 1979) akin to tenets latently espoused in the early punk song "Autonomy" by the Buzzcocks, offers metatheory and transcends hometown issues at play in Portage la Prairie, Manitoba, Canada. Its *Less Talk More Rock* (Fat Wreck Chords, 1996) album packaging lists its perspectives: "Pro-feminist, animal-friendly, anti-fascist, gay-positive," which was almost immediately lampooned by Everready, which listed its own counter-slogans on advertisements for its album *El Vato Loco* : "pro-beer, anti-punk, hot dog–friendly, and girl-positive."

Meanwhile, a single song title by Propagandhi—"Nailing Descartes to the Wall/(Liquid) Meat Is Still Murder"—alludes to both the rationalist French philosopher Rene Descartes and the vegetarian-espousing band the Smiths (*Meat Is Murder*, Rough Trade/Sire, 1985) in an approach that appears syncretic, intertextual, ironic, and translocal: the band serves as a conduit between communities sharing similar orientations, including fans who donated money to activist organizations supported by the band in exchange for two songs released during the *Supporting Caste* album promotional cycle, which raised $7,500 for Partners in Health, the Sea Shepherd Conservation Society, and Peta2, according to the band's website. Also, proceeds of their earlier record sales were donated to Food Not Bombs, People Acting for Animal Liberation, the Winnipeg Homeopathic Society, and AK Press Distribution, which its label Fat Wreck Chords matched dollar for dollar.

This was especially poignant after the band's sour dealings with Robbie Fields of Posh Boy Records, who wrangled with the band concerning rights to a song used in a compilation. The group's larger sense of community building and ethos-based commitment is not surprising, since bass player John Samson's musical inspirations were industrial music agitprop icons Consolidated and college rock heroes Midnight Oil, known for longstanding humanitarian and social justice efforts, including a Stop the Drop anti-nuclear benefit, Jobs—Every Home Should Have One benefit, and Beat the Grog alcohol abuse benefit campaigns in Australia.

In 2010, Propagandhi followed up with the digital-only *The Recovered* benefit EP, which aimed to help Partners in Haiti. The eyes of the world media were likely to fade, the band posited, while outside pressure from former colonial watchdogs would only increase as the nation attempted to regenerate and rejuvenate its infrastructure. "Haiti will still face the incredible challenge of rebuilding their impoverished, fragmented cities," vocalist/guitarist Chris Hannah told *Exclaim!* website, "while very likely having to fend off political and economic interference from the usual suspects: Canada, U.S.A., and France" (Pratt 2010). The EP featured the track "What Price Will You Pay?"—a song featured on the *Not So Quiet on the Western Front* (*Maximum Rocknroll*/Alternative Tentacles, 1982) compilation by the inventive hardcore provocateurs Code of Honor. During a song break, both singers declare "smash it up" not long before the last monologue bemoans the "fascism, racism, sexism" that society breeds. Not to be overshadowed by such older colleagues, the Class War Kids from Newfoundland, Canada, released a digital EP, too, benefiting the Batay Ouvriye Haiti Solidarity Network. Targeting issues relating to post-disaster relief business, singer and guitarist Patty O'Lantern was even more pointed than his elders in his assessment of the recovery situation. He wanted to channel money into appropriate efforts, in which it would be "for the poor and working class to organize themselves against the multinational corporations that have helped to solidify the poverty that Haiti is buried underneath" (Cram 2010). Such bands desired to help "nation build" from the bottom up, centering on close-to-the-ground organizations outside the manacles of corporate policy making.

Still others like Good Riddance used proceeds from its CDs, like *Symptoms of a Leveling Spirit* on Fat Wreck Chords, to benefit the

Multiple Sclerosis Service Society and the Second Harvest Food Bank of Santa Cruz County. Fat Wreck Chords also released *Protect: A Benefit for the National Association to Protect Children*, featuring an array of contemporary punk bands like Hot Cross, BARS, and Coalesce, as well as punk-affiliated singer-songwriters like Joey Cape and Matt Skiba in 2005.

Though detractors abound, NOFX is an important case study. "One thing to separate out, and to get time correct: NOFX made a lot of the musical tropes for modern pop punk, for better and for worse," argues Todd Taylor, editor of longtime fanzine *Razorcake*, who also penned the liner notes to the *Protect* compilation, but "don't blame them for the legions of copycats and their awful fans" (Taylor 2015). Plus, the band remains viable, even in the scrutiny of the public eye, "mostly because of Erin's business acumen" and because it remains steadfastly DIY. "They never lapsed to a major label and did it largely themselves without systematically fucking others over. I'm sure some have business complaints with Fat, but it's not . . . systemic," Taylor continues. "Blindly following Chomsky *is* a cop out. Either people fall asleep listening to Chomsky or, when they actually learn something from him . . . they apply some of his principles to how they operate, which brings me to the operations of Fat and their contracts with bands, like non-onerous royalties." They pursue "genuine artist development with bands other labels would have discarded because the numbers weren't there. That stuff I find highly political. Would people rather a band/label say all the right things in public and then rip everyone off/treat them like shit, like Lookout Records?" Taylor asks.

The previously mentioned *Rock against Bush* campaign harnessed the power of punk and neopunk bands that had reached a significant commercial scale—those selling records at box stores and shifting units by the millions, like Green Day, Foo Fighters, and the Offspring, in the case of *Rock against Bush*. This suggests that national politics was the domain of punk, just as Ronald Reagan, who appeared on innumerable flyers and in songs in the 1980s (like D.O.A's "Fucked up Ronnie"), became a meme upon which punk's vehemence was projected and disseminated. The liner notes to the *Rock against Bush, Vol. I* CD reveal the regime-change agenda quite clearly: "It's Not about 'Let's Be Punk Rock and Hate the Government'; It's about 'Let's Be Punk Rock and Change the Government.' . . . It's about uniting against a Common

Enemy." The songs, videos, and "Reasons to Hate Bush Jr." lists compile the punk rock threat—by no means merely local—with determination and vigor. Still, some critics within the punk community felt that the Bush campaign money could have been rerouted to other, more long-term efforts, "like fighting the right-wing agenda across the board, not just focused and squandered on one election campaign" to elect "a liberal figurehead," argued Daniel Eloquence in *Profane Existence* (2000, 33). Other critics have attempted to elucidate punk stratagem by focusing on an individual's sense of volition—the power of choice. Kevin Dunn's analysis is attractive and potent in this sense, for he posits, "The power of punk rock is that it encourages its audiences to become active forces for articulating their own critiques and responses to the politics of daily life" (2008), but in cases like this campaign, Fat Mike was trying to coordinate a unified response, specifically voter registration and turnout. Some politics transcend local dynamics, and some punk practices, attitudes, and philosophies are readily and richly translocal, disseminated freely in the digital era; hence, the public commons and social platform of the Internet has replaced the local gig, mall, record shop, bar, suburban tract, or street corner.

The Internet is a thriving hive of punk-mediated activity across the globe. Reagan and Bush became almost interchangeable tropes of the unwanted and despised, inspiring songs from Dead Kennedys' "We've Got a Bigger Problem Now" and D.R.I.'s "Reaganomics" to, again, NOFX's "Franco Un-American," in which the art for the single features a cartoon depiction of George Bush as a sad, frowning clown. "It might be particular to those of us who grew up under Reagan's legacies of social hysteria and brutal discipline (disguised as a moral majority and tough love)," tells Mimi Thi Nguyen, now an associate professor of gender and women's studies and Asian American studies at the University of Illinois, Urbana-Champaign, who once took part in the counter-memorial for Ronald Reagan in San Francisco upon his death. "But punk rock did pose a challenge . . . to the short-circuiting of the civic imagination" by addressing "the intimate levels of consciousness at which identification with or against authority was lived and felt (whether manifest as a boy in eyeliner in a Southern small town or as the brick in hand at the anti-war riot)," including how "nationalism and democracy are lived and felt" (Nguyen 2010).

Reagan and Bush have been replaced by other memes of total power, such as Russian premier Vladimir Putin, castigated by Pussy Riot, who were imprisoned for "hooliganism"—officially described as "rude disruption of social order," referring to its political and religious protests, videos, and performances—after undertaking a breathless, hectic, and truncated punk prayer provocatively titled "Mother of God, Drive Putin Away" in a Moscow cathedral in 2012, which rankled the Russian Orthodox Church. The case quickly spurred international headlines and made martyrs of the three members, who were tried by the taciturn, uber-bureaucratic, and absolutist state, echoing innumerable "show trials" from the Soviet Union's not-so-dusty past. Recently, punk bands like 7 Seconds had to consider this atmosphere when planning global tours. As Kevin Seconds informed me, "We carefully considered all the reasons to not go before we finally decided to do it. Russia doesn't have a good track record on gay rights, and that concerned us greatly. We talked with friends of ours from other bands, bands like Madball and H2O, and they all had great things to say about Russia. What really sold it for me was getting this incredibly warm, passionate, thoughtful letter from the promoter trying to get us to come over. He expressed how much it would mean to all of the people in the punk rock and hardcore community there who do not agree with their government's views and laws. It seemed more important for us to play there and share our music and views than to be just one more band boycotting an entire nation for the fucked-up deeds and views of politicians. I mean, coming from the U.S., it's pretty hard to rail against the bad shit other governments pull when ours isn't much better" (Ensminger "7 Seconds" 2014).

The case of Pussy Riot places the band squarely in the contentious "punk as political pulpit" strain that is deeply rooted in the lineage of punk and easily crosses borders. Equally pithy, Joey Shithead's maxim has always been "Talk – Action = 0." This propelled the band to release multiple benefit singles and lend songs to benefit record causes, including the Direct Action political prisoners known as the Vancouver 5 ("Right to Be Wild"); mass strike action in Canada ("General Strike"); evictions in the wake of Expo 86 hosted by Vancouver, also highlighted at a live gig in Vancouver featuring an acoustic D.O.A. with legendary Pete Seeger and Arlo Guthrie (*Expo Hurts Everyone* featured "Billy and the Socreds"); the preservation of old-growth forests in Clayoquot Sound ("The Only Thing Green"); a memorial to deceased D.O.A.

drummer Ken Jensen (the *Ken Jensen Memorial Single* featured "Knots"); and the decriminalization of marijuana (the *Cannabis Canada* split single featured "Marijuana Motherfucker"). They played innumerable benefit gigs as well, most notably putting aside punk elitism to join the likes of mainstream heroes Bachman Turner Overdrive and Bryan Adams to support Environmental Watch, which fought paper industry degradation of the ecosystem.

UNDEAD LEGACIES

At the helm of D.O.A. since 1978, Shithead—who told a fan at a recent stop in Houston that he wished to be even 10 percent as effective and productive as recently deceased folk activist Pete Seeger—exercises a hybrid style of populist protest music. "Early punk was the heir to folk music as was early hip hop. They all tried to say something about society and the 'human condition,'" Shithead explained to me in 2015. D.O.A.'s style, a meld of cross-fertilized punk, reggae, ska, and classic rock (their acute choice of covers have included "War," "The Midnight Special," "Eve of Destruction," and "Fortunate Son"), seems tethered to working-class toughness or resolve while also incorporating "green" environmental issues simultaneously. In doing so, they balance rowdy sportsmanship, punk savagery, "real Canadian hockey rock," aggressive politics, and worldly wisdom that deplores both corporate madness and indifferent public attitudes.

During a four-decade-long career, the band has used royalties from albums and songs like "Dwanga" to aid causes around the world, including the African National Congress, and has played more than two hundred benefit gigs, including concerts supporting El Salvador's Radio Farabundo Marti, OXFAM (which provided money for an ambulance in Soweto, South Africa), Expo 86 evictees (raising $10,000 alongside Pete Seeger), preservation of the Stein Wilderness in British Columbia, Rock against Radiation, anarchist prisoners the Vancouver 5 and K. Omori, the British Columbia Solidarity Coalition strike, *Overthrow* magazine, fair-trade efforts, Refuse and Resist, the striking White Spot workers, the Qualicum and Parksville Youth Centers, End the Arms Race, and myriad others.

At the helm, Shithead has always stared down power and culled the hefty history of leftism, right up to the Occupy movement (at a concert in Houston, Shithead wore a tee shirt and patch emblazoned with "D.O.A. We Occupy" on his torn jeans). "Occupy opened up [the] debate. It could not sustain itself as a movement," he insists, "but it has done its job. It all boils down to the same thing, education equals empowerment, and that brings all fortunes up together, not just a few. There will always be wealthy people, let's just level the playing field a bit. One issue I will try to promote over the next number of years is cooperatives, where people have a chance at partial ownership of where they work. People work a lot harder when they have a stake in something, but let's stress [that] this is something that you would have to bust your ass for—it will never be a gift—but people can better themselves and their families with hard work and a little entrepreneurship" (2015). In such pointed cases, Shithead doesn't seem to favor dismantling capitalism but forging alliances and networks to create voluntary, self-organizing, and sustainable fair-wage partnerships that offer a just reward to workers—human-scaled capitalism rather than a corporatized liberal laissez-faire system.

"Real Records, the record store owned by partners Ronnie Bond [singer of Really Red] and Jim Crane, was key in connecting all sorts of indie bands to Houston clubs in the early 1980s," drummer Bob Weber of Really Red recalls. "Ronnie got calls and letters from everywhere asking where to play and who to talk to. So, as a consequence, Ronnie had names and phone numbers for the bands, clubs, and promoters that were valuable in booking cross-country tours for Really Red, Mydolls, and other local acts. Joey Shithead would set up a date in Vancouver for D.O.A. and Really Red to do a show together. Then when they came to Texas, Ronnie would book a show for the bands here. It was collaboration.

"D.O.A. was coming this way right after a Really Red West Coast tour in 1982. I have a leaflet from a show in Dallas on Friday November 12 for D.O.A., Really Red, and the Hugh Beaumont Experience playing the infamous Studio D. And another a couple days later on Sunday the 14th for D.O.A., Marching Plague, Really Red, and the Mystery Dates at Villa Fontana in Downtown San Antonio 'under the tower.' We bitched about Houston being remote from a lot of scenes, which made it hard to get exposure outside of Texas. Well, D.O.A. had a similar challenge being from Vancouver, Canada, but they seemed to get out on the road more than we did. I asked how they got away from work. Dave said they worked long hours on fishing boats that went offshore for days or weeks and came back loaded with tons of tuna in the hold. They got paid well and couldn't spend it, so they stashed it. That way they could take off for months to do D.O.A. tours across Canada and the United States.

"D.O.A. and Really Red traveled together for a few shows one year, probably 1982. When we got to the mountains—maybe it was the Continental Divide—there was lots of snow and we were road weary, so we got out to cool off. Before you knew it, we were in a big snowball fight, the Canadians against the Texans. I guess Ronnie was in the middle because he always claimed dual citizenship. A few of us switched vans to see if the D.O.A. van smelled fishier than Really Red's van. It did. The D.O.A. guys were surprised to hear Carlene Carter in the tape player. They didn't realize that we listened to everything from the Red Crayola to Soft Machine to Throbbing Gristle and homemade shit like the Hugh Beaumont Experience. We had a huge cardboard box of cassette tapes sitting on top of the cooler between the front seats" (Weber 2014). Though politics might be the backbone of bands like D.O.A., they were still road warriors, and music was their currency shared in the informal punk networks dotting the landscape.

As of late 2015, Shithead was putting more punk praxis into action by running in a by-election in the provincial electoral district of Coquitlam-Burke Mountain for MLA (member of the Legislative Assembly) for the BC Green Party in the Legislative Assembly of British Columbia. An e-mail he sent to potential supporters outlined his platform: "In D.O.A. I have always been an informal politician, so now I am taking the plunge into formal politics. Here's what I will fight for: affordable tuition; real democracy—elected Greens vote for the people and not just the party line; lower cost for day care; protection of our environment; help for our most vulnerable citizens; job growth through green technology" (Ensminger 2015). His Gofundme campaign was even more specific: "I will fight for $15 minimum wage, free tuition for post-secondary education, and good jobs through green technology. I will also work to stop bitumen oil pipelines from running through BC and to get the 1 percent to finally start paying their fair share." In all, Shithead represents a continuum of punk's conscience that stretches from the first wave to the here-now battles.

Longtimers like T.S.O.L. might be construed, ideologically speaking, as a left-to-libertarian axis band due to lyrics like "abolish the government" and "property is theft." Singer Jack Grisham, who enjoys subverting people's fear, prejudices, and misjudgments, explained to me in 2012, "I try to deal with underlying conditions, not players. Freedom comes at a price. 9/11 unified America like Pearl Harbor, but we surrendered some freedoms. We need responsibility and discipline to achieve ideals, but there is no quick goal or plan. Like Martin Luther King said, 'We now have guided missiles and misguided men.'" T.S.O.L. acts not like teeth-bared soapbox orators denouncing disquieting times these days but also reminds listeners that conscience *and* liberty need to be guarded and guaranteed. Even its recent record releases embody such a mission. For instance, *Life, Liberty and the Pursuit of Free Downloads* might have been offered free through the website of clothing company Hurley, but the band encouraged fans to donate money that they would have been spent on a such an album to help fund not-for-profit organizations Midnight Mission, Surfrider, Orangewood Foundation, Orange County Food Bank, and others. Hence, the band offered listeners the liberty of free access to music while simultaneously encouraging a call to action.

In late 2013, Mike Magrann, singer and guitarist for Channel 3, informed me that their band navigates similar lyrical intentions: "We like to deal with the politics of the individual, and 'Truth and Trust' is just another song about the individual's confusion. I would think it is just a little too easy to say, 'I'm a punk therefore I'm liberal left at the least, fuck the government, blah blah.' That sort of immediate reaction without thought is as bad as the Tea Party Republicans. . . . Most people shouting the loudest don't really look into the issues before spouting off. Of course, I would like to think the punk political ethos would always be liberal and for the individual vs. the powers that be, but it just doesn't boil down to such easy answers" (Magrann 2013). At times, punk seemed to reduce politics into pathos alone, but the steadfast nature of D.O.A., T.S.O.L., Anti-Flag, and NOFX, all of whom still play gigs and make fresh music, prove the long-term vision, insight, and adaptability of punk veterans. What seemed no more than truncated screams from the gutter has remained a persevering outsider sensibility that has not retreated.

2

KNOW YOUR ENEMY

J. J., a fan of and columnist for *British Columbia's Blackout*, described the essential enemy of punk as multifold and varied—that which "stands in the way of freedom," everyone from the communists, capitalists, police, and fascists to "new age liberals" and "hardcore straights." His remedy: "Investigate, feel the spirit," especially the voice of punk, which had become "the only autonomous revolutionary expression today of people too young to have consciously participated in the struggles of the late sixties and early seventies" (Say 1978, 3). Punk's discourse continues to ripple with candid and ongoing references to war and violence, unemployment and poverty, pain and dissatisfaction, anarchistic allusions and associations, and alienation and taunts. Each punk wave survives the crash of new generational changes and shifting vantage points. Even bands like the Ramones shifted from referencing B-movie-style teen angst on their first few albums to examining the blunders of Ronald Reagan's presidency on the tune "Bonzo Goes to Bitburg" from 1986, written during the ascendancy of more militant hardcore and competing for attention with the likes of *Smoke Signals* by M.D.C. and *Bedtime for Democracy* by Dead Kennedys that same year. So even during the first decade of the Ramones' career, their social context greatly changed. "The world is a different place now. . . . Now things are heavier," Joey Ramone told Jim Farber. "All you hear about is Stars Wars since Reagan's taken office. The world nowadays is a scary place, so our stance is more serious" (1986, 17).

For writers like Daniel Traber, punk's self-marginalization seemed revelatory, for it articulated a "politics of dissent" that spoke to the core, in his study, of the Los Angeles punk scene: "To resist meta-narratives they found static and repressive, in order to form an independent sense of self, a small fringe of youth pursued a life based on that inner-city underclass denied access to the American dream, an identity," which he terms the "sub-urban" (2001, 30–31). Traber's sense of politics was not rooted in the roles of readily identifiable political strains: "Punk may best be understood in terms of a Foucauldian micropolitics: the localized effect of crossing boundaries contains the potential to spread" (2001, 56). Punks projected personas and practices based on a kind of mimicry of those they felt were authentic outsiders, like blacks, Hispanics, and others, which disturbed and perturbed the powers that be in their lives, thus loosening and fragmenting the restrictive web of their interpersonal narratives.

Still, punk did seem to have a politics flexibly rooted like a ductile anchor in some ideological affiliations, though allusions and references to nihilism and leftism in general throughout punk's trajectory have often clouded punk participants' actual hands-on work in communities struggling with issues from homelessness and hunger to medical needs and animal welfare. In effect, punk's ethos may be more closely tied to humanitarian aims and worldviews—the DNA of punk conscience often realized in close-to-the-ground efforts—rather than simply as endless rhetorical tropes reeking of chaos and dystopia.

Granted, punk was not always strictly oriented to the left, although punk fanzine columnists like Lefty Hooligan of *Maximum Rocknroll* regularly covered such fare, including the struggles of French labor unions publicly striking during the mid-1990s; the role of publications like *Labor Notes*; and steps toward forming a new labor party, all while exploring various strains of left philosophy, including vanguardist and social democratic traditions. Bass player Jason Useless of the band the Volatiles, who also penned columns for the same zine, discussed the dilemmas facing unions, too, especially their lack of a guarantee to organize in America, in contrast with their Canadian comrades. Useless advocated using "a simple, automatic authorization card system," rather than "political and/or armed solutions" to let workers decide upon union participation. This approach, he argues, is much more fair than employers hounding them by delaying elections and committing illegal acts—firing employees seeking union representation—which often break "even the most discontented worker's spirit" (1996).

In broad terms, other punks seemed like fellow travelers. Andy Gill of Gang of Four attests, "We were sympathetic to the SWP [Socialist Workers Party], we had done some benefits, but we didn't make our own approach in those broad political terms. It was more to do with living in a late capitalist society" (Savage 1996). The band members were not stout party loyalists but loosely concerned with the effects and pitfalls of a shared economic system. "Many punk rock bands distorted and twisted politics into simplistic empty slogans, and disappointingly, much of the music devolved into neofascism," argues D'Ambrosio, recognizing that punk's vehemence was essentially a strategy and vehicle that could be steered by a diverse political spectrum.

Punk's perceived right-wing indulgences have long been the concern of critics evaluating its shock tactics and rhetoric: as early as 1978, Dave Laing argued "both progressive and reactionary elements appear in the work of the same musician, sometimes in the same song," which reveal the "contradictory aspects" of punk rock (1978, 123). He does, however, acknowledge that the National Front despised Johnny Rotten, who despised the "ridiculously inhumane" policies of the National Front (Manzoor 2008), plus Laing singles out the "God Save the Queen" media fanfare as "the most effective political intervention of a song since the 'protest' era" (Laing 1978, 124). Hence, it was far more than a piece of vinyl; it was a cultural standoff.

Malcolm McLaren himself insisted the silk-screened image of the Queen remade in flat Andy Warhol style with a strategic safety pin placed in her nose was a way to "authenticate our beliefs, move away from American culture, resist . . . vacuous, gilded Hollywood . . . and fight it and come up with a culture of our own. That was punk rock" (Adams 2008, 471). And actually quite Warholian, for McLaren, too, symbolized "the demystification of art through appropriation," according to Paul Taylor of the New Museum (Gross 1988, 28). Hence, the rebellion actually shored up a sense of cultural identity of Englishness and the modes of Warhol, rather than undermining either, although the art attacked "a particular version of English nationalism, the monarchical, jingoistic, xenophobic sense of superiority" widely felt in consensus-dominated Britain (Adams 2008, 474). Hence, the song, based in the often common-as-mud vernacular of punk dramatizing the decline of

Britain (and by extension, America), was a counterculturally sanctioned rallying cry to wake and seize one's fate from the overweening forces of the complacent and dismissive establishment status quo (Adams 2008, 477).

Laing also understood "Oh Bondage Up Yours!" by X Ray Spex as "an attack on social bondage" that also "jolts" audiences, making them aware of their own "position in the leisure apparatus" (1978, 126–27). So although he seems to laud punk's potent potential to at least distress the capitalism's systemic framework momentarily, he offers no evidence of its reactionary or right-wing biases or tendencies. The dialectic seems to be missing one side. Looking back, writers in 2014 like John Spong singled out "God Save the Queen" as a blistering song declaring the "prim monarch" as "fascist and inhumane." Hence, for forty years, he notes, most writers agree the band's most pivotal songs remain acerbic "embodiments of underclass unrest" (Spong 2014).

CLASS WAR ON 45

What some in the press disregard as right-wing, reactionary, chrome-dome skinhead factions in punk might actually embody a different set of ideologies altogether, as Oi enthusiast Garry Bushell purports. "We'd been talking strike benefits, not National Front marches. No Oi! Band had sported swastikas, as the Sex Pistols had done" (Bushell, "Carry on Oi!," 1981). Support for such causes has not waned in the intervening years. In 1979, Angelic Upstarts, led by former apprentice miner Mensi (Thomas Mensforth), whose song "King Coal" narrates the woe and solidarity felt in "Satan's hole," played a benefit gig for *Guttersnipe* fanzine at a time when the band earned £25 per week, less than the unemployment rate of £27.50, as reported by *Red Star73* fanzine online (Bushell "Angelic Upstarts," 2006). Even as late of 2006, Mensi still asked "for a truly socialist government," telling the interviewer his unbreakable belief was that people should "1. Join a Trade Union. 2. Vote Labour. 3. Never Trust a Tory" (Bushell "Angelic Upstarts," 2006). As part of the class-cultural lens of the Oi! genre lauded by Gary Bushell of *Sounds*, Angelic Upstart's cockney-inflected, overly proletariat, and populist short and sharp sing-along tunes contained confluences of "youth cultural antagonisms, work (or the lack of it), football violence, petty crime, police harassment, and suspicion of authority in all its forms" (Worley 2013). Bushell lauded Oi! because it stemmed from a readily identifiable landscape in which people "lived and worked," which distanced the genre from less-than-shocking colored hair, trendy Mohawks, and decaying false promises of retro-minded punk, which seemed "formulaic, ghettoized, and fatalistic music" by the mid-1980s (Worley 2013).

Mensi, having first been attacked by the Young National Front in 1978 and by no means a supporter of neofascism, does regret not addressing right-wing elements more decisively. As the fanzine *Red Star73* tells, he backed down from vocalizing his concerns aggressively in lyrics until right-wing fans mustered too many threats and violence. His pro–working class, pro-tolerance sentiment held firm over subsequent decades. In 2002, Angelic Upstarts played an Anti-Fascist Action (also supported by the Welsh punk band The Oppressed) benefit gig in Ireland with Runnin' Riot (Angelic Upstart also played another at the Bolton Labour Club in 2005), and in 2005, the band played a gig supporting the left-wing IWCA (Independent Working Class Association) and Release at the Dome Tufnell Park. Since 1967, Release, as advocated on its website, has believed "in a just and fair society where drug policies should reduce the harms associated with drugs, and where those who use drugs are treated based on principles of human rights, dignity, and equality" (www.release.org.uk). Still, bands like the Angelic Upstarts, which in 1982 slagged the Meat Puppets for playing a Rolling Stones cover, are more known for their "pro-active defensive" stance—sniffing out fascists prior to gigs in order to sideline right-wing plans of disruption—hence, roadies were prized more for their fisticuff potential than their ability to string guitars (Spence 2013). For instance, Pete Frame remembers the Catacombs club in Willenhal being such a contested space: "There wasn't a glass or neon tube left in the place after the Angelic Upstarts took on some local fascist thugs" (1999, 197). The power of the band was not limited to power chords, as critics are apt to argue.

Trade unions have often been lyrical terrain or part of the social consciousness of multitudinous punk bands like Red London; Test Department, which invited a miner's brass band to join them on tour; Redskins, notable for such gigs as its Rock 'n' Roll against the Dole benefit for the Birmingham Unemployed Workers Association; and

D.O.A., including its benefit seven-inch single, "General Strike." Others include The Dils, which played the miner's benefit New Wave against Black Lung documented in the film *Louder, Faster, Shorter*, at Mabuhay Gardens in 1978, a two-day event organized by Howie Klein and Tony Kinman (bass player/singer for the Dils), featuring fourteen bands inspired by the likes of Joe Strummer, as well as a benefit for striking Norfolk & Western Railway Workers, and Newtown Neurotics/ Neurotics, which played a Socialist Worker miner's support gig in front of a poster reading "Stop Apartheid Terror: Black Workers to Power" and received death threats from the British Movement, as did Gary Bushell (Hahn 2006).

The zine *Wake Up* (n.d.) chronicled The Neurotics' groundbreaking tour of communist East Germany, in which Attila the Stockbroker and Billy Bragg (often concluding with raucous joint versions of "Garageland" by the Clash) joined them. Their live performances were documented on vinyl, which came with the fanzine, whose sales proceeds supported a miner's support group. Recorded in East Berlin, such live tracks as a cover of Ben E. King's "Stand by Me," the band, with "slight yet deft lyrical dexterity," converted key lines to "As husband and wives join together on the picket lines / Darling won't you come and stand by me," the zine attests. The band also modified "Shake Some Action" by the Flamin' Groovies to become "Take Strike Action" in Dresden, later releasing a recorded version on its album *Kickstarting a Backfiring Nation*. Years later, Billy Bragg would record with Wilco a rollicking version of "I Guess I Planted," a Woody Guthrie tune about union battles inspired by the strike of maritime laborers.

The staff at *Wake Up*—active supporters of Direct Action against Apartheid, Anti-Fascist Action, Nicaragua Solidarity Campaign, and the State Capitalism Forum—viewed bands like the Neurotics and Housemartins as the vanguard of social consciousness in pop music. From its vantage point, the connections between the oppression of miners in the United Kingdom, the harms of nuclear energy, and the exploitation of miners in Africa were self-evident. Closing local mines meant propping up slave-based South African ones, whose dirty energy was then imported as cheap product back to the United Kingdom, while uranium mining, backed by Western powers and a crucial component for U.S. cruise missiles used in Cold War deterrence, "rape[d] Namibia" (*Wake

Up n.d.). Hence, the period between 1984 and 1985 became a fulcrum of intersecting global concern.

But Joe Strummer also came to the aid of miners as well, most notably gigging with Latino Rockabilly War (a covers-heavy outfit with Zander Schloss of the Circle Jerks) as part of the Class War "Rock against the Rich" tour, which took place during an era in which he also gigged for Amnesty International. This support for the radical direct-action group raised some disparaging eyebrows as "a misjudged romantic gesture" (Gray 2010, 447), but key facts remain: he played for such organizations as the Brodsworth Miners Welfare, which benefited unemployed miners, earning Strummer a Hatfield NUM [National Union of Mineworkers] badge, which he regularly wore. "It was gonna be the 'White Riot' tour all over again—with the added malevolence of Class War behind it," Darren Ryan states in a memoir about the tour. "We presented the idea to Strummer that it was going to make his return to his Clash roots—back to Garage land—back to the streets. I think that he thought he would get some kind of political street cred from associating with us. The reason he thought that was because we concocted an incredible scenario for a tour for him; each gig was to be based around a local issue of class warfare. . . . Do a benefit for Red or Green Wedge and you were comfortably hip and acceptable. Do it for Class War and you were an outrage. We were very comfortable with this. As far as we were concerned, the left were every bit as bad as the right, politically and culturally. [Strummer] was sick of being surrounded by sycophantic wankers that were nothing more than rock 'n' roll trainspotters. To him this was real" (Ryan 2015).

Even Williams S. Burroughs, avant-garde Beat Generation writer and proto-punk guru to the likes of Patti Smith and Kathy Acker, understood the importance of unions to modern music. "I'm always asking rock 'n' roll people if they know who Petrillo is, and none of them do. Well, they wouldn't make a dime if it weren't for Petrillo, because he organized the musician's union way back at the end of the '30s. And that is why they make money on their records" (Morgan 1979, 22). On that note, the release of Blondie's *Eat to the Beat* videocassette, an entire video conceptual album, was delayed by such union business after the American Federation of Musicians (AFM) attempted to negotiate a 5-percent rate on the novel format debuting at a more expensive consumer cost than LPs, which garnered musicians only 1 percent of the list price, *Rolling Stone* reported in 1980 ("Union Dispute Delays Blondie Videocassette" 1980, 28).

The Redskins (whose previous incarnation was called No Swastikas), a skinhead band still idolized by red/left-wing skinheads, entered the top-40 English charts with its husky vocals and dexterous, danceable "Motown-meets-1977 punk" hybrid: half were adamant members of the Socialist Workers Party who helped to sell the party's periodical and collect money at gigs for striking workers, who wrote such defiant pro-labor tunes as "Unionise," and who were "the most politically oriented musical act since Paul Robeson," according to *New Music Express* writer Steven Wells (1985). Wells (also known as Seething Wells and Susan Williams) was a long-time punk writer, video director, and poet associated with acts like the Mekons, who publicly denounced the right-wing sympathies of the singers of Warzone and Slayer in *Maximum Rocknroll* while insisting American readers "learn your history." In 1987, he believed the only "real agent of change in society" was the working class, which in the United States might be mimicked by punks "building an alternative culture" that could go beyond "challenging and stimulating spit in the face of authority" (Wells 1987). Even though punk music in 1977 catapulted the youth of England into a culture of their own creation that they could control, it was "still pissing in the wind" compared to the amount of social transformation needed. "Go get organized," he pleaded (Wells 1987).

Redskins gigs held during the miner's strike in 1984 and 1985 acted as a network of stalls for miner support groups, Women Against Pit closures, the Labour Party, and the Socialist Workers Party. Despite the band admitting that it represented "abstract propaganda," it did seize and subvert the image/trope of skinhead iconography, a lasting victory: "The one important thing is we have stolen their symbol, we use up their symbol, their strongest symbol of cropped young men with big boots that are violent," tells Paul Hookham, short-lived drummer for the band. "By being a skinhead band, being left-wing, you diffused, you diluted the strength of their one bonding sort of image. Even if we have not won any converts from the National Front type of skinhead at least we have done one thing and that's robbing off the potency of their symbol" (Kowalski 2014).

For years, bands gigged at labor halls, both active—like the UA Plumbers and Pipefitters 469 hall in Phoenix, Arizona, which hosted gigs by Bad Religion, and the United Food and Commercial Workers hall in Goleta, California, featuring gigs by the likes of Lync and Phooey—and inactive—like W.O.W. Hall in Eugene, Oregon, a former Woodmen of the World lodge. In Vancouver, punk bands ranging from locals like the Modernettes and Death Sentence to touring bands like Black Flag and Alien Sex Fiend gigged at the Waterfront, situated below "Bows and Arrows," the hall of the Local 38-57 International Longshoremen's Association, headquarters of a 1935 docker's strike in which nine hundred dockers were locked out, many of whom were attacked at the "Battle of Ballantyne Pier." Years later, shows took place in other Canadian labor-affiliated community centers, such as the Carpenter's Union Hall in Calgary, which hosted shows with Sparkmarker, Crash 13, D.B.S., Falling Sickness, What Remains, and others.

Other gigs routinely took place in granges across America, including Eugene, Oregon (Irving Grange); Danville, California (Danville Grange Hall); and Olympia, Washington (Black Lake Grange Hall). At the Grange Hall of San Bernardino, California, touring bands like Agnostic Front joined acts like Infest, Visual Discrimination, and Offspring, and regional showcases featured Pillsbury Hardcore, Liberation Crutch, Malicious Intent, Civil Defense, Reason to Believe, Side Effects, CRX, P.O.W., Pitchfork, Walk Proud, SDI, STC, Apathy, Twisted, and others. Granges are both fraternal organizations and advocacy groups focused on rural American sociocultural, political, and economic needs. Krist Novoselic—a former member of Nirvana, Sweet 75, Flipper, and Eyes Adrift—is "master" of Grays River Grange No. 124 in Wahkiakum County. The historical struggles of the organization have included fending off railroad cartels, supporting free rural mail delivery, temperance, direct election of senators, women's suffrage, food banks, immigration, and much more.

By no means were granges free of law enforcement pressure and suppression. In Hesperia, California, the police targeted a show featuring Pillsbury Hardcore, Ice-9, 13 Stitches, and C.U.R.S.E. A flyer distributed with phrases like "B.Y.O.B." and "all ages" catalyzed the sheriff department's attention, which became concerned about potential overcapacity issues, proper licensing, and lax security measures. According to Captain Michael O'Rourke, who found the moment ripe for hyperbole in the local paper coverage, the forced cancellation "averted a disaster in the making" (Snyder 1987).

"I approached the Hesperia Grange Hall in order to put on a show with my band, C.U.R.S.E. and Pillsbury Hardcore," tells veteran punk Greg McWhorter, who has played in bands since 1983 as a member of Signal 30, which shook Plano, Texas. "When I approached the manager of the hall, they seemed eager to get my business and didn't seem to mind in the least that I was putting on a 'rock show' with several bands. I probably didn't use the label 'punk,' but I made no secret that rock bands would be playing and they told me that bands had rented it out before so no problem. I left my deposit and proceeded to book the bands and flyer the High Desert. I printed up somewhere between 400 and 500 copies of the flyer. The original flyer didn't have N.M.D. (Nude Male Dancers from Hesperia), but they were added to subsequent flyers that were printed. I had contacts with punks at all high schools in the area, and we left about 150 flyers at Victor Valley High School, Apple Valley High School, Hesperia High School, and even at a few local record stores.

"My flyer campaign was too successful. Somehow the Victor Valley Sheriff's Department contacted me at school on the same day that the show was supposed to happen. They told me that I needed to report to the Sheriff's Department right away. I went and they told me that the Hesperia Grange Hall was canceling my show at their insistence. They told me that they didn't want the punk element in the High Desert and tried to scare me that I would have been liable for all damage, injury, and a potential riot that the sheriffs felt would happen if the show went on. They handed my deposit back and sent me away. The nice people from the Grange didn't even have the nerve to face me or return my calls. They let the police do their talking for them.

"I was devastated. The show was supposed to happen that night, so I rushed home and called all of the bands and my friends and told everyone to spread the word that the show was off. That night I was so upset I decided to drive over to the grange just to see if anyone showed up, so I could apologize and tell them it was off. When I drove up to the hall, there were several police cars around it and a lot of punk kids driving by. They were being told to leave the area. I was surprised to see so many cars loaded with punks driving around it, and I wanted to talk to them, but I was told to leave the area too or I would be arrested. Since the show was off, I gave up and went home to get drunk. I didn't book multi-band shows again until I started booking at Spanky's Café in

Riverside and Munchie's in Pomona during the 1990s" (McWhorter 2015).

In Washington state, granges attracted "a smorgasbord of conservatives and socialists, Christians and free-thinkers. . . . Farmers formed alliances with organized labor. The Grange was instrumental in the fight for an initiative and referendum amendment . . . and the formation of public utility districts" ("Krist Novoselic" n.d.). Such longstanding civic service to the community, plus a resonant history, attracted punks like Novoselic, who considers himself a lowercase democrat; who in 1992 formed the Joint Artists & Music Promotions Political Action Committee, a free speech effort; who has campaigned for Instant Runoff Voting for years; and who penned the book *Of Grunge and Government—Let's Fix This Broken Democracy!* in 2004.

The politico-labor consciousness has continued with contemporary bands, such as Street Dogs ("Up the Union," "Unions and the Law"), whose singer Mike McColgan covered "There's Power in a Union" by Billy Bragg (not the version of IWW songster Joe Hill) for a 2012 "Get Out the Vote" rally. Tim McIlrath of Rise Against also took the stage with McColgan to sing "Ohio" by Neil Young, in Madison, Wisconsin, under the banner "Reclaim Wisconsin." Bragg himself sang the song at a late-summer 2014 benefit gig at the Royale tavern in south St. Louis to raise funds for the Food Pantry at St. Stephen's Episcopal Church, serving families deeply affected by Ferguson, Missouri, riots over the death of an unarmed black man at the hands of local police. He delved into his own catalog, plus covers of Woody Guthrie, George Perkins, and Bob Dylan. He also discussed issues with striking railway workers in Galesburg, Illinois, sang with teachers at a nearby picket line, and gigged at the Iowa State Penitentiary as part of Jail Guitar Doors, an organization he cofounded with ex-prisoner Wayne Kramer of the MC5 (Durchholz 2014). "We find people who work in corrections that are willing to use music as a tool for rehabilitation, and we provide them with guitars," Kramer told *Razorcake* (Proctor 2014). By supporting partners in reentry programs and setting up opportunities in key locales like Chicago, Austin, Philadelphia, and Los Angeles, such measures amount to a transgenerational effort to help reform a small sliver of the prison-industrial complex and offset the suffering resulting from the war on drugs. "It's an abject failure and the human cost is incalculable. Ten million Americans under direct state control . . . wrenched out of the mainstream of American life . . . a crime against humanity," Kramer insists (Proctor 2014, 73).

Other bands, such as the Strike, the Flying Folk Army, and Dropkick Murphys, ardently supported labor causes. In 2010, Dropkick Murphys released a video titled "Tomorrow's Industries," with actual caregivers playing their own roles, as an official sign of solidarity with the Local 1199 branch of the Service Employees International Union. They released the "Take 'Em Down" single in support of Wisconsin unions and supporters, with tee-shirt sales benefiting the Worker's Rights Emergency Response Fund in 2011. In 2013, they visited Ohio with a similar intent—to bolster union sympathies, especially appreciated by the likes of the International Association of Machinists and Aerospace Workers, who documented the visit on their official website. The single remaining original member of Dropkick Murphys, Ken Casey, intones, "Unions are often seen as villains, and if you look at what happened in Wisconsin in 2011, the rich people in control successfully pitted the workers against each other. The union workers were making $4 an hour more than the non-union workers were, and instead of the non-union members asking, 'How do I get that extra $4?' they were saying, 'I can do the same job as the union guys for $4 less per hour.' It's tough for unions now, but bands like ours, who speak out through our lyrics, try to point out a side of the story that many people aren't getting to hear on the news or reading in the papers" (Dearmore 2013).

"In the early 1990s, I left my parents' house and moved north from Rockford, Illinois, to Minneapolis with two of my best friends Ted and Joe," says Tad Keyes, show promoter, singer, and graphic artist. "It was refreshing to be around the rich scene of anarcho-punk bands, zines, and bookshops in the Twin Cities. I was a fan of the *Profane Existence* zine and record label and respected political punk bands like Destroy and Misery, but by then our crew were punks who didn't dress particularly punk, and our politics were a little less overt. We soon met others like us who were motivated by the more real-world issues of our lives.

"Bands emerged that were more tuneful but still very punk with a hint of hardcore and pop," Keyes recalls, "and it was exactly what I wanted to listen to. The Strike, Dillinger Four, and Man Afraid also had the politics to educate and show me where political ideology is really put into action. They presented the struggle as a class struggle, not a dystopian fantasy or existential malaise. These people had an understanding of the Spanish Civil War, the Minneapolis Bus Strike, and could write amazing songs! I have lived in Los Angeles for almost twenty years and have worked as a graphic designer for a labor union for fifteen years. I came into the union with Joe and Ted, the same two guys I moved to Minneapolis twenty-four years ago. Working for the union is my dream job. I work with people I respect, I feel useful, I feel fulfilled, I feel challenged, and I feel like I didn't have to sell out to earn a living.

"Plenty of punks end up working for unions and it makes sense: you get paid to be a bit of a troublemaker. Everyday I put the skills learned from years of DIY punk into action—I feel like I am just doing another version of what I did for all those years of putting on shows, making flyers, writing zines, and forming bands," he asserts. "For me, punk was most interesting at the fulcrum of intellectual ideas and working class ideals. The labor movement is another intersection of ideas and action—where ideology meets work" (Keyes 2015).

Likeminded stalwart community organizers Positive Force D.C. felt the pull of these issues as well. In November 2011, it hosted Ted Leo (of Chisel and Citizen's Arrest) and the Pharmacists for a "benefit concert for immigrant rights, union organizing, and community-building," their digital flyer announced. In related efforts, some art-punks lent their work to labor organizations, like illustrator Cristy C. Road, who grew up in the multicultural Miami punk scene of the early 1990s and later sold works to *Bitch* and *BUST* but donated others to INCITE! Women of Color Against Violence, and the Coalition of Immokalee Workers, a human rights coalition founded in the worker-based tradition, which continues to focus on social responsibility, efforts against human trafficking, and gender issues in employment sectors.

During the late 1980s, punk–labor relations were nuanced and complex in places dusting off years of anemic state autocracy and emerging from the Soviet/Eastern Bloc system, including Poland, where state radio played Sex Pistols ("Pretty Vacant") and New Model Army ("51st State"). Homegrown punk bands like Maanam, Dezerter, Trybuna Brudu, U.O.M., Kasaya, and Brygada Kryzys thrived despite circumstances. International punk bands like No Means No (Canada), UK Subs (United Kingdom), Instigators (United Kingdom), False Prophets (United States), the Brigade (France; "No Communists in the Kremlin" was popular at the University of Wroclaw), and Soul Side (United States) gigged in the country as it experienced a social, political, and cultural thaw.

"We all grew up in Washington, D.C., so we were all exposed to images of Lech Walesa and the demonstrations that were going on," described Bobby Sullivan from Soul Side, who sang there six months before the Berlin Wall fell. "It was something America supported so it was very present in our media. The music scene we were part of in D.C. was very politically aware with many collective discussions on any issues at hand. Once we got there, our eyes were wide open the whole time. All the Communist imagery on the streets and the difference in architecture were new to us. But the spirit in the underground scene there in Poland was similar to what was going on in the United States," (Kozielski 2011). Although most Westerners like Sullivan believed the Solidarność (Solidarity) trade union movement was a liberating force instigating positive change, not all Poles held the same high opinion.

Some decried Lech Walesa's movement as another form of "greedy power," decried "independent trade unions support[ing] communist party way of thinking," and leaned more in line with WiP (peace and freedom movement) and the Inter-City Anarchist Group, a national collective of agitators (Marczynski n.d.). Sullivan seemed to recognize this restlessness: "I suppose the subsequent rip-off by the IMF was apparent on the street and especially to those who were expecting worker ownership, a goal of the Solidarity movement. The punks, of course, with their DIY movement weren't fooled. The ones we talked to could see, even in the early stages, that there was a huge difference between democracy and capitalism" (Kozielski 2011).

Other bands mined a similar vein of discontent with Solidarity as well, including Kolaborancji. "We deal with the daily fear, which still exists though the government is now run by Solidarity," they told a *Maximum Rocknroll* reporter (Dussutour 1990). Even though rock 'n' roll performers held benefits to help Solidarity, punks were wary—their bullshit detector was highly attuned to the pitfalls of switching from one autocratic government to another, and they were aware of the sometimes tenuous and fissured solidarity between workers and punks. "Poland is a so-called workers state, but workers just think about their working conditions. They aren't too open-minded, don't think we have anything in common. They have this kind of pride that makes them think that pun[ks] are stupid, are drug addicts. . . . There is no communication between them and us" (Dussutour 1990). Years later, Poland attracted American punk activists like Richard Kramer, former punk entrepreneur behind Lumberjack Distribution, who began to teach human rights and refugee law in Krakow by 1998, which he announced in *HeartattaCk* (Kramer 1998).

Other punks have immersed in labor activism on an individual basis—like *HeartattaCk* columnist Helen Luu, who participated in activists groups Food Not Bombs and Students against Sweatshops—but have bemoaned their mostly "overwhelmingly white" cadres. Only after joining efforts to aid groups like a local Windsor, Canada, union attempting to organize the workers for a large Toronto paper and then becoming involved with the Movement for Justice in London, England, where people of color were an integral part of the discussions and outreach, Luu discovered a much broader multiracial, grassroots, and antiglobalization base that appealed to people beyond the punk crowd. Still others, like Eric XXX at *HeartattaCk*, favored radical unionist cultural heroes like Phil Melman, soapbox orator for the International Workers of the World, who spent decades spreading the word, even while living nearly penniless at a flophouse.

Others, most famously Chelsea ("Right to Work"), Propagandhi (who make a metaphor of fat "union bureaucrats" in the tune "Gamble"), and the Avengers ("Open Your Eyes"), have been more ambivalent when examining the nature of unions. Virus X, a noted politically minded drummer for Articles of Faith, penned a letter to the editors of *Flipside*, declaring, "I happen to be a Revolutionary Communist musician . . . revolution being a very important first step in destroying the political/economic/social relations that maintain the present degrading and oppressive state of human existence. . . . You've decided to announce to us your discovery that music won't change the world. No shit Sherlock. Even less will doing 'union work' for that matter" (1983). Still, the Avengers did join the New Wave against Black Lung effort aiding miners, and singer Penelope Houston placed a solo folk track on the *Devouring Our Roots* benefit album for Food Not Bombs in 1990, a disc partly honoring United Farm Worker organizer Dolores Huerta, who was beaten by police. The organization attempted to give away free food until a 1989 San Francisco court order banned it from doing so without proper licensing, leading to the 1994 conviction of Robert Kahn, even after the group obtained said license. Likewise, both Chelsea and Propagandhi have been avid, longstanding supporters of left-liberal causes.

Writers often use a distorted, ill-informed lens to view punk politics, which some punks have worked diligently to balance. John Robb, a well-known music journalist and member of the Membranes and Goldblade, describes the dilemma at length: "Of course, there were people with right-wing attitudes involved in punk, but there are probably more people with right-wing attitudes at an Oasis concert, but that doesn't make that band right wing. Punk was a lot of fucked-up teenagers squashed into a hot sweaty room, a lot of chaos and wild ideas, and some stupidity and naivety thrown in. A lot of the kids into punk were kids, and they were carrying around opinions they didn't really understand inherited off their parents. . . . Most people were apolitical. . . . People always try and claim that the Oi bands were right wing, but which ones?

"Most of them were singing about getting pissed, and some of them were more left wing, like the Business—more working-class street politics. I think it's very easy to tar everyone with the same brush. People seemed to really want to believe the *Daily Mail* version of events, and whether you like Oi! music or not, please don't just swallow the party line that they were all 'Nazi bands.' . . . It's lazy to claim this stuff, and I find it annoying that if you actually try and get close to the truth then you can leave yourself wide open to being called Nazi yourself. When the story comes from people who were there, it's vastly different from what the press wanted it to be" (Robb 2007).

RACE AND REAGANISM

Robb suggests misinformation accrues partly due to the normative master narrative of national papers, which writers and academics tend to amplify. Due to an etic perspective—an outsider's viewpoint—writers often do not understand the rousing class solidarity and skinhead subculture of bands like the Oppressed, who have played benefits for Anti-Fascist Action, WesGAP (an anti-poverty organization), No Borders South Wales (a "transnational network of autonomous groups advocating freedom of movement and equality for all" operating "on a non-hierarchical, anti-authoritarian basis"), and UNITY (a support organization for asylum seekers). They also helped to share Skinheads against Racial Prejudice (SHARP) movement ideals discovered on a November 1988 trip to New York City, where singer Roddy Moreno stayed with members of the Toasters, NY Citizens, and the Radicts. Bands like the Oppressed resisted and reproached xenophobic, nationalistic, and anti-communist skinheads, the likes of the British Movement, and "white noise wankers" and have never apologized for its staunch stance ("The Oppressed" 2005, 6–7). Female bands have also confronted the same right-wing cadres: "Bully Boys" by the band Poison Girls addresses hyper-masculine chauvinism and violence, while Delta 5, who played benefit gigs in support of Rock against Racism and gigs against the Corrie Bill, an antiabortion legal effort, tangled with right-wing cadres on the street.

In the article "Not So Quiet on the Western Front," Brock Ruggles single-handedly surmises "the politically radical punk bands of the Reagan era and beyond drew heavily from the politics of the New Left and the music that carried the message of the movement" (2011). This might have been somewhat true in regard to Rock against Racism gigs organized by the Socialist Workers Party and Anti-Nazi League in the United Kingdom (whose posters read "Socialist Challenge: Self-Defence against the Fascists!" and "Ban the BNP" on yellow placards shaped like lollipops). They rallied to stem the surge of the National Front in Britain and the racist sentiments of colonizing rockers like Eric Clapton, who openly appropriated blues and reggae into his music and yet embraced right-wing Torry Enoch Powell and warned of Britain becoming a "black colony." Partially spawned by a letter-writing campaign in such periodicals as *New Musical Express*, *Melody Maker*, *Sounds*, and *Socialist Worker* by the likes of activist and photographer Red Saunders and others, Rock against Racism gigs eventually grew to number more than three hundred and included the Buzzcocks, Clash, Steel Pulse, Slits, X-Ray Spex, Tom Robinson, Sham 69, Stiff Little Fingers, and Elvis Costello. Five carnivals were held, including in Victoria Park, a fixture of London's multicultural East End, where a mosaic crowd gathered, defiant and proud, a merging of "punks spilling out of coaches in leather and safety pins to join vicars, hippies and trade unionists," waving flags and banners, including "Queer jew boy socialist seeks a better world" (Manzoor 2008). This directly contrasts the vision of rock 'n' roll emphasized by the likes of Keith Richards, who deadpanned to *Rolling Stone*, "Once rock & roll gets mixed up in No Nukes and Rock against Racism—admirable causes though they are—it's not for rock & roll to take things up as a full-time obsession. . . . [Because] they really don't obsess your *crotch*. Rock & roll: it's a few moments when you can *forget* about nukes and racism and all the other evils" (Flippo 1980, 42). Punk was the leading edge against that escapist charade of cock rock and passivity.

More important, as Mark Bedford implores, Rock against Racism events were responsible for helping to turn the tide against fascist youth programmers attempting to steer working-class kids into being part of the rank-and-file hate network. Tim Mardell argues, "The National Front had been trying to influence youngsters by leafleting football matches and were starting to find a way into the music scene as well, but Joe [Strummer] gave us a figurehead for what became a stand against racism, and his involvement with Rock against Racism was fundamental to retuning whole swathes of [white] working class music fans in London to the anti-fascist and anti-racist stance" (Bedford 2012). This was supported by sample research, performed by Bedford, of longtime Clash fans, most of whom also had family affiliations to the Labour Party. Some such fans eventually became trade unionists, anti–death penalty workers, and Amnesty International activists. Hence, Strummer and crew weren't solely speaking into a middle-class mirror; in fact, they tangibly reached vulnerable segments of the population that could have become the front line for fascism but instead often adopted the band's concerns for social justice and inalienable rights. Or, as Mardell surmises, "We were lucky to have a figurehead in Joe, which meant you could go the other way and be in Joe Strummer's gang" (Bedford 2012). Punks were also members of the organizations. According to Stewart Home, bass player for Crisis (an adamantly anti–National Front band whose lyrics heralded fighting at Lewisham and Grunwick), Tony Wakeford "was a dues paying member of the Socialist Workers Party," while rhythm guitarist Doug Pearce "belonged to the International Marxist Group" (Home n.d.). Such affiliations helped cement the punk-political crossover, even though such people and bands were later left soured by a movement that seemed "self-seeking."

As Don Letts, longtime Clash supporter and working ally, reminded *Socialist Worker*, the threats were not existential but very real: "There was quite a lot of racial tension as I was growing up. We had Enoch

Powell with his 'rivers of blood' speech and we had the National Front with their swastikas. In west London, where I lived, 'KBW' [keep Britain white] was painted in big letters on the walls all over the place. . . . We had the police on our backs too" ("Voices from Rock against Racism" 2007). In 1979, such police bludgeoned people protesting a National Front election meeting opposed by the Indian Workers Association and the Southall Youth Movement at the Southall town hall near a Woolworths at which local activist Blair Peach was injured and later died at the local hospital of a head injury likely at the hands of the Special Patrol Group. The headquarters of People Unite was raided, as well, ending with the manager of Misty in Roots beaten into a coma. That reggae band had joined punk icons Alternative TV for a Rock against Racism gig at the Albany—a club whose axiom was "Today the Albany, Tomorrow the World!" perhaps a pun on the Ramones song "Today Your Love, Tomorrow the World"—in Deptford, which was firebombed no less than two weeks later. During the Southall melee, police in riot shields used truncheons and a heavy cordon with horses while youth flung "missiles" or Molotov cocktails, according to eyewitnesses in police reports. This was the acrid landscape of street politics between 1978 and 1979. To commemorate Southall suffering, a benefit concert for Southall Defence Fund and People Unite was held at Trinity Hall Old Market featuring the Spics, Revelation Rockers, and the Stingrays, which was announced on a flyer reading "Southall Kids Are Innocent," a surefire reference to the Sham 69 song "Cockney Kids Are Innocent."

Later, in the heat of the summer in 1981, Southall once again witnessed an uprising: this time, Asian youth revolted against the presence of skinheads, some riding coaches emblazoned with National Front banners, descending upon a gig with 4-Skins, the Business, and the Last Resort, which resulted in nearby Asian youth attacking and firebombing the pub, confronting thirty local police, and then battling more than six hundred police reinforcements, as told by *News of the World* ("Britain's 1981 Urban Riots" 1981). Mathew Worley suggests that this melee helped provoke or reshape the Oi! movement's recording enterprise by catalyzing more left-wing-leaning bands like the Burial, Newtown Neurotics, Attila the Stockbroker, and more to be included in compilation albums celebrating the genre and lifestyle (Worley 2014, 12–13). As the article "Carry on Oi!" recounts, the disturbance actually led to a ban on Oi! gigs and to the album *Strength thru Oi!* being deleted by its record company (Bushell 1981). Yet Steve Pear, guitarist for the 4-Skins, bemoaned the misunderstanding at the heart of the matter: " I am a socialist, I believe in socialist principles. . . . And I would never have any time for a band who propagated racialist or Nazi ideals. . . . None of our black fans have ever been harassed at our gigs. That's not what the 4-Skins are about" (Bushell, "Carry on Oi!" 1981). Subsequent Oi! compilations, like *Son of Oi!* (Syndicate Records, 1983), featured the League of Labour Skins singing "Jerusalem" (later also covered by Billy Bragg) and Angelic Upstarts performing "I Understand," a reggae song originally released in 1981 that protests and bemoans the fate of Rasta Richard Campbell in prison.

As 1978 slipped into 1979, Rock against Racism organizers galvanized forty bands to appear on its behalf at twenty-three concerts stretching across two thousand miles, which also helped to gestate bands like the Specials, who headlined the Leeds Rock against Racism gig in 1981 (Manzoor 2008). Member Jerry Dammers sincerely believes Rock against Racism helped knock down the National Front right at a time when it attracted growing votes: in fact, Rock against Racism "played a huge part in defeating them" (Cripps, Naylor, Mugan, and Brown 2008). Such efforts seemed to influence future endeavors, including the mammoth mid-1980s humanitarian effort Live Aid (U2, Boomtown Rats, Ultravox, Sade, Sting, Queen, Who, and many more) and the Red Wedge tour of the late 1980s, in which Billy Bragg (who also led the 1985 Jobs for Youth tour, sponsored by the Labour Party's Jobs and Industry campaign), the Communards, and Paul Weller, as well as The The, Captain Sensible (The Damned), and the Blow Monkeys led anti-Thatcherite concerts. A revived Rock against Racism effort under the new moniker "Love Music Hate Racism" in the early 2000s tried to inaugurate a new era.

The Rock against Reagan tours in the America were organized by Yippies/Youth International Party in the United States, which had bicoastal influence. Its New York City headquarters sat just down the street from CBGB. On the West Coast, Tim Yohannon, who wrote for the Yippie publication *All You Can Eat* in the 1960s, became the editor and, many argue, dictator of the potent groundswell *Maximum Rocknroll*, which debuted in 1982. The newsprint fanzine quickly became, even to cofounder Jeff Bale, a steadfast reflection of "the sectarian, intolerant, left-wing milieu of the Bay Area," led by its editor, dubbed a Maoist and a communist by friend and foe alike (Boulware and Tudor 2009). It still elicits feverish worldwide readership, even though its editor ate meat, didn't read, was a Giants fan, and never attended a demonstration when fellow zine writer Aaron Cometbus knew him (Boulware and Tudor 2009).

By examining even a single issue of *Maximum Rocknroll*, one can glean some understanding of its political and editorial policies. Issue 97, June 1991, features an overview of the political action group Positive Force; meanwhile, the editorials vehemently debate lifestyle choices versus legislative and law enforcement history (straight edge, the war on drugs, and prohibition), technology (the effects of reviewing CD and albums only), sexism (via a discussion of Kim Colleta, bass player of Jawbox), faith (Krishna religiosity in hardcore), and modern global conflict (Gulf War). Columns discuss the efforts of Catholic antiwar activist Daniel Berrigan, sexism and microeconomics in the music of Go!, coca trade and history, and the legacy of Chinese political-economic systems. Long profiles probe the "New World Order: The Gulf War and American Culture," and news articles outline "Organized White Supremacist Groups in Law Enforcement Agencies" and describe alarming assassination hit squads used against Kuwaiti citizens.

For most readers, the fanzine served as a conduit of such impassioned ideas—an accessible meeting ground in the pre-Internet era, a translocal community bulletin board, a compilation of tour itineraries, a network of product and distribution outlets, a nuanced contested space in which sectarian politics broil, and a news agency that imparted, with a sense of urgency, focused anger and semi-democratic values (articles and advertisements could be denied and material censored)—the voice of punk just as the countercultural magazines of the past also represented often-segmented youth culture and politics. It was like *Creem* merging with a left-liberal-libertarian broadsheet, helmed by an editor that valued self-reliance, open communication, motivation, a zeal for history, imagination, persistence, and responsibility, as he notes in his appeal for "shit-workers"—"a few good women and men!" residing in the Bay Area and already holding part-time jobs—who could live (not communally, though) at the *Maximum Rocknroll* house and reshape the zine.

Yohannon was not the only fanzine editor with ties to the Yippies and the pre-punk era. In Houston, campus radical Henry "Wild Dog"

Weissborn led the Direct Action Committee at the University of Houston. He was "an early supporter of the Houston punk scene," tells U-Ron Bondage, singer for Really Red. "I can say that even though the Yippie scene was fading and the punk scene was emerging, there was a certain anarchist anticapitalist area where they overlapped ideology-wise" (Ensminger 2005). Two bands especially convened at the gigs sponsored by Wild Dog: "I can't speak for Jerry and the Disease," Bondage continues, "but I remember both bands being in full support of what the Yippies were on about at the time. While Legionnaire's Disease's politics were sheer chaos and shock, Really Red's politics were somewhat more focused and defined.

"We loved what we were doing . . . trying to make high-energy rock that might be a small catalyst to inspire people to start thinking and to start standing up for social justice and political change. We tried to practice and not just preach." Like so many punk bands working to fill the void left by the vacuous pomp and insipid indulgences of mainstream music, Really Red hitched its music to causes. "We did benefit gigs all the time, for everything from the John Brown Anti-Klan Organization to KPFT radio to raising money for an operation for someone's dog. One of the times we were playing Vancouver in Canada we headlined a benefit concert for the legal defense of the infamous anarchists the Vancouver Five. Great gig with Greg Ingraham, guitarist of Avengers and Subhumans fame, as well as a slew of others. The Royal Canadian Mounted Police paid a visit just as we started into playing 'Teaching You the Fear.' It couldn't have been more ironic if we had scripted it. If it was a worthy cause, then we would usually do it. It was part of the gig. Social conscience. Civic duty, if you will," says Bondage. The idea seemed simple enough: punk was about removing the suspension of disbelief that overlaid the music of bands like Rush. They didn't want to enter an illusion or fantasy, a mythology or literary realm: bands like Really Red wanted to inject everyday street politics of an American kind into rock 'n' roll's circuitry. Other local bands like AK-47 followed a similar model. They released "The Badge Means You Suck" (rather than "care"), a 45 record that listed victims of police violence on its front cover, earning a legal suit in state district court from the Houston Police Officers Association claiming it libeled local officers "by exposing them to public hatred, contempt, ridicule, and injury" ("Police Group Files Legal Suit" 1981). Both bands took aim at a police force that they deemed vicious, uncontrollable, and intent on cracking down on citizenry, especially minorities, dissenters, and punks.

Yet even Really Red itself has a prolonged civil war among members who "disagree to disagree" with each other regarding contemporary political issues. "Really Red was all four of us, the band could not exist without all four of us. The band died in 1984," argues bassist John Paul Jones. "Maybe that's fitting now that the real Big Brother is watching over all of us. It turns out that it's the Marxists and Communists (also known as Progressives of both parties) in our own government that are destroying the American way of life. I was told once by a judge that I would go to jail for not cutting my hair by the time he left his chambers. I went ahead and cut that hair but swore that I would never let 'the establishment' control my life. At that time, it was the police and the corporations that were coming down on me, but the greed and thirst for power of this government is truly massive.

"The present thirst for power among 'elitists' from music to politics crosses all boundaries. The leftists in power right now were probably supported by the 'punks' out of their hatred for Bush, but in return they are having their rights and freedoms taken away by Obama. The days of big government and victim entitlement are upon us, and those jealous of successful people are choking the life out of this country because they think they 'deserve' what other people have. The plan of redistribution will make us a third world country. I stand up against that. Government should leave me alone to make it or break it. I don't want what you have, and I want you to stay out of my way. Quit taxing the hell out of me and get off my back" (Ensminger 2010).

Other iconic punks see Obama as essentially a descendent of Reagan himself. "I mean if you look at the way we have been treated in this country, now every single national leader that has been pressed in front of us, every single president, dressed in front of us on the TV set, has been one more flavor of Reagan," rails Jello Biafra. "And that very much includes Obama. I now realize, compared to a lot of people that listen to my stuff, I am so damn old I actually have visual, tangible memories of when there were actual differences between the Democratic and Republican parties. I have actual memories of when even the big three TV networks took real pride in their news departments and attempted to out-scoop and out-muckrake each other because they hadn't all been swallowed by global corporations who then decreed that the news must make a profit" (Biafra 2014).

For Biafra, instead of ruining the free market, Obama is actually zealously propping up the market's wealth addicts. "That's one of the main Reagan entrails that's really poisoned our society and look no further than Texas for the very idea that there should not be any idea of a community whatsoever. It should be about everybody for themselves; they don't need to do anything about, 'well, I'm not going to call it climate change, let's call it climate collapse,' but the reply is, 'no, the markets might not like that.' Instead of Islamic fundamentalism or even Christian fundamentalism, I think maybe market fundamentalism is fucking up this country and this world even more. We can't put any of these bankers in jail; they're too big to fail. The market might not like that. Fuck the market, put the fucking market in jail. How many decades has it been now since I took up the cause in the California Green Party platform of enacting a maximum wage?

"These market fundamentalists are basically like crack addicts. Only instead of crack addicts, they are money addicts. They are wealth addicts. I mean how much more money do you need if you've made your first million? You can live really well off that for the rest of your life. But no, these addicts are like, 'now that I've made this, I've gotta make more, more, more,' and start shaking like they need their needle of whatever: more, more, more, and more. So, I think the maximum wage would send the clowns into rehab. Sorry, Ron Paul, I am very pro-tax. I just think the people with money should be paying it. Our payback, of course, would be a free education for all, free medical care for all, clean transportation, including airfare. You can have some high-speed rail built and hop on the train and go from Houston to Austin in an hour. Sure, Europeans pay way more in taxes, but you can see the benefits all over the place" (Biafra 2014).

More importantly, perhaps, the Tea Party offers no progressive challenge. "More and more I think [the Tea Party is] showing their true colors. Back when I was a kid in grade school, they had another name—they were called the Ku Klux Klan. Now they are smart enough to leave the hoods in the top drawer, plus they have vastly more money, both in oil-stained Texas billionaires like the Koch brothers and whatnot. . . . People seem to be forgetting another moneyed family that helped get a lot of that going with money and influence was named Coors. It's harder to boycott the Koch brothers because you can't just go out and boycott a refinery or something, just doesn't quite work that way. Sure, you can avoid Georgia Pacific paper towels, but for most part their money is not in consumer industries. Coors, for the most part, was a different matter. I got hip to what that was when I was still in grade school because my parents kicked Coors out of the fridge and out of the house and never let it back in because of Joe Coors' political activities. Later, he was in Reagan's kitchen cabinet and was credited to be the one that planted James G. Watt in the Interior Department" (Biafra 2014).

In Biafra's eyes, Republican cabinets proved to foster deadly collusion between private industries gone amok and diehard reactionary politics, stoking outright obvious environmental distress, sometimes underpinned by religious zealotry. "Before that, Watt worked for a nasty little right-wing legal watchdog called the Mountain State Legal Foundation, which specialized in suing environmentalists. He was also involved in actions against the Colorado utility company giving rate breaks for poor people and another against a school district in Phoenix trying to get dropouts back in school. Watt was Joe Coors' guy. Keep in my mind, Coors was not just beer; there was a whole other side of the company called Coors Porcelain [CoorsTek, Inc.], so in order to get a hold of the kind of ingredients needed to make their porcelain . . . it's in your best financial interest to strip-mine the country as much as possible. Thus, the cabinet office you want to control is the Interior Department. And you remember Watt was that wacky space alien who in his first press meeting said there was a need to go whole hog with strip mining, clear cutting, and turning our whole coast into a big orgy of oil drilling, like the Gulf coast. A reporter asked Watt, 'What about our children?' His reply was, 'By then we will have seen the Second Coming of the Lord.'

"People don't believe me, but I tell them that's part of the motive of these people is that a lot of them are reconstructionists or dominionists, as they are called. I believe Perry is another one, and Palin another one, too, and W. may have been one, too. They believe it is the End Time, and Jesus is going to come back, and when he does, he's going to put all the forests, all the natural resources back, and even all the money that has been looted out of Washington that created the deficit because Jesus loves America. They believe this shit. Watt came right out and admitted it. So then Clown Prince W. gets into Washington and takes another Coloradoan, Gale Norton, to be interior secretary, and guess who she worked for, the Mountain State Legal Foundation, another strip-mine, clear-cut, drill-baby-drill fetisher" (Biafra 2014).

Reagan, as punks tended to portray him, was indeed the venal embodiment of things to come, the photogenic septuagenarian puppet wearing an immovable grin, as Biafra attests. "The tipping point, in many cases, began in the Reagan years. I think at least he knew he wasn't president. His genius, if you could call it that, was that he could look at any page of a script—and he had a photographic memory, he could remember it like that [snapping fingers] and regurgitate the lines for exactly the kind of acting role that was required. Thus, he was so effective when he had his cue cards in front of him, and when he didn't, you know, things came out of his mouth that were almost as bizarre as what came out of Clown Prince W.'s mouth for the same reason. The danger of the Clown Prince later on was that at least Reagan knew he wasn't president; he knew he was just there as an actor to portray the president while his friends looted the country. I think W. actually thought he was president" (Biafra 2014).

The overall legacy of Rock against Racism efforts, which John Paul Jones might not equate with the politics of identity and victim's rights/entitlement, may be understood as a backlash against media efforts to depoliticize 1970s youth culture. As Lester argued in 1990, the media attempted to "proclaim the definitive death of the '60s counter-culture values and along with them, the commitment to fighting social injustice," but such coordinated music-cum-political actions proved these notions wrong. A decade's worth of similar militant, independent, underground music happenings used "music and art as active catalysts for social change," which served to "undercut" the New Right's attempted "new Dark Ages" (Lester 1990, 13). For the likes of Lester, youth culture staved off the forces of repressive hegemony.

For instance, Reagan Youth, Dicks, M.D.C., and the Dead Kennedys played a Rock against Reagan gig in San Francisco in front of five thousand people in 1984. This soon led to between one thousand and fifteen hundred of those people marching to the local hall of justice on Bryant Street, where many encountered legions of police, and chanting lyrics from a T.S.O.L. song, "America / Land of the Free / Free to the power of the people in uniform," reported Tim Yohannon in August 1984. Yet even such gigs, related tours, street actions, and left-wing idealism often became mired in disappointment. As the Republican National Convention descended on Dallas in 1984, the Dead Kennedys headlined a Yippie-organized Rock against Reagan gig on a stage outside the Dallas County Convention Center next to a banner reading "Eat the Rich." One concert goer during the afternoon held up a folded, homemade sign urging "Free the Vancouver Five," referring to the aforementioned member of the Subhumans and members of Direct Action. The orange flyer for the event, though, spelled out the real cause: "A Rally against the Reagan War on Marijuana Smokers and Growers."

Torry Mercer, a longtime punk and political activist from Houston who fronted bands like Beatless, Naked Amerika, and Anarchitex, played impromptu "guerrilla" gigs during those few momentous days by using gear that could be unloaded off the back of a truck in five minutes. He also joined dozens of protestors in street theater and confrontational actions, like sweeping through a Niemen Marcus shop at the nearby Galleria while asking, "Where is the punk department?" in a nod to Stop the City ("Carnival against War") and No Business As Usual rallies, which stretched as far south as Houston by 1986, where supporters with searing, sardonic signs like "U.S. Foreign Policy Is Bomb!" held a die-in downtown at Tranquility Park.

"The Dead Kennedys weren't on tour and didn't want to spend all that gas money just to play one gig, but they changed their minds at the last minute and came, but did gigs ahead of time in other Texas cities to make money, which had the fucked-up opposite effect of keeping local Houston punks in Houston," Mercer recalled in e-mails to me in 2014. In effect, the Dead Kennedys concerts became magnets that drew people away from the convention in Dallas—the epicenter of direct action. "A lot of marginally inclined folks that may have gone to Dallas to protest stayed in Houston to see the DKs. It really annoyed me that they would choose money over strategy. There were more punks from San Francisco, New York City, and Washington than from Houston. I complained to Jello about this after their gig in a parking lot, [with] him on crutches, and he didn't seem to care at all. They didn't stick around to protest, either, just rolled off to the next gig" (2014).

According to Frank Campagna, who booked gigs at local space Studio D, Biafra also struck down local act the Assassins for the opening slot due to potential problematic publicity, yet he faced off with rank-

and-file Republican conventioneers by helping chant "Fuck off and die!" and singing "Kill the Poor" as delegates passed nearby (Liles "Echoes" 2008). Although Greg ("Joey") Johnson, a member of the Revolutionary Communist Party, was arrested for the desecration of an American flag, someone else actually lit the fabric in front of city hall caught on video by worldwide news crews. This footage eventually became part of Supreme Court evidence in 1989 when the court (Texas v. Johnson) narrowly sided with the state of Texas in finding the state's implemented punishment—a $2,000 fine and one-year jail term—appropriate and justified.

During the throes of the moment, though, the Dead Kennedys, who itself would be the subject of legal battles regarding its album *Frankenchrist*, chose not to engage. "We were right there in the belly of the beast," Biafra attests, "but we were also in the middle of our own tour at the time, so we didn't have to time to freak out on what might happen at that one show" (Liles, "Echoes," 2008). To some fans like Mercer, this business-first attitude amounted to a disappointment; meanwhile, in 1999, Johnson offered this prescient reminder, "One of the first acts taken by the Nazis was to outlaw desecration of national symbols—to make it a crime to speak against the swastika, let alone burn it," notes Philip Taylor (1999). For Johnson, burning the flag spoke much louder than words and was not an exercise in anarchism as much as a litmus test for freedom. Two years later, Jello Biafra openly confided to *Maximum Rocknroll,* "We are not as hardline or grassroots as M.D.C., BGK, or Crass," yet he hoped the band did catalyze a positive impact (Yohannon 1986). So in hindsight, the Dead Kennedys' reaction in Dallas seems less severely detached, although others, like Samuel Charles Salmon of the band Circle Kaos has continued to point out the hypocrisy of a politically conscious band earning $1,000 at gigs in nearby Austin at the Ritz and paying openers, such as his own band and Scratch Acid, a mere $50 for the night. When pressed to explain, the Dead Kennedys replied that they are "lucky to open for the Kennedys and . . . the publicity should be enough" (Salmon 2014).

Still others like Eugene Robinson, singer of Whipping Boy and Oxbow, challenge common perceptions of the Dead Kennedys' politics. They "were pretty apolitical, strangely enough. I mean it's easy to not see that given their name and their songs and how their whole history played out, but knowing them, with the exception of Jello, these guys were much more excited about the prospects of what they could do musically and artistically than they were in any sort of agitprop. *Except* for Jello" (Ensminger *Mavericks*, 2014). The caterwauling, skirmishing singer seemed to "shoulder the shaping of the thematic thrust of the band, which, in his hands, always seemed a little newspaper-headline driven. I mean, Jello is a voracious listener to music. I've never been able to get a pause in edgewise with the guy. So, [he's] not so much a listener to people, also not so much a voracious reader of anything other than newspapers, which will eventually shallow your approach to whatever themes you're drawn to, I think" (Ensminger *Mavericks*, 2014).

Yet others like Mike Watt of the Minutemen were equally driven by newspapers: "I'm addicted to newspapers—that's my problem, I can't stand the TV. That's what's in the newspapers, we all feel so helpless like we're all on a big bus ride to the edge of cliff so we're gonna shout" (Al and Peter 1982). Notably, the wordplay and craft of the Minutemen's bassist have a much wider berth of influences, from rock writer Richard Meltzer, with whom he recorded an album as Spielgusher, to Dante's *Inferno*, which he reimagined in his rock opera *The Secondman's Middle Stand*, to the painter Hieronymus Bosch, who influenced his back-to-jam-econo opus *Hyphenated-Man*. So although the Minutemen at times felt permeated with politics and news of the day ("Fascist," "Joe McCarthy's Ghost"), Watt has proven then and now that such diatribes were merely the tip of an iceberg loaded with a mashup of other subsequent cultural influences.

In Washington, D.C., Tomas Squip, singer for both Beefeater and Fidelity Jones, decried Rock against Reagan as merely a stomping ground, not for the decriminalization lobby itself, but for a much broader swath of casual, innocuous, and generally misguided pro-drug concert attendees. "We came on and made a bunch of statements and a big furor about the disguise of how it's supposed to be Rock against Reagan. . . . We were making fun of everybody out there stoned and getting busted, laughing in their faces for them thinking they were unifying under some banner. They had no militant views about anything" (Yohannon and Martin 1989). Squip considered his own band a "message-conscious" band attempting to "spearhead and help create a new level of underground music" that drew upon world beat—"punk-oriented that . . . would be a very ethnic, dance-oriented type of music" as diverse as Chocolate City itself (Yohannon and Martin 1989). To have that music and message mired in vague ruminations about police tactics and drug laws seemed pointless.

Squip was not alone in harboring such borderline repulsion. "There were remnants of the Yippies around, the 1960s radicals, the ones Jerry Rubin and Abbie Hoffman were a part of, and we mostly saw them as people that wanted to get stoned, whether it was Rock against Reagan, Rock against Racism, or Rock for the Legalization of Pot," admits Mark Anderson. "It seemed to feel like it was outside of our scene. These were groups that did collaborate and did have a presence in the punk scene. The Bad Brains worked closely with the Yippie folks in New York City and Washington, D.C. That was kind of an exception to the rules. Although I should say, for me personally, it goes back to the MC5. I could recite word for word the opening rap from . . . 'Ramblin' Rose,' so they were certainly a big inspiration, as were Jefferson Airplane and Hendrix, and the Doors. But we were trying to do our own thing, and honestly I was more touched by examples of the original Rock against Racism in England, which to a certain extent was married to the Socialist Workers Party there," a synergy that did not sit square with all participants (Anderson 1991). "I really believe in RAR [Rock against Racism]," bassist Paul Dean of X Ray Spex told *Zigzag*, "We did the gig at Hackney because we are all totally against racism of any kind, but a lot of Socialists used that event for their own political reasons. I am not a socialist and I just want to say that I was not there for that reason" (Anger 1978, 29). Others, like Glenn Matlock of the Sex Pistols, confided, "A lot of the bands who were saying they were the most socialist have turned out to be the most capitalist of the lot. . . . They become like cardboard cutouts singing about revolution in the end" (Anger and Thrills 1978, 12). And in the end, the Sex Pistols itself, led by trendy liberal-loved "cause celebre" Johnny Rotten, as he was described by filmmaker Julien Temple, ended up no more "threatening than retreaded Chuck Berry," and eventually became integrated into the "rock vernacular" even after shredding the form and the community's sense of complacency (Gilmore 1980, 20, 21).

Rock against Racism efforts in America—which drew punk bands from Bad Brains and M.D.C. to Mydolls, AK-47, and Really Red—were led by the John Brown Anti-Klan Committee, at least in Houston and Chicago, with longstanding ties to radical political posses such as the Weathermen. One gig benefiting the group at On Broadway in the heart of San Francisco featuring acts like M.D.C., Dicks, Slugords, and more took aim at racist elements operating within the Bay Area: "The Cowboys are a KKK-type gang inside the Richmond police. They carry out racist terror against the Black community with the full support of the Police Chief and city government," read the event flyer. The grassroots organization was not opposing mere ground-level racism, such as racial language used by police forces, but endemic police corruption and conspiracy. Hence, their benefits, gig flyers, and stage banter became a micromedia campaign to turn the tide against such forces.

As its flyer from a Houston gig declares, the group seeks to "fight white supremacy in solidarity with the New Afrikan Independence Movement" and was organized to "stop the KKK, killer cops, and mercenaries through educational forms, mass work demonstrations," and the media. Houston, with the "highest rate of citizen murders per officer in the U.S.," according to the flyer, was a seething epicenter of police issues, recounted in songs like "Teaching You the Fear" by Really Red, which describes the violence suffered by Hispanics, African Americans, and gays in the city undergoing an oil recession. The John Brown Anti-Klan Committee responded by reaching out to grassroots efforts like People United against Police Brutality, an umbrella group featuring "over 20 local organizations." Benefit gigs at clubs like the Island drew in a wide array of multiracial support and cemented the marriage between punks and activists that continued to flourish.

"Outside of L.A., the police department that scared the shit out of people more than anywhere in the country was in Texas, especially Houston," tells Jello Biafra. "It seemed like Biscuit, Gary, Really Red, and AK-47 with that 'The Badge Means You Suck' single were challenging some of the most out-of-control, violent police departments in America. They were one step away from being full-blown Latin American death squads, meaning they were risking life and limb just to say this shit and play this music. Nowadays a lot of people take the whole underground independent scene for granted—there's always going to be bands and message boards and blogs and endless things to entertain us, but it was very different earlier on" (Biafra 2014).

In Austin, the work of the John Brown Anti-Klan Committee was embraced by the likes of the Dicks and the Stains/M.D.C., one of the foremost incendiary political punk bands in America, and by many others in the community as well. "Just about everyone in Austin, except the cops, rednecks, frats and certain politicians hated the Klan and made it clear they didn't like them any way they could," argues Ron Posner, guitarist for M.D.C. who gives much credit to Gary Floyd for being a powerful mentor to anti-Klan efforts. "I went to the Anti-Klan march in the early 1980s, and we all converged on the Capitol Building steps, where the Klan were there making a speech, all the pomp and circumstance included" (2014). As in many locales across the states, such events amounted to bristling face-offs between enraged locals, right wingers seeking publicity at any cost, and police forces. "The Klan had their own large security patrol with Plexiglas shields, etcetera, as well as the Austin police force in riot gear," tells Posner, "only to protect them from the protestors." The authorities often used such opportunities to document left-wing organizations at odds with police forces exhibiting racist policies as they were with the KKK. "The police had video and film cameras and were filming the protestors in the crowd, never mind the Klan," avows Posner. "Their interest was entirely devoted to who was protesting the Klan."

Violence became routine, normalized, and seemingly stirred by local authorities keeping rank-and-file left-liberal "rabble rousers" in line. "In the end, the only people that were injured that I know of were the protesters due to police brutality," Posner continues. "I personally saw a Chicano woman being beaten by a large group of police with riot batons and hickory sticks, like vultures on top of prey. There was one policeman who couldn't get a hit in until a couple of them backed off. That was when he gave her a couple of full force swats himself" (Posner 2014).

These events shaped the profound sense of agitation seething in bands like M.D.C., propelling them toward ever-sharpened attacks on the system at large. "We later went over to a large puddle of blood on the street where she had lain, dipped our hands in the blood and made blood imprints on our T-shirts," states Posner (2014). This moment of ritual, in which her sacrifice was announced with solemn, self-styled media, like spray-can graffiti rendered from the harmed body, reveals a continuum in punk conscience. For instance, as James Stevenson (Chelsea, Gen X) and Mick Jones of the Clash wandered into a Notting Hill carnival in 1981, they confronted "a mixed race battle against the authorities," remembers Stevenson, who quickly turned to Jones and urged, "See, this is our battle too!" (Ensminger 2007). In *New Musical*

Express, Joe Bowie of Defunkt concurred, "When the social riots come this time, they are going to be different. The economic situation is starting to hit the whites too," he argues presciently a year before major miners strikes, "so there are going to be a lot more people in the streets" (*Rude Times* 1982). Such riots, whether in central Texas or multicultural England, often affirmed punk's passion for political and economic justice, freely defined self-determination, and broad and fair equal rights. These did not amount to marginal struggles: they were felt broadly and deeply by citizens of color and lower classes physically struggling with biased, uneven, and aggressive law enforcement.

M.D.C. identified racist rants, rallies, and episodes as part of the sheer evidence mounting in its defense of radical change. "As it says in our first LP," says Posner, "'the police are the Klan, are the Mafia, so you better take your stand' . . . 'big, bad and blue, they're in the Klan too.' . . . Boy, [that was] true at the time. I would tend to think the John Brown Committee welcomed support wherever they could get it, but were a radical subversive group, so hence, the secrecy" (Posner 2014). So if the relationship between the organization and punk seems a bit gray, murky, or unclear, that might have been a veil wittingly used by the organization in order to preserve its mission while under constant surveillance.

On the other hand, Gary Floyd of the Dicks, who also supported the John Brown Anti-Klan Committee by playing benefit gigs, epitomizes some of the issues that arose from the meeting ground between New Left party activism and more nontraditional punk rock attitudes in which the only meeting ground might have been Reagan as a meme of intense dislike and loathing. As Floyd describes his initial enthusiasm, "The Reagan error/era was insane, so meeting up with people around the country who felt the same way seemed like a perfect idea. Plus, though a lazy guy on the outside, I did live for the music. I also lived for the dizzying shows, the endless songs, and meeting people—friends and foes—so I was on board. . . . Little did I know, I was about to begin the Tour of Hell" (Floyd 2014). To Floyd, the caravan of beat-up cars, barebones vans, and large yellow buses loaded with turkey dogs (hotdog substitutes), eager punks from D.R.I., M.D.C., and Crucifucks, and agenda-led Yippies constituted a ragged, motley collection of punks being directed by "leftover, extremist, hippie weirdoes. . . . Dealing with the RAR [Rock against Racism] crew was a trial in itself" (Floyd

2014). Even the punk audience members became a source of letdown and frustration, especially after the Dicks "worked up the old stirring soul song 'Love Train,' . . . some of the punks thought it was lame, too pre-punk, black music from the age of dinosaurs. So, we excommunicated them, moved them into the category of damn-ass hippies and stupid, no-humor punks. A big 'fuck you' went out to the boys with no sense of history" (Floyd 2014). The rancor was real, vivid, and legitimate.

Floyd might have been sympathetic to the Revolutionary Communist Party, the John Brown Anti-Klan Committee, and the Black Panther Party, but he was also a ribald gay performer who often dressed in drag. "We are for a party of the proletariat that is not dogmatic and freaks out every time something bad happens," he told one paper during the Rock against Reagan tour. "We're for the Communist Party that liberates everyone; sexually and politically," so some songs were geared toward "fun and dancing" ("The Dicks Interview" 1984–1985). Floyd also learned lessons in "inner-city politics," not merely from reading the *Communist Manifesto*, but from listening to friends and coworkers as well, like Elwin, with whom he worked as a janitor at Jefferson Davis Hospital in Houston during the early 1970s. As he recounts in his memoir *Please Bee Nice*, "We talked for hours about imperialism, war, and racism. In the stairways of that hospital, I learned a huge lesson about personal pain coming from his life that he laid in front of me almost every day. Coming from a pretty damn poor family myself, we shared with each other more than I can even write" (Floyd 2014). Manifestos commingled with personal storytelling, lore, news headlines, and empathy in his life.

M.D.C. and Floyd "shared similar ideologies and a taste for cranking out sharpened, bellicose, and gutsy music—I sang 'Anti-Klan' and they sang lyrics like 'No KKK, no fascist USA'—so we got lumped together as the benefit bands. We played so many shows for cause after cause: we were banner bands for groups of hardworking people that needed not just soap box voices but sheer power. . . . I was always happy to do shows and provide money to things I believed in. I am especially proud that we played for the John Brown Anti-Klan Committee" (Floyd 2014). Yet Floyd was far from doctrinaire, far from being a run-of-the-mill, rote spokesperson of New Left causes. His ideologies were drawn in part from his own biography—a poor, gay, and smart man from rural Texas.

Joe Strummer's politics were equally fluid and personal. Early American interviews, like those in *Punk* fanzine, insisted that his politics past and present were "to the left. . . . I'm not into fucking people working away in factories doing useless boring jobs" for the sake of company profits (Jolly 1979). That entrapment within a Fordist system became a central focus of transgenerational punk songs like "Day by Day" by Generation X ("I feel like a robot / on the production line / ain't got no tomorrow"); "Hate Work," a bristling meditation on "stolen years," by M.D.C. ("never gonna work in a factory / or sweat my life in misery"); and the Clash song "Clampdown" ("The men in the factory are old and cunning / You don't owe nothing, so boy get running!"). Strummer, though, eschewed the stringent lines of any sectarian ideology. "I don't wanna say that I am a socialist or that I am a communist 'cause I fuckin' hate parties and party doctrine." Instead, he acted more or less as a free-agent soapbox orator of everyman issues yet felt he might be seen as a "rip-off artist or a liar" (Jolly 1979).

His disdain for party lines, as well as his sense of martyrdom for being misunderstood and an easy target of entrenched ideological camps, became fodder for the song "We Are the Clash" ("right wing, left wing / I want something / to see me through the siege"), found on the band's often ill-regarded swan song *Cut the Crap.* Many listeners understood the literal, implied, and even metacritical vision of Clash songs, including a knot of songs deciphering the repercussions of marginalized work. "Career Opportunities," as Steve Shelley of the Buzzcocks understands, is "about not wasting your life working nine-to-five in a job you hate" ("Clash City Rockers" 2003, 47). If anything, punk embodied a counterculture to the routines of daily work life and party politics—representing the regimes of conformity and stifling groupthink—and instead offered a participatory culture rooted in a kind of folk politics, populism, and intuitive rebellion.

"I believe in the counterculture, and I believe in people politics. I have no interest in political parties anymore. Labour and Conservative are like Tesco or Wal-mart. They are corporate concerns," argues John Robb of the Membranes and Goldblade. "They don't speak to me at all. I vote for the Green Party. It's the closest anyone gets to where I am. It's a great idea for people to get organized to try and change the world for the better but with all the selling out that has to be done by political parties, people have become cynical. Trouble is that while we are all being smart and cynical, the corporations are getting even more in control.

"No political party speaks the truth anymore," continues Robb. "They are too concerned with their public image. In a sense, politicians have become prima donna pop stars, so the politics that I believe in are different. They are the politics of antiwar marches, the politics of issues not supporting a whole party. . . . We have the communication, we have the ideas, and we have the energy! We are bored of being told to work our whole lives to buy a twenty grand car. The spirit and ideas that came out of punk rock are still around" (Robb 2007).

Those who envision Crass as an unconditional supporter of left-wing causes would err, as well, for Penny Rimbaud wrote the condemnatory "Bloody Revolutions" after a Persons Unknown organization benefit gig. According to Vi Subversa of Poison Girls, the cause revolved around the "Irish problem"—the detainment and trials of unnamed people caught with weed killer and sugar, homemade bomb components (Landstreet 1985–1986, 19). The gig featured hardline Dutch Maoists the Rondos and a group of Red Brigade members assaulting skinheads friendly to Crass, which was later misrepresented as an attack by the right-wing in the paper the *Guardian*. The song spouts the line "Freedom has no value if violence is the price." As Rimbaud declares, "Soon after the release of our first album, we had realised we were in the very real danger of becoming 'leaders' of a new movement for social change. It was a role that we refused to play; the revolution we sought would be without leaders" (1998). To worsen matters, even after Crass released a benefit single to aid the Anarchy Centre raising $12,000, the organization soon collapsed, and the headquarters was marred with graffiti like "Crass? Capitalist wankers!" (Rimbaud 1998, 119, 121–22, 124).

Crass and the Poison Girls suffered a stubborn rift after the Poison Girls' single "The Offending Article"—which discusses a woman castrating a man and attempts to link cruelty against animals to cruelty against women in lines like "All butchers are men"—led to Crass sending back their art and records while Poison Girls were on tour (Landstreet 1985–1986, 5, 19). More importantly, on many occasions, the New Left disavowed punk, and punks disavowed the New Left, just as many punks questioned each other. "We're aware of the anarchist groups such as Crass and I liked some their stuff," declared Hugo Burnham of Gang of Four, "but it's kind of pathetic really 'cause they'll never accomplish anything with an anarchist line. . . . The government won't be brought down or changed by anarchy. It's actually very destructive and directionless" (Gibson and Springer 1981). Punk's sectarian lines seemed helplessly entrenched, yet both bands did not merely spur and sprout devout fans and followers. Instead, such bands galvanized the conscience of musical acts such as Toxik Ephex (whose track can be found on *Bullshit Detector*), who, despite their disillusionment with Crass and followers, still supported "animal rights, [the] special baby unit," and various groups supporting the unemployed, left-wing causes, homeless, and the elderly (Lance Hahn 2006). Other citizen-organizers, even abroad, felt the Crass momentum.

"Crass was very much about getting up and making things happen. They were a band. Positive Force began to exist right at the end of the era when Crass existed as a band," Mark Anderson recalls. "One of their slogans at the end was 'It's not time to be fucking nice, it's time to act!' We knew they were involved with the Stop the City demonstrations, the creative, disruptive blockages that were intended to disrupt the financial district of London. It was very clear that while you might think that certain bands, even if they were interested in the right things, were more interested in doing something more than just talking. Certainly that was the sense with Crass and everything they did. It was essential *to act*. Words were worse than nothing, basically, because they disillusion people. You talk big and you don't do anything, so why care at all?" (2014).

Others felt more keenly critical. Ken Lester, the manager of D.O.A., wrote that Crass followers "often wear their anarchy [symbols] and . . . emblems as talismans to indicate a moral superiority and distinctness from the unenlightened rabble. Unfortunately, the symbols do not translate into fresh or creative actions" (1984). Later in the piece, he also questions the Clash and Gang of Four, who played Rock against Racism in Manchester in 1978 and a miner's strike benefit in Wakefield, pointing out the "shortcomings of music as a social force . . . all protest is absorbed and converted into commercial trends and style," which highlights his own self-aware metadiscourse about punk. Though D.O.A. and Crass both appeared on the P.E.A.C.E./War Compilation

(R Radical Records, 1984) and both likely drew inspiration from at least the early era of the Clash, replete with "grand gestures of defiance and the myths that surround them" (Davis 1980, 56), punk rock internecine fault lines seemed omnipresent throughout punk history, even among fellow travelers with sympathies toward similar goals, like fostering more inclusive, democratic societies. Yet this was lost on activists like M-50, who in March 1980 passed out leaflets in Detroit that read the Clash "sold out" even as the Clash were playing a benefit gig for Jackie Wilson that night (Whitall 1980, 41), or Gang of Four, who faulted the Clash for "regurgitating the old myths of rock 'n' roll" even as Gang of Four came close to appearing on *Saturday Night Live*—"must-see" mainstay media during the era—a year before the Clash (Young 1981, 30).

Contemporary punks tend to be wary of organizations that share punk values, but they may not value punks themselves. Groups tried to mount national anarchist organizations and gain a toehold in America, but even workers from *Profane Existence* ("Making Punk a Threat Again!"), often generically linked to anarchist agendas, were wary of such groups, who they argued often demean punks, even though the magazine was a fount of anarchy-related news. The summer 2000 issue alone contained news about Minneapolis May Day demonstrations; anarchism on the Internet; rallies in Windsor, Ontario, featuring Food Not Bombs against the Organization of American States; smashing the World Trade Organization; raids against Amsterdam squats; support for the Universal Shelter Association; and much more. When punk bands like the Dead Kennedys appeared in anarchist publications like *Kick it Over*, they specifically stressed their own version of "anarchy of the mind, personal anarchy, as opposed to collective anarchy" ("The Only Good Kennedy Is a Dead Kennedy" 1982, 5). They by no means welcomed the fault line of sectarian politics or the agendas of groupthink.

Some of those fault lines existed as delineators between the new (hardcore) and old (punk) genre forms, while anarchist punks like Graue Zellen from Germany operated in a third space because it felt as if "Hardcore was created by various U.S. sportswear manufacturers to increase sales" ("Graue Zellen" 1995). When appearing in the zine *Profane Existence*, they differed with their own interviewer over such issues as solidarity for PKK (Turkish resistance fighters), whom the band favored (unless the PKK was guilty of the oppression of "other nationalities"), whereas the interviewer considered the PKK no more than "scum" whose support by the band amounted to a "classical radical-left mistake." Despite these differences, Jan of Graue carefully delineated the space occupied by likeminded bands, which inhabited a network of "independent, non-commercial . . . squats, youth centres, and self-run places" in such locales as Switzerland, Greece, and Norway, which seem to resist "U.S. cultural imperialism" embodied by more mainstream hardcore bands, at the time likely identified with labels such as Epitaph and Fat Wreck Chords ("Graue Zellen" 1995, 15–16).

Hardcore punk tethered together a bruised and battered sense of self—the consuming language of victims (take, for instance, band names like VKTMs, song titles like "Society's Victim" by Discharge, and album titles like *Victim in Pain* by Agnostic Front)—and fused it with an intrepid disregard for institutions—the state, the workplace, school, and domestic life. By unleashing a startling syntax of blasphemy and anguish that made punk look quaint, hardcore punk distressed the routines of a pleasant, mannered way of life by amplifying and aggregating a simmering underground youthful spirit. As Matt Diehl of *My So-Called Punk* touts, "Crass, in particular, was less a band than a collective espousing the most radical, anarchist, vegan politics ever: Crass released albums, yes, but those served as manifestos for the underground" (2007). In the crucial 1980s era, offering more than mere music mattered; hence, during hardcore's salad days, the messages and subtexts, symbols and signifiers of bands ranging from the Misfits and Corrosion of Conformity to Septic Death and D.R.I. became more hardened and grisly.

Writers look at the first wave of punk and observed clichés that shouldered borrowed, hijacked, and reworked formulas seemingly rooted in 1950s bombastic rock 'n' roll but that was equally schooled in avant-garde art movements from Futurism and Dada to street theater and Fluxus. Yet punk seemed like a momentous unshackled poetry, too—crackpot chaos using the distorted microphone pulpit to riddle so-called truths with holes and tear fissures in hollow normative lifestyles. Punk was not just a way to rebel against economic decline in Manchester and Los Angeles, acting as desperate music for a desperate time; it was more than a measure of the dissatisfaction of "no future" that the Sex Pistols howled. "That's what the government had in store for people like me, from the working class," admonishes Rotten. "The school system kept you in the same social condition" (Davet 2013). For the likes of Rotten, punk was vehemently attacking the status quo of a system destined to bolster the affluent and privileged, not create doors of opportunity. As *Socialist Worker* observes, "no future" decried "economic recession, mass unemployment and the threat posed by racist police and the fascist National Front" ("Voices from Rock against Racism" 2007).

Punk was a joint sphere, a convergence culture in which fashion became a marker of politics and identity ("like trousers, like brain," once quipped Joe Strummer), lifestyle was a mode of ideology, and music was not mere entertainment (no wonder Gang of Four called its first album, ironically, *Entertainment*), but a form of guerrilla-war-simulation engagement, a sharpened sense of the *good fight*. Jon Savage dubbed the Clash's sonic and lyrical onslaught of the early versions of the Clash as multitiered, for it acted as reportage unveiling "instant snapshots of current events" drawn from a "social realist . . . sociological" perspective in such tunes as "White Riot." The end result was a sound akin to "the cry of the abused child," while their program, worn real as a second skin, demanded a do-it-yourself, keep-it-small-and-authentic austerity that rallied the "culturally dispossessed" (Savage 1996, 84–85). At least that's how the beginning felt to some, before CBS Records became their uneasy launch pad. Still, to others like Johnny Rotten, the Clash were always simply "sloganeering, taking quotes and turning them into choruses . . . a very lazy attitude" (Di Perna 1996, 61).

GOD SAVE THE SEX PISTOLS

Yet punk rhetoric may also be the Achilles heel of punk. Punk might have charged furiously, noisily, and hungrily into the bitter nights, but how it actually practiced what it preached becomes a bit murky, blurred in fragmented lore and dimly recalled memories—the fog of culture war. Easy targets—from Ronald Reagan, nuclear war, and conflicts in Biafra and Cambodia to Margaret Thatcher and the Falklands crisis—were ruthlessly examined by a torrent of sniper-honed song grammar: each vowel seemed to shudder with a kind of destruction of good taste, and each slogan became a keyhole in which fans could peer into the punk's relentless flanks and help to brutally bash icons, heroes, and darlings.

Johnny Rotten, who once assaulted royalty ("God Save the Queen"), faith and worship ("Religion"), lurid fame ("Public Image"), public history ("Belsen Was a Gas"), and more, rejected the political parties as essentially conformist institutions. "I'm not a revolutionary, socialist, or any of that . . . an absolute sense of individuality is my politics. All political groups that I am aware of on this plant strive to suppress individuality . . . it's replacing the same old system with different clothing" (Albiez 2003, 367). In addition, Rotten attacks the sense of punk as a movement with equal invective and disdain: "There is no punk movement. . . . Once you start mobbing up into little groups, that's separatist, and it's anti-human" ("The Sex Pistols Return to the Road" 2003).

Still, despite derisive rhetoric from Rotten, the Sex Pistols did play a Christmas benefit, about six songs, including a "clean version" of "Bodies," for the children of striking miners (themselves perhaps a "mobbing" collective) in 1977 at Ivanhoe's in Huddersfield. According to gig goers like Jez Scott (soon to be a veteran police officer), the record company provided "loads of freebies from the record company: badges, skateboards, posters. I got a yellow skateboard with pink wheels—like the *Never Mind the Bollocks* album cover—by winning the pogo-ing competition. I soon swapped my jumper for a yellow T-shirt with the album logo on it. Then I got two handkerchiefs with the Anarchy cover printed on them" (Scott 2007). In this space, the world of punk theater (replete with a straw hat on Rotten and a Sex Pistols cake), late-capitalism promotional trinkets, sympathy for the working class, and a media circus converged in an uneasy partnership.

Despite the fanfare at such gigs, Rotten still maintains, as of 2003, "We've had no help from the music industry. Never. Never. We've been disenfranchised from the day we started and we still are. The system does not care for people. It cares for left wing or right wing, and there's no common sense in between" ("The Sex Pistols Return to the Road" 2003). His rejection of labels, groupings, ideologies, groupthink, and segmentation remains palpable and potent, despite having appeared as spokesperson for Country Life butter in 2008, which supposedly netted him $8 million, enough for him to jumpstart a record label and reform Public Image Limited ("Never Mind the Bollocks" 2013). This was not out of character for the frontman. In the mid-1990s, he also appeared in advertising work for Schlitz beer and Mountain Dew, in which he recorded a version of "Route 66." Yet as late as 2013, Rotten maintained that he donated a portion of his income to charity—orphanages—which links to his father's own efforts. After Rotten's mother died, his father would "shelter orphans at home on weekends, so they could enjoy a family atmosphere" (Davet 2013). Unfortunately, as the notoriety of the Sex Pistols gained steam, the "authorities forced him to stop." Hence, even if Rotten himself is guilty of commodifying punk, he has retained a conscience.

In addition, in a 30 December 1977 official Warner Brothers memo that coincided with the band's soon-to-be-notorious appearance at the $3.50 per ticket Longhorn Ballroom in Dallas, Texas (where Patti Smith would soon appear as well), artist development head Ted Cohen declares the "groundbreaking . . . controversial . . . raw" band akin to early-era Rolling Stones. They could become a "viable and saleable commodity" but not without the "cooperation and support" of regional staffers ready to take "full advantage" of "various merchandising aids" in "high visibility, window and in-store display space." To say labels did nothing is a bit disingenuous. They simply worked within the framework of their market protocols—business as usual, except when dealing with press junkets on the tour. At least at Randy's Rodeo in San Antonio, Texas, the label refused to offer any complimentary press tickets for journalists; instead they "were happy to sell journalists a $2.50 ticket at the door," says Bill Bentley, who became a vice president for Warner Brothers-Reprise (Moser 2003).

Jack Perkin, correspondent from NBC, witnessed the band's sold-out, five-hundred person American debut in Atlanta. Sid Vicious and Paul Cook, in a "strange mood, flaky," demanded $10 before doing any "bleep bleep" interview. "Denied that, they stomp off," he narrates, later describing all four as "outrageous . . . vile and profane" who left spit and cigarette butts on the local hotel floor as well as booze and Clearasil boxes, the sundry material of their "raucous rebellion called punk rock," a "music as ugly as the men make themselves" ("NBC News Report" 2007). To that end, photographer Roberta Bayley recalls, "They had skin like reptiles that had been underground their whole lives, like salamanders, beyond even the standard English pasty look. And they looked freaky, especially for Texas" (Spong 2014). Yet one female fan attested, "they're not half as hardcore as people really expected. . . . There's nothing to be scared about." Hence, what labels could not do—spin and spread the narrative of punk into millions of common homes loyally devoted to nightly news—media like NBC could, acting as a conduit, channeling punk much like they channeled Vietnam's conflagrations. As one Texas writer says, looking back at the Longhorn scuffle where Vicious was punched by one female fan and scrawled "gimme" across his emaciated chest, "Local news affiliates were on hand to document the proceedings and scare the hell out of viewers at home" (Liles November 2008). The fog and detritus of a cultural war was now a facet of everyday life in 1978 as the Sex Pistols roamed the landscape of a Jimmy Carter–led America attuned to *Battlestar Galactica, Dallas, The Incredible Hulk*, and *Diff'rent Strokes*. Their punk amounted to a human cry: however unlikely, the music of the Sex Pistols and its concomitant critiques escaped from the margins and confines of each member's background—from the snares of school and work systems, media branches and law enforcement—and continues to rattle listeners decades later.

Not content to exist as a lone treadmill of style, not succumbing to success beyond first-generation chart-toppers mostly in the United Kingdom like the Jam and the Clash, punk remained choleric and unkempt, astonishing in its array of vented anger, always a barbed figure hurtling through pop culture's mild traffic. As Johnny Rotten belted in "Problems," "You won't find me just staying static / Don't you give me any order / To people like me there is no order." Perhaps these searing sentiments drew in the likes of Lawrence Grossberg, who in 1983 penned, "The politics of rock and roll is not the production of an identity but the constant struggle against such identities, even as it creates and politicizes them. . . . [Rock and roll] locates itself within the cracks of hegemony, the points at which meaning itself collapses into desire and affect" (1983–1984, 109). Yet the walls of hegemony have remained intact even as the Clash tried to stir a "White Riot," bemoaned the Spanish Civil War and the Falklands War, and united graffiti artists and punks in Time Square. The Clash played benefits for Sid Vicious' legal costs (Camden Music Machine, 1978)—which spurred a counter-benefit for Nancy Spungen by the Cash Pussies, who cut the one-off single "99% Is Shit" and featured members of Security Risk at the Bedford Corner Hotel in England—miners (Brixton Academy, 1984), New Youth Productions (Fillmore Theater, 1979), legless Vietnam War veteran Larry McIntyre (Agora Ballroom, Cleveland, 1979), homeless people (Geary Temple, 1979), Jackie Wilson Medical Find (Motor City Roller Rink, Detroit, 1979), and the people of Kampuchea (Hammersmith Odeon, 1979), and even partially united on behest of striking fire fighters (Fire Brigade's Union) from Harlesden and Willesden (Acton Town Hall, 2002). In terms of New Youth Productions, the group amounted to little more than twenty-five people who sought to "open up a music club and cultural center to serve the needs of all fledgling bands in the area" and provide space for "an after-hours club, all night films, gallery space and other types of live performances," their flyer insists. Each of these acts seems to represent what Lester Bangs termed in 1977 the "persistent humanism" of the Clash under their "wired harsh landscape" ("Joe Strummer 2002). To this end, in the liner notes to *The Story of THE CLASH: Volume I*, Albert Transom, alias of Joe Strummer, penned, "The benefit shows seem to stick out maybe because they were a bit more special than the average gig night and you took a definite notice of it." To Strummer, the impetus was heartfelt and memorable, not just a matter of routine.

By no means did the outreach of Joe Strummer, who once said, "Punk rock is exemplary manners towards your fellow human beings," end there (D'Ambrosio 2012, 176). To that end, Strummer released a version of Jimmy Cliff's "The Harder They Come" for an album benefiting the campaign to free the West Memphis Three, a struggle also avidly supported by Henry Rollins of Black Flag and the Rollins Band, who produced *Rise Above: 24 Black Flag Songs* to benefit the West Memphis Three in 2002. Joe Strummer also gigged on behalf of Amnesty International at Milton Keynes Bowl with his late-1980s outfit Latino Rockabilly War. Even the name of Clash songs become fare for humanitarian goals: Wayne Kramer, Billy Bragg, Boots Riley, and Tom Morello formed Jail Guitar Doors, named after the Clash song, a group providing much-needed instruments to people attempting to rehabilitate prison inmates with music therapy. Bragg, for one, understood how one guitar can matter so much. Pictured wearing a "Silence = Death" tee shirt in a *Guitar Extra!* layout, Bragg said, "During the miner's strike of 1984, when we went to the north of England to play in the coal fields, not only were the folk singers there before us, but they were far more radical than anything we had to offer" (Pollock 1992). Such a tradition was borne of "the history of the people that has never been edited, that's come down raw and powerful" (Pollock 1992, 96). One guitar could muster that heritage and hope.

Hence, the ethos of punk has not collapsed into vapid affect alone; punk does not act as a flickering desire rooted in no more than "passion is a fashion." Glocalized and reinvented over the last four decades, forever mutating and hybridizing, punk promulgates *effect* as well; it becomes a mobilizing medium, a soapbox and critical-thinking tool kit, not just identikit. It allows participants a way to interact on behalf of not just discourse but action-politics and humanitarian aims. It becomes a magnifier of conscience that maps out or becomes realized in different forms and functions. That's why in 2006 Le Tigre and Sleater-Kinney, in support of the organization Freedom to Marry, placed songs on the *Wed-Rock* album as a way to boost efforts to normalize and legalize gay marriage.

3

ZONES OF INFLUENCE

Washington, D.C., and San Francisco

Few cities in America have chronicled the rise of restless punk politics more than the nation's capital and San Francisco, the West Coast nexus of counterculture that sprouted the Beats, the hippies, and the left-wing community surrounding the magazine and radio show *Maximum Rocknroll*. In Washington, D.C., shaped by post-hardcore punk variants that let bands explore more diverse sonic palates, Revolution Summer in 1985 became a bellwether of change, hope, and action. Soon, understanding their proximity to institutions of power, bands like Embrace, Beefeater, Scream, and Rites of Spring began to coordinate activities with Positive Force, a community organization by punks *for* punks that became a grassroots epicenter, not just for formulating gigs, but also for catalyzing candlelight marches and percussion protests in front of foreign embassies, as well as citywide antigovernment poster campaigns, which married music with messages.

In San Francisco, bands like the fiery, polemical Avengers soon gave way to the even more ideologically driven Millions of Dead Cops, who lived at the Vats—the actual vats of a former beer company—with the likes of the Dicks, featuring the gay, cross-dressing, self-styled communist Gary Floyd. Some of those residents eventually decamped to a punk-friendly squat once occupied by the Hotel Owners Laundry Company (HOLC), where drugs were shunned; food was distributed; and ongoing links to Bound Together, an anarchist bookstore, were maintained. Skateboarders avidly used the ground floor, and Reagan Youth, D.R.I., and others visited (Goldthorpe 1988). These bands joined genre-warping Colorado exiles the Varve, post-hardcore rockers Frightwig (both contained all female members), plus art-damaged Tragic Mulatto, helmed by Flatula Lee Roth, to redirect conversations and attitudes about the roles, limits, and ramifications of dissident politics, queerness, sex roles, and gender identity in punk.

"To me, the initial 'punk scene' [in Washington, D.C.] comprised the folks who played at or came to shows on 'punk night' at a bar called the Keg on Wisconsin Avenue, north of Georgetown," tells Howard Wuelfing of the Nurses. "The bands that made appearances were Overkill (not the metal band), Slickee Boys, the Look, and I'm sure there were others. All these folks were white, but it seems that that was due to only white folks being interested in '60s garage rock and new music evolving from that basis, which is how punk started. That being said, I was initially brought to the Keg by black rock-writer Gordon Fletcher (now deceased); he never went to another show but that's because he didn't really like the music he encountered (being more of a hard-rock/metal aficionado). The owners of the Keg were from Iran. I never sensed that any of the regulars at Keg 'punk nights' were racist and certainly never heard racist talk in casual conversation. So if it was a white scene, it's because garage rock collector nerds tended to be white.

"Early punk was relatively idealistic," he avows. "We felt like we were a community and tried to function in that community in ways we felt were a bit hipper, more constructive, and respectful of our environment than the general populace. It had a nice anticonsumerist strain. We were into thrift-store clothes—they were cheaper, it was less wasteful, and they often looked a lot cooler and were made better than what you'd find in your typical department store.

"The original punk wave was so determinedly diverse and could encompass the Real Kids and Suicide and Pere Ubu and MX-80 and the Ramones," Wuelfing recounts. "And that seemed naturally to evolve into acceptance of alternative lifestyles (gayness, vegetarianism, collectivism, etc.). . . . There are *always* exceptions to every rule, and I'm sure you'll come across testimonials that flatly contradict everything I've stated" (Wuelfing 2008).

"I was in a few bands during my teenage years," recalls Alec MacKaye. "When I was fourteen, I definitely felt encouraged by Slickee Boys and Tru Fax. I liked going to see them play and was excited when I saw Kim Kane at Untouchables shows or when Diana Quinn asked us to open for them on a couple of gigs. Tru Fax even bailed on a show once, when the club wouldn't let us (the Untouchables) play because we were too young. As I recall, when the manager said we couldn't go on, Diana said, 'If they're not playing, we're not playing!' as sort of a threat, since they were the headline act. The manager of the club just said, 'Okay. Then you're not playing either.' So, they took a hit for us—pretty cool. By the time Faith started playing, there was a little distance, I suppose. We were heading into a more intense, less carefree or quirky kind of approach to music than the Slickees or Tru Fax. Our audiences were different than theirs, our music was different, even our intent was different.

"I think those older bands recognized somewhat the conventional rock approach and worked within its framework more than we did, even if it was not straight up rock-biz stuff," MacKaye continues. "The Untouchables and Faith and other bands like us completely ignored the music industry. In fact, we worked in spite of, and in many ways, against it. So, philosophically, there was some distance. I always liked those bands and the people in them, though! 9353 were not an older band—they were around when I was in my twenties. . . . They were interesting and pushed an envelope, but they weren't part of my formation, per se. I was pretty friendly with them . . . though" (MacKaye 2011).

"When the center of the D.C. underground music scene moved to the 9:30 Club, the audience was a bit more racially mixed," recalls Wuelfing. "There still weren't a lot of black rockers, but the ones there were [were] definitely accepted as part of the family; some went on to become house DJs at the club, join bands, et cetera. Honestly, the race issue seemed nonexistent at the time. I can't speak for how black rockers felt themselves about the situation—it's always tough to be the odd man out—but it always appeared to me that they were accepted without a second thought as part of the scene. Now things could have been different in the hardcore punk scene that followed, but I wasn't an integral part of that scene and couldn't really speak to that. I do remember angrily lecturing some kid out of Iron Cross on this topic one time. I must have thought they seemed a little too into the proto-Fascist stance; that memory's a little foggy—it was in a park somewhere.

"There are certainly some thuggish elements. Some of them were the really young kids who saw this scene as an opportunity to project some of their own inner turmoil. Some were older folks who really focused on the antiauthoritarian strain in this scene as validation of the kinda white trashy, 'fuck-you' solipsism—I remember they started calling themselves 'Bent Edge.' Meaning they'd get drunk, go for as much promiscuous sex as possible, et cetera—basically old school rock 'n' roll excess," Wuelfing remembers (2008).

"By and large I never saw these negative aspects really getting out of hand because the overall culture did *not* support or encourage those kinds of attitudes. There could have been little groups that formed in this kid's basement or that one's, but when they had to interact with the general population, they found that homophobia, racism, et cetera, was not considered cool. At least that was my perception. But remember, the hardcore scene was mainly teenagers who experienced things with the drama that colors everything at that age. I was in my mid-twenties. So when I saw kids acting stupid or ignorant, I just thought, 'Stupid little kids!' If I were a sensitive teenager and saw Iron Cross sieg-heiling—I'm not saying that I ever did see them do that—I'm sure it would have had a much greater impact," says Wuelfing.

"I can only speak for myself when I say that 'straight edge' was for me at that time not as much of a scene (the lyric sheet should have had quote marks around the word 'scene' to indicate sarcasm—we didn't know we would have to be explaining it in decades to come!) as it was a reaction to a tired sort of nihilism that was not going to serve me/us well," attests Alec MacKaye (2011). "Drinking cheap beer and fighting over nothing was too time consuming, at the very least. I had energy and wanted to get things done and not step in someone else's quicksand along the way.

"Young people pursuing things with an unclouded mind is not the worst way to start out, I'd say," MacKaye continues. "The vagaries of life will destroy them soon enough—why make it easy on the destroyers? Some people have made a good career of being drunk in public and that's good for them, but I'd wager that many more people are spending their days, grouchy as hell, fixing air conditioners for a living when they'd rather be doing something else and riding the bus to the dialysis center three times a week.

"We were pretty young when we were in the Faith, still in high school. What was happening to us directly was the most important thing to us. By the time we were in Ignition, we were old enough to be drafted, drive cars, and influence policy by voting, if we were so inclined. Driving around in a van, seeing the world, talking to people in other places, listening to more music, will enlarge your view" (MacKaye 2011).

"I grew up going to those early Positive Force shows," admits filmmaker James Schneider, "So my early exposure to any kind of political consciousness came from those events and the bands that were singing about issues. Then I could go see other local bands or out-of-town bands and get a totally different flavor—there were choices. It's worth pointing out that even before Positive Force D.C. began, harDCore was on the outs and a lot of people in that scene were looking for a new direction. Positive Force became part of that evolution" (Ensminger, "*Punk the Capital!*" 2014).

Positive Force, whose motto was "be more than a witness," echoed punk social consciousness. The organization was rooted in everything from the ethos of the self-declared "Revolution Summer" and D.C.-area No Business As Usual activism to the Bethesda–Chevy Chase High School Student Union to Promote Awareness and local punk circles. Positive Force acted as "a collective in the fundamental meaning of that word," Anderson avowed to me in 2014. According to a flyer for a Fugazi gig at the Smithsonian Folklife Festival, Positive Force works for "radical social change and youth empowerment through artistic expression and political action." As *WDC Period* fanzine recounted in 1985, the group's efforts involved myriad issues and mediums: it showed films like *The White Rose* by Michael Verhoeven depicting an underground group of students opposed to Nazism during World War II; it held teach-ins about Nicaragua; it created a "War Zone" tour held before a Rock against Racism concert aimed at disrupting business associated with nuclear weapons, including staging mock die-ins and guerrilla street theater; it commemorated the fortieth anniversary of nuclear blasts in Hiroshima and Nagasaki with a concert; it hosted poetry readings and speakers, followed by another die-in in which some of the three hundred attendees participated in front of the corporate buildings of Honeywell and United Technologies; it held a zombie walk replete with fake blood and leafleting and staged more die-ins during the Fifth

Annual Arms Bazaar; and more ("An Introduction and Short History of Positive Force D.C." 1985). Positive Force also supported the Big Mountain Legal Defense Fund and Survival International.

Punk's inherent restlessness, flexibility, and fluidity reflects participants' willingness to choose different paths as well as to evolve or transfer feelings. A case in point is Ian MacKaye, who once told *Maximum Rocknroll*, "I've been desensitized to politics to the point where I don't have any interest in politics," then formed Fugazi, a band that played numerous sociopolitical benefits and became intensely associated with Positive Force (Bondi, Dictor, and MacKaye 2011). "We definitely want to bust the [punk] genre, we want to break out of the established ritualistic patterns," MacKaye told *Maximum Rocknroll*, "because those are the patterns that will be the death of any underground community" (Brian 1988).

"Certainly, I, and members of Fugazi and Positive Force, were inspired by the MC5 and the White Panther Party, their energy and the way they wanted to marry music with message," argues Mark Anderson of Positive Force. "Obviously, our politics ended up being somewhat distinct, given that Positive Force and Fugazi would be loosely aligned with straight edge, and MC5 was anything but. What was their slogan—'dope guns and fucking in the street'? So that was associated with them, and obviously straight edge had some critiques of that 1960s idea, both on the drugs and sex level. They also tended to have an uncritical embrace of violence as a means to change things."

"I was always into high energy music anyway. Before the punk thing happened I was already into the Stooges and the MC5," points out Scott "Wino" Weinrich of the Obsessed, St. Vitus, and Spirit Caravan. "I was familiar with *Raw Power* way before the Pistols and all that. We were listening to the Dictators. We had them all. I had *Go Girl Crazy* and *Manifest Destiny*. When *Blood Brothers* came out it practically blew our mind. It's the quintessential fucking rock record. . . . We were into Radio Birdman, the Saints, and all that kind of stuff. Then of course the Pistols happened, whom I dug. . . . I think that everybody felt the energy with the punk thing because people were pissed off. Of course, the kids in England had it a lot worse than the kids in America, but the kids in America appreciated the anger, too.

"Right around that time, the Bad Brains started doing their thing," Wino continues. "The Bad Brains were a fusion band from a bad part of the world out here. They started off in Prince George's County, which is known for being a really rough police kind of county, with a lot of low-income folks being brutalized by the cops all the time. The Bad Brains were basically these pot smokers and low lifes that never cut their lawn and lived in Prince George's County and played fusion. I have some really early Bad Brains stuff, and they're playing a song called 'Redbone in the City,' which is a total take on 'God Save the Queen.' They went radically from this progressive fusion band to kind of imitating the Pistols a bit, then they realized that they needed to combine the energy of their fusion stuff with a dramatic punk delivery, so that became the Brains that we all know and love.

"We still weren't 100 percent accepted by the punks back then," Wino admits. "They loved our originals, but they hated the fact that we played punk rock covers. We were kind of outcasts then, although we had a big suburban following who would come to these shows downtown with all these punks. So the crowds would pretty much clash. Once we canned our lead singer and went down to a three piece and played all originals, that's when Iron Cross started liking us and playing shows with us. That's when I became friends with John Stabb and we played with Government Issue. That was when Ian started paying attention" (Ensminger *Left of the Dial*, 2002).

"First I will say that I am not a principled pacifist," avows Mark Anderson. "I don't reject violence in all its forms. I mean, there's a long discussion about where self-defense sits in there. I think Ian from Fugazi is much more a principled pacifist, though other members of the band might not be, but certainly we share a general sense that violence is an extremely limited and crude tool. It was not something that would generally work in our favor against the awesome force of the corporate military governmental structures—the real monopoly on tanks, guns, and bombs—but also the money. Although I would hasten to add, Positive Force or Fugazi were anarchist in the sense of seeing the state as the enemy.

"The state was an enemy within certain circumstances, but corporate power was just as important in our mindset, so it was less of an ideologically anarchist vision, but we did understand it as a corrective to the authoritarian left, like the Revolutionary Communist Party, which was quite active, but that group was widely rejected by the punk scene at least in D.C. because people felt they were trying to exploit our politics, our scene, for their ends and their revolution, and they didn't consult with us about what the revolution should look like," Anderson notes (2014).

One band aligned with Positive Force was Scream. Associated primarily with Dischord Records, Scream originated in Bailey's Crossroads in Virginia. It brandished titanic hardcore hooks that later merged with traditional hard-rock habits. Its breathless tunes testify to the band's inchoate, sinewy, musically finessed take on short, sharp, fast templates. "U. Suck A.," named after a line in a poem by singer Pete Stahl's father, rages at the "intellectual poverty" and "suburban luxuries" that wilt the nation from "slimy sea to sea." Unwilling to settle for such stagnation, the band sought confrontation and youthful regeneration. With jaunty reggae inflections and echoing, wiry guitar, "American Justice" looks at legal prejudice on the streets of everyday America, where down-and-out citizens are subjected to search and seizures while police fill jails with the "poor and black." In this faulty America, in which a person's dignity becomes impugned and fairness goes unheeded, "justice has just been faking."

As Stahl informed me, "I wrote it after being arrested in New Orleans. The cops set us up, proceeded to threaten us on the way to jail, and beat up my friend when we got there. I spent a night and day that I won't forget in Parish Prison" (2012). During Hurricane Katrina, the prison, considered a completely lawless hellhole by *Mother Jones*, notoriously became the symbol of an overly harsh, broken penal system after authorities abandoned the facility, leaving prisoners without food or water as filthy water poured in, sometimes chest high. In 2012, the Southern Poverty Law Center charged the prison with gross management problems, including putting inmates in severe risk of rape, beatings, and medical misconduct, including withholding drugs from mentally disturbed inmates for weeks (Ridgeway and Casella 2012).

Stahl spent the "next few months dealing with the justice system in New Orleans" (Stahl 2012). Like Johnny Cash, the man in black who enjoyed reggae and gigged at prisons, Scream spoke for those suffering at the bottom of the economic ladder, for those lost in the penal system, and for marginalized voices deserving recognition, which led them to play gigs benefiting the Martin Luther King Center of Arlington. "The entire benefit . . . told the people present that one doesn't have to be superhuman and superrich to realize the dream of equality, justice, nonviolence, and human dignity," wrote an enthralled reviewer in *WDC Period*. "All it takes is the vision and hard work through conscience and persistence. An understanding of this was so powerful and so evident in that room" (Burris 1986). The vibe, intent, and proactive messages that one witnessed at such an event, the writer felt, counterbalanced mainstream notions that punk youth were greedy, destructive, and ineffective protestors.

Scream also placed the song "Feel Like That" on the *Viva Umkhonto* benefit album supporting Umkhonto weSizwe, the military wing of the African National Congress, and "Ameri-Dub" on the *State of the Union* benefit album supporting both the Community for Creative Non-Violence and the American Civil Liberties Union. Such efforts formed a modus operandi that seemingly inspired a contemporary generation—like Bluebrain, Protect-U, and Painted Face—to commit to Positive Force outreach, too, by playing gigs for organizations like the D.C. branch of the Brain Injury Association. Others, like Benji Madden of Good Charlotte, donated $15,000 to We Are Family senior outreach network, started by Positive Force. Perhaps Scream's most compelling benefit, though, occurred in July 1987, when the band shaped a song set specifically for the night's purpose: a benefit and march for Amnesty International, which netted $500 for the cause. After the gig, Positive Force passed out candles to the gathered audience, which marched with leaflets detailing human rights abuses through D.C.'s myriad embassies and finally rallied at Sheridan Circle to commemorate the site where Chilean socialist politician and educator Orlando Letelier and his aide Ronni Moffitt had been assassinated in 1976, the year that punk broke.

"In hindsight, it seems that most of the shows in D.C. between 1987 and 1990 were Positive Force events held in community centers, churches," recalls Jason Farrell of Swiz, Bluetip, and Retisonic. "The music scene was healthy and growing, as was the social scene supporting it. Everyone would turn up to see bands, hang with friends, flirt, socialize, whatever. The main interest was social, but many were open to the causes Positive Force supported. The July 1987 Amnesty International benefit was a cause anyone could get behind, and the candlelit march on the nearby embassies had an added sense of action and activism beyond paying $5 and watching bands you'd come to see anyway. My band Swiz was asked to play, along with Scream, Kingface, and 3.

We were a new band (our fourth show, our first being just a month prior), so we were excited to play with bands we loved, and we were honored to be involved.

"Like many Positive Force shows that followed, this show was held in the day," he recalls. "I always found this to be awkward; as a viewer, sunlight coming through the window has a way of pulling me out of the moment, reminding me that a day is happening. It saps energy out of a show. Dark windows pair better with loud music, but anyway the show was fun and people felt really good about being involved and making a change (or at least making an effort). As the bands finished and the sun started to go down, the John Hopkins center was trying to usher everyone out the door, including the bands and all their equipment. People hastily got their candles ready, though it seemed like the march had already started without them. I grabbed a candle and was looking forward to my first moment of political activism: marching, chatting, socializing, making plans for the night, but we had to stay back and load up all of our shit. I don't know if any of the other bands got to go, but the march was long over by the time we finished throwing everything into our cars. I recall the show as being one of the best Positive Force events.

"Shows were the hub of a large, loose social circle," Farrell continues. "A wide range of ages and interests that weren't necessarily in sync could be found at any given show. Most of these fifteen to twenty-five year olds were there simply to listen to music and engage with their friends. Their most pressing political issues were social: goofy golf-jacket punk or fresh skinhead trying out his/her glare, and then traditional skinhead vs. the slightly less violent 'Sharp Skin' (Skin Heads against Racial Prejudice), whether or not you slam dance, were you straight edge or not. The causes Positive Force championed were generally in line with the mentality of the kids at the shows (Apartheid = Bad), and sitting through an impassioned/awkward speech by Mark Andersen seemed a fair trade to watch your favorite band. But sometimes they ventured into realms that not everyone felt comfortable with. The benefit concert for the Gay and Lesbian March in Washington, D.C., was one of the first Positive Force shows where the atmosphere was a little off.

"The show was on September 26, 1987, a few months after the Amnesty International benefit," Farrell remembers. "Fugazi was brand new at that point (I don't think Guy was even in the band then), but people were obviously interested and excited. If I remember correctly, they headlined. Darkness at Noon (a new band in the vein of Rain Like the Sound of Trains), opened the show, followed by Swiz. We were pretty much traditional hardcore, a sound that was in stark contrast to the rest of the bands on the bill and to what was going on in D.C., so we attracted a bit more of a macho element. There may have been a brief moment of slam dancing during a particularly moshy part (generally frowned upon at a Positive Force event).

"Usually, you recognized all the bands on the flyer. They were bands from the scene, or musically similar bands from out of town. But I don't think many people at the show had heard of Sarcastic Orgasm when they started playing next. I don't remember what they sounded like. I do recall their two shirtless male dancers in hot pants aggressively humping the air through the entire set," says Farrell. "Not everyone was ready for that. Acceptance of homosexuality was not as prevalent as it is today, and even now, twenty-six years later, not everyone feels comfortable with hypersexualized gestures thrust their way (gay or straight). But even with those caveats, I was surprised by some of the reactions and comments we heard later—people being disappointed that we would play a show with a band like that, how far we'd fallen, or whatever. These comments sounded stupid and started to distance us from some of the few people who actually liked our band. It made Swiz question what we were doing musically to attract the kind of people who couldn't deal with something as ridiculous as Sarcastic Orgasm. They were funny. The name is awesome. I don't remember them being any good, but still, if you felt uncomfortable you could just go outside until Fugazi came on.

"I remember at the time thinking the grander gestures of the Anti-Apartheid Punk Percussion Protest and the Amnesty International candlelit march felt more important, more substantial than those with a more local focus, or those that were not as politically clear-cut," Farrell tells. "It's hard to remember what effect any of these benefit shows might have had, but I imagine the smaller entities like the Gay and Lesbian March, H.I.P.S. (Helping Individual Prostitutes Survive), along with the hundreds of other shows helping people in the immediate community had a proportionately larger and more immediate impact on the day-to-day lives of people in need than the bigger stabs at global issues. Exposure to issues that don't affect you, that you don't see, or that you actively avoid can force you to acknowledge, analyze, and possibly reassess your way of thinking. I would hope that the impact on some of those former kids going to those shows has somehow lasted to this day" (Farrell 2014).

Breaking molds happened not just musically, but also in terms of playing gigs in spaces outside traditional rock 'n' roll venues. This meant arranging concerts in galleries, an old Safeway store, theaters, a roller-skating rink, church basements, Lafayette Park in front of the White House in the rain, and even the Lorton Reformatory (prison) in the heartland of Virginia in front of predominately African American minimum-security inmates (Kim 1991, 83). Fugazi's hope was to convey one inherent element: "this band is moving in a different kind of network and . . . things can happen in a different fashion" (Brian 1988). In addition, the band also attempted to play a free event at Lafayette Park—joined by the likes of False Face Society and Dan Littleton—in order to prompt discussions about the American prison system, but it was cancelled due to rain. Luckily, other benefits occurred, including a March 1990 effort at the Citadel Sound Stage (a former Derby dome refitted for the likes of films including *Pelican Brief*) with Sonic Youth, Fugazi, Geek, and Unlimited Groove, which raised $4,000 for Washington Inner City Self Help, a group that focuses on the well-being of people in the core of inner-city Washington, D.C.; the alternative school Roots Activities Center; and the decades-old Sasha Bruce Youthwork, dedicated to "improving the lives of homeless, runaway, abused and neglected youth," according to its mission statement.

Such efforts multiplied across the country, not without occasional friction. "The second time I booked Fugazi, I did a canned food drive for a shelter," tells Robert Medina, a former promoter in Denver. "The skins showed up with homemade racist labels pasted over the real ones. There was even a can-throwing fight. It was pretty surreal. In terms of punks doing benefits . . . it only happened early when one of the moms of a band member tried to open an all-ages club [Kennedy's] and had benefits to keep the place open. I think benefits started to happen when punk grew up. I think when scenes are young and barely surviving, it is difficult to focus on having motives to help other organizations. I remember there being a couple of benefits for organizations like peace centers, bookstores, generally things that were left of center. This occurred toward the mid- to late 1980s and beyond. Dead Silence was behind a lot of that" (Medina 2015).

Maintaining the status quo, as observed by Dead Silence, was simply not an option. The band released an EP to benefit Denver General Hospital's sexual assault volunteers, which links it to Fugazi's extensive efforts in the D.C. metroplex area. "I would say that 95 percent of the shows we play free there always benefits [the recipients]," MacKaye insists. "That money is solid, factual money that goes to causes that we believe in . . . for soup kitchens to buy food, for AIDS hospices [and] education" and myriad other issues close to the core of Fugazi's ethos (Ciaffardini 1990, 36). Punk praxis was far more important than punk rhetoric.

As one of the founders of Dischord Records, MacKaye released a benefit album, too, *State of the Union: D.C. Benefit Compilation*, in 1989, in support of both the American Civil Liberties Union and Community for Creative Non-Violence, while Fugazi has steered fundraising efforts for innumerable campaigns, including Housing Now! (Middlesex, New Jersey, Interfaith Partners); the Free Clinic of Washington, D.C., in which the No Means No gig netted $5,000 in donations after expenses; the Washington Peace Center; the gay and lesbian march on Washington, D.C.; Outreach Services, Inc.; and Freeze the Drug War, an effort to "fight poverty and redirect governmental priorities"; all documented via flyers.

One of the those involved at the Community for Creative Non-Violence was future labor educator and activist Marc Bayard, son of Haitian immigrants who cut his teeth on punk in the mid-1980s when bands like Ignition, Verbal Assault, and especially Soul Side, which "dealt with issues of race and Apartheid," offered up more than music. "It was about making a difference in a community setting—getting up and making a difference," Bayard notes, an ethos later echoed by 1990s bands like Propagandhi (Rooks 2000). In fact, Bobby Sullivan, Soul Side's lean, evocative singer who worked at RAS Records and later led Rain Like the Sound of Trains, was an active member of the local Food Not Bombs and Anarchist Black Cross affiliates. Until this day, he remains committed to prison outreach (via the Rastafarian UniverSoul Order Prison Ministry); manages a food co-op in Asheville, North Carolina, and continues to advocate for coops on the national level as a board member of National Co+op Grocers and is attempting to coordinate a larger transnational cooperative network.

For Bayard, punk politics' center of gravity remained "the communitarian anarchist or collective work ideas" as well as the idea of agency: "you can take responsibility for some things that happen . . . the whole DIY ethic is useful in political work" (Rooks 2009). Such activism supplants merely generating an independent record label or distribution network. For instance, the singer for Verbal Assault, Christopher Jones, was deeply influenced by the 1971 book *Rules for Radicals* by Saul Alinsky, a primer that argued "if you want to make a change and you really want to get involved then it's going to involve a little bit of compromise, a little bit of trickery, it's going to involve playing in the real world" (Quint 1993). For Jones, that meant distributing material for Greenpeace, Amnesty International, and Sane/Freeze at his band's gigs. Hence, idealistic bands understood pragmatism and praxis as well as historic roots of engagement.

Bayard received a master's degree in political science from Georgetown University and committed his efforts to organizations like ACORN, the New Party, United for a Fair Economy, and the Solidarity Center within the Internal Affairs Department of the American Federation of Labor-Congress of Industrial Organizations (AFL-CIO). Once there, he used Brazilian progressive educator Paul Freire's concepts of co-intentional education to "develop education curriculum . . . within trade union federations" across the globe, including "Brazil, Indonesia, and South Africa" (Rooks 2000). Punk's influence, though sometimes intangible, remained potent. "A lot of the things in punk rock are organic things that you can't label. It's easy to spot punk rockers who have become organizers. You can smell it on them" because of their unique approaches and habits, a template and playbook of ground-level actions that do not derive from "standard organizer trainings or . . . role plays" (Rooks 2000).

Dave McClure, former bassist of Downcast, also found a home in education and labor initiatives. Inspired by punk rock from the likes of the Clash, Los Crudos, Spitboy, Fuel, the Ex, and (Young) Pioneers, whose Adam Nathanson supported Food Not Bombs and a Society without a Name, for People without a Home, an advocacy group for the homeless, McClure volunteered with Frontline Foundation to help provide meals to skid-row residents, then joined the Labor/Community

Strategy Center, which produced the document "L.A. Pollutes the Air" in 1990. The organization sent people to Mexico in solidarity with a prolonged bus-driver's strike and propelled efforts like the Bus Riders Union project, which pursued a class-action lawsuit against the Los Angeles Transit Authority. Such efforts provided him a meaningful, proactive education and helped galvanize his work as a social worker even today.

One of the more creative and turbulent affairs in D.C. was the Punk Percussion Protests in front of both the White House and the South African embassy, which partially inspired the band Scream to write the song "People People." One flyer for the event by Kweli emulates graffiti scrawls emphatically testifying "protest and survive"; "It's not the color of the skin, it's the color of the hate"; "Show you care / their shoes could fit / your feet too"; "America means nothing only you matter (and others)." Fugazi played in front of the White House under a banner reading "There Will Be 2 Wars" in front of 1,500 massed people in the drizzling sleet while the promo material for the gig stipulated that the protest meant: (1) decrying the Iraq/Middle Eastern war (while also condemning Saddam Hussein's invasion of Kuwait) and calling for peaceful alternatives; (2) pushing the Bush administration to alter budget priorities from a war stance to one that worked to "fight homelessness, hunger and other forms of poverty and injustice"; and (3) pushing to bridge the antiwar communities across the United States and to foster grassroots activism in order to offset the Bush administration's "ego- and profit-driven barrage in the Middle East."

In the 1990 flyer for the Positive Force action "Oppose U.S. War in the Middle East," attended by roughly two hundred people, the language both forewarns regional conflict spinning into "nuclear or chemical warfare" (often the theme of No Business As Usual, too, whose pamphlets warned of "instant global incineration: fire, and radiation . . . followed by the long winter") and provides the phone number to the White House, while also urging participants to help plan the next demonstration because Positive Force could use each person's "energy and creativity." Bands attracted to the cause found common ground; in the case of Scream, that included apartheid, censorship, health care, and adequate housing and food, which became readily apparent after gigging in often-socialist Europe, leading guitarist Robert Lee "Harley" Davidson, whose family descended from "dirt farmers in Alabama," to declare "your health care is only as big as your wallet" in America (Greene 1988).

Another poster that disrupted the civic politics was "Meese Is a Pig," designed by Dischord cofounder and graphic artist Jeff Nelson, who also drummed for Teen Idles, Minor Threat, and 3. "I did the anti-Meese posters because my rage over Reagan, the Iran-Contra business, Oliver North, Attorney General Meese, and the NRA boiled over to the point where I felt I had to make the strongest public statement possible. A large poster was the only vehicle I could think of for my message—I knew I could produce it myself and get friends to help put them up. The whole operation was a wonderful collaborative effort, and I could not have printed all those posters nor put them all up without the help of many friends and many volunteers from Positive Force.

"If someone had at some point printed a poster with a message that I agreed with and they wanted my help, I'd like to think I would have chipped in and helped them," Nelson adds. "But I think we all must pick our battles, and for me, there are *way* too many wrongs in the world to try to right all of them. I personally can only get involved deeply in political stuff when I really care about it or get really angry about something (Meese posters, later fighting Oliver North when he ran for senator in Virginia, and making large yard signs here in Toledo against the Iraq War and against Bush). I cannot immerse myself in political stuff all the time, or I get burned out. I felt (and still feel) that there are many in D.C. who fight every fight and expend their energies trying to right every wrong. That is noble, but not for me. I feel that such an uber-awareness of injustices in the world can also lead to being a politically correct party pooper.

"When I made flyers, I was just working with whatever images I could find, limited to magazines and such that you could cut up (only an asshole would cut something out of a book)," Nelson tells. "Certainly the hostage note graphics of the Sex Pistols were very inspirational, and the aggressive, crude-on-purpose nature of punk allowed one great freedom. I had been drawing logos of imaginary bands and beer cans for years, so things I came up with would have been the product of a seventeen to twenty year old who was really just coming into a sense of style and layout. I would guess the precursors that come to mind for me (not as influences, but as predecessors) are Dada and Russian Constructivist stuff. Certainly collage was an art form practiced by many in their scrapbooks, if not for public consumption. The Nation of Ulysses guys, Ian Svenonius in particular, were very much influenced by Russian Constructivist art" (Nelson 2010).

Flyers and posters become a microcosm. In the case of "Meese Is a Pig," the poster acted as a blunt, evocative shortcut explaining the dangers of the administration and encouraging people to take action; hence, such acts recognize the inherent worth and value that each person can bring to bear on various struggles—the value of crowdsourcing a reaction to the fullest. Nelson also used a readymade image in the design aesthetic for his band 3, which incorporated the pink triangle used by ACT-UP (AIDS Coalition to Unleash Power) and its motto, "Silence = Death," on the band's eponymous LP for Dischord. "We put the . . . emblem on the 3 record because we hated how the Reagan administration and the Moral Majority refused to take the AIDS epidemic seriously and how marginalized and vilified the gay community was back then" (Nelson 2014). Hence, the decision drew attention not merely to gay rights, social justice, and safe sex, but also to the lumbering right-wing bureaucracy that neglected, derailed, and exacerbated the issues.

Positive Force openly acknowledges influences as well, like the band Crass: "Positive Force began to exist right at the end of the era when Crass existed as a band. One of their slogans at the end was, 'No time to be nice. It's time to fucking act!' [from "Nagasaki Is Yesterday's Dog-End"] We knew they were involved with the Stop the City demonstrations—the creative, disruptive blockages that were intended to disrupt the financial district of London," declares Anderson. "It was essential *to act*. Words were worse than nothing, basically, because they disillusion people. You talk big and you don't do anything, so why care at all?" (Ensminger 2014). For such believers, defeatism was not an option.

Instead, aided by Shudder to Think, Holy Rollers (whose drummer Maria volunteered with Positive Force, participating in acts of civil disobedience and the March on Washington), Jawbox, Fly, Desiderata, and the local youth organization Students for Peace, under the banner of "Resist Bush's War," the bands raised $3,000 for War Resisters League and American Friends Service Committee. Another benefit featuring Cringer, Fugazi, Citizen Fish, and Autoclave raised $4,300 for the Washington Peace Center and FAIR (Fairness and Accuracy in Reporting), offered outreach to local coalition forces like the Dorothy

Day Catholic Workers, Quakers, and Unitarian Universalist Committee to protest Desert Shield/Storm (Anderson 1991).

Positive Force's ongoing political commitments resist pigeonholing as well. "PF, by and large, has resisted being affiliated with any specific left-wing tendency or group, whether socialist, communist, or small 'D' democrat or anarchist. We left that intentionally vague," Anderson avows (2014). The organization's goals are not to offer up rapid and vapid slogans and rhetoric: instead, it aims to catalyze and encourage. According to Anderson, "We wanted to create space for people to find their own definition and arena to act within. It seemed to be using the punk ethos" (2014). Other punk antecedents existed, too: "7 Seconds was crucial because people in and around the band formed the first Positive Force out in Nevada that we heard about," Anderson continues. "It helped catalyze not only our group but more than a dozen across the country for a time. The idea was: wherever you were, whatever punk scene, there was something you should be doing. . . . Bands impact people politically first and foremost by being really good bands. The art is really important: you have to move people with your art; otherwise, it's just like me standing on the street corner spouting off," says Anderson (2014).

With that goal in sight, over the decades Positive Force continued to harness post-1980s-era groups like Bikini Kill, Edsel, Lifetime, Ted Leo, Crispus Attucks, and myriad others to support a plethora of causes, yet Fugazi remained perhaps its greatest asset and ally. "Without seeming silly and self-aggrandizing," Anderson continues, "the alliance of Fugazi and Positive Force is one of the more significant and fruitful artistic and political collaborations . . . certainly in punk rock but also music in general. I worked with literally hundreds of bands, and I've never found a band as committed to a political vision as Fugazi. I will also say they were also as committed to their art, and that was part of what made our collaboration with them so powerful" (Anderson 2014). That powerful marriage, which eschewed commerce in favor of conscious commitment to action, remains a steadfast punk trait, rooted in the punk era's earliest efforts, such as closing-night proceeds of the Electric Circus (which hosted the Anarchy Tour in 1976, as well as the Rezillos, the Slits, Buzzcocks, and more) in Manchester, England, being funneled to cancer research in 1977.

One of the supporters of Positive Force was Tomas Squip of Beefeater, also known for his artwork on Scream albums and flyers. "If there ever was a true punk, Tomas Squip was one of those at the head of the pack, for real," tells Fred "Freak" Smith, guitarist for Beefeater. "Tomas really didn't give a shit about living beyond menial means—food, shelter, lifestyle. He lived at the Dischord House for a while in a room, shared a bathroom. He slept on the floor with no furniture. His pillow was a medium-sized rock and he had a blanket to cover himself. He was always reading and constantly on top of all the news, local and global, and on every political issue on the grid. That fucker probably doesn't even know it, but he taught me so much about the world, the system, and us as human beings.

"He really wondered why punks were doing the same things as everyone else did—get fucked up, do stupid things resulting in altercations with law enforcement, and not really trying to distinguish themselves from the norm they were rebelling against, other than clothing and music association," Smith says. "He wondered why people, including myself at the time, didn't try to alter their eating habits to respect animal rights, to change daily aspects of their lives to respect the Earth, to be aware of things that are said at times that are racist and sexist and homophobic. He always thought a lot of punks weren't really trying to make change at all. No rebellion or real anarchy at all. It saddened him all the time. It was very tough for him. He really wondered if anyone, aside from a very small faction of the scene, were any kind of real alternative society at all! I thought it was definitely an alternative society then, and I still think so now. But then again, a lot of things would make an observer looking in totally disagree with me. Like everything else, it basically comes down to what a certain individual is going to do with it—with that punk rock ethic" (Ensminger *Left of the Dial*, 2013).

"Positive Force is not going to change the world, and they know that," fanzine editor Ken McClard noted in 1989. "The point is that while punk and hardcore has always cried out against a world gone sour, punks have not always gone beyond that outcry" (McClard, "Positive Force D.C.," 1989). McClard, like so many other punks tired of empty promises, wanted punk to be more all encompassing, to stand up beyond rhetoric, to achieve something concrete and viable. He was impressed by the group's wide-ranging activities, whether protesting in front of the National Rifle Association office or living communally, promoting recycling, or regularly volunteering in soup kitchens. "Positive Force puts action behind the words. They offer an alternative to words. . . . Protesting can be fun. Hardcore is for real. Positive Force is serious about change. Revolution from the inside out" (McClard, "Positive Force D.C.," 1989).

One of those carrying the Positive Force creed forward in the Deep South is Osa Atoe, journalist, singer, community activist, and organizer. "I grew up in the suburbs of D.C., so the D.C. punk scene was the first one I experienced, starting in the late 1990s. So yes, Positive Force was influential to me (I even tried to join at one point!). Because I grew up around the D.C. punk scene and that was the first one I was exposed to, I always assumed that punk was a political thing. I didn't understand that punk could be nihilistic for awhile.

"My entrance to punk rock was Riot Grrrl. I'd heard the Sex Pistols, the Clash, and NOFX before that, but it didn't make me feel like being a part of punk. Riot Grrrl did. So, I've always connected punk rock to issues of social justice. Positive Force and Fugazi were just more ways in which punk and politics were shown to me to be inseparable. My political awakening and my love for punk rock kind of grew concurrently. I wasn't ever introduced to apolitical punk. I very naively did not realize that there were people out there that thought that punk was just about getting wasted and offending people.

"In 2007, my band New Bloods played a benefit show I set up for the New Jersey Four, a group of black lesbians who were sentenced to prison for defending themselves against a homophobic and racist attack," Atoe messaged me. "I do ongoing benefits for Community Kitchen, a Food Not Bombs–like group that serves free meals underneath city hall every week here in New Orleans. Plus, I run No More Fiction as a way to get more women and LGBTQ [lesbian, gay, bisexual, transgender, queer/questioning] folks to participate in DIY and punk music making. If the show I set up isn't to support a touring band, it is a benefit for a local cause. Our next show is a benefit for Black and Pink, an LGBTQ prisoner support and prison abolition group in New Orleans" (Atoe 2014).

For the likes of Atoe and myriad others, Positive Force is not a history lesson scrawled in stone somewhere out of reach; it is a living lesson, a life blood, which provides a reason to make music, to gather, and to steer the community toward better alternatives than the clanging jostle of green and brown beer bottles at the local dive bar with its enforced age barriers, profit-aimed bottom line, cavalier apolitical vibes, and business-as-usual practices. Atoe believes in punk's transformational credentials and potential, not just its "resting on its laurels" countercultural lore. She is the front line of hope.

SAN FRANCISCO: NOT SO QUIET ON THE WESTERN FRONT

Examining the lineage of punk, the lyrics, and the dress and gear do not convey punk's full impact. Even a quick survey of punk sites—Chagarama in England to CBGB in New York City; the Deaf Club (a deaf social club that hosted punk shows) and Mabuhay Gardens in San Francisco; the Masque in Los Angeles; Raul's in Austin, Texas; Paradise Island in Houston, Texas; and Oz in Chicago—suggests that each locale embodied more than blaring music, hectic multicolored graffiti, fetid bathrooms, and drink-splashed floors. Each became a conveyor belt of performances, subculturally coded behavior, and ideas that tried to overturn antiquated, self-serving notions of rock-industry standards.

"I came to San Francisco in March 1980 and found a bunch of other young people who seemed to feel the same," tells Mia dBruzzi, guitarist for Frightwig. "The music scene and the art scene were one and the same. It was just a huge raging monster of creativity, out-of-control energy producing out-of-control art and music. I don't think anyone gave a shit about pleasing the critics, if you know what I mean—unapologetic creation" (Ensminger "Interview with Mia dBruzzi of Frightwig," 2014). Such bands simply did not toe the line of craven local entertainment industries or feign interest in the hype, skill sets, and attitudes of mainstream musicianship. "When we started Frightwig, we did not know how to play our instruments," she continues. "And here's the important part. We didn't care, and we still don't care, but we did learn how to play. We sounded like things were dying, exploding, being torn apart. 'Sounding good' just wasn't on our priority list. We needed to express our condition (still do), in any way we could. Viscerally and without censor" (Ensminger "Interview with Mia dBruzzi of Frightwig," 2014).

The Bay Area, with its long, undeniable lineage of countercultures (conscientious objectors, Beatniks, and queers) seemed like a microcosm of punk-at-large, too, a perfect home for such bristling and barbed bravado and acrid atavism. "The time and place, Bay Area late 1970s, early 1980s, that I first discovered the punk movement really coincided with the anger and rebellion I was feeling against the status quo of what was going on in America at the time," dBruzzi attests. "Saying 'fuck you' to all the things the media, politicians, and authority figures were trying to cram down our throats as a society really felt like the correct and true thing to do. One of the wonderful things about the San Francisco Bay area is that it's totally acceptable to be a freak here. No one really cares that much if you differ from the 'norm.' That's been my experience, anyway. We have a great history of social commentary and expression. I wish it were more like that today, let me tell you" (Ensminger 2014).

Bands like the Nerves, Dils, and Avengers seemed to straddle two cities—fog-entrenched, hemmed-in, City Lights–backdropped San Francisco and southern freeway-addled, smog-laden, stretched-out cinematic Los Angeles, where the punk scene seemed to spread like hissing prairie fire through diverse communities. "San Francisco is where I ended up to attend San Francisco Art Institute, and it was there I met Penelope," tells Danny Furious (Danny O'Brien), drummer of the Avengers. "For us, San Francisco was the all-important punk music/art scene, simply because we all lived and studied there. We 'grew up' there and held no allegiance to anywhere else except Los Angeles, where we played as often as we did in San Francisco.

"I loved the Hollywood scene, the people and the bands," he confesses. "Not all the San Francisco bands felt this way, but we surely did. We loved playing L.A., we loved playing San Francisco. It was two sides to the same coin. We always remained a San Francisco band heart and soul. I love San Francisco and always will. It has always been a nurturing locale for artistic growth. There is a certain sense of abandon and freedom you won't find elsewhere in any major city anywhere. It's a town where anything can happen and we certainly did happen . . . in San Francisco!" (Furious 2014).

In 1978, the Avengers joined the Nuns as openers for the Sex Pistols' notorious last live gig. Yet in songs like "We Don't Need the English," the Bags, one of Los Angeles' more cantankerous coterie, seemed to attack the fetish of British punk often displayed by homegrown audiences eager to relish visits by the Damned, Clash, and Sex Pistols, onward to Discharge, GBH, U.K. Subs, and Chron Gen in the hardcore era. Danny Furious sees pride, rather than bile, in the song's lyrical craft: "Why did we open for the Sex Pistols' very last show at Winterland? Why wouldn't we? What an amazing opportunity. The Bags would have opened, too, had they been asked, but they weren't asked to open. We were asked and accepted. The Bags' single 'We Don't Need the English' was nothing more than a rallying cry for our local scenes, a rebel yell of pride. Nothing need be read into those lyrics aside from a beating of one's chest to exclaim how proud we were of what *we* were doing" (Furious 2014).

The forceful, wit-infused, and slyly sentient lyrics of the Avengers on the likes of "We Are the One" seem to sweep away any sentiments for machine politics, parent-teacher-media scrutiny of youth, and the passive roles of previously neutered generations. "Our 'politics' were uplifting positive 'messages' to those who cared to listen to what Penelope was singing. Most did not," Furious attests. "Either way, I believe us to have been 100 percent honest about everything we did on stage as well as in our personal lives. Nothing's changed. We are the same people we were in 1977. That's the beauty! We were called pretentious by some older and bitter journalists. Nothing is farther from the truth. We did exactly as we wanted: we looked played and lived as if life depended on it. And it did" (Furious 2014).

Do-it-yourself (DIY) was the destiny of the band. "No one had jobs, so our band was our job. We just barely made rent," admits Furious. "We lived frugal lives, and that's where DIY comes to play here. DIY means you haven't a choice because if *you* don't do it, it don't get done. No one else was gonna do it for you. We did it all ourselves, young and resilient. So damned obstinate and positive, hopeful and determined. Success was viewed in terms of, 'Did we get them up on their feet?' If so, then we did what we came to do! We came to incite. Many people have told me over the years that seeing us for the first time changed their lives. No exaggeration. People have said this to me! Am I proud of that? What do you think? Punk changed the game plan forever. For the better? Who knows, some days I think so. Others, definitely *no*! (Furious 2014).

"Before I got to San Francisco in 1973, at the age of eighteen, I was already a participant in the antiwar movement and had a rock 'n' roll band called Pig Nation in the Buffalo area that attracted some attention for our radical anti–status quo antics," tells Peter Case of the Nerves, the first independent band to tour America, three years before Black Flag. "I'd left school after completing ninth grade and moved in with a bunch of like-minded young freaks. At one point, about sixteen people lived in a six-bedroom ramshackle house for $200 a month. The economy was on the side of youthful culture and insurgents back then, compared to the present.

"My political attitude was formed by growing up in the years of the civil rights and antiwar movements," Case reflects, "watching all of our greatest leaders get murdered; the lyrics of Bob Dylan, Frank Zappa, Jefferson Airplane, MC5, and Phil Ochs; the music of the Plastic Ono Band and Captain Beefheart; and the books of Allen Ginsberg, Abbie Hoffman (*Revolution for the Hell of It*, *Steal This Book*) and *Ramparts* magazine, a radical monthly, which at the time was available at newsstands coast to coast. I was also a big fan of deep blues and country blues musicians, which led me to conclusions at odds with the prevailing culture.

"A lot of people exactly my age or a little older were on a similar path, fed by the same things, and revolution was in the air," he continues. "So, when I got to San Francisco, it was still happening, and things were changing: the much-hated President Nixon resigned, and the last American troops were pulled out of Vietnam on March 29, 1973. J. Edgar Hoover, the arch-vile FBI director who had run the evil COINTELPRO operation to spread confusion and discord that effectively destroyed the political underground, had died in 1972.

"I would say the 'real sixties' ended in late 1974," Case argues. "Before that, there had been a counterculture vibe on the streets, all kinds of kids doing all kinds of interesting things, poetry, music, protest, but after that: zip! The whole thing just kind of dried up and blew away. Where was everybody? Where was my generation? I felt stranded in a dead town in 1975. As we started the Nerves going, it was in a rock 'n' roll vacuum. There were no venues for people our age. One of the only places we could play was the Garden of Earthly Delights, a super-sleazy bar beneath a flophouse at the corner of Eighteenth and Mississippi in Potrero Hill. Another was the Frisco Club, on Sixth Street, near Mission. We did a residency there, but the clientele was mostly drunks, street people, and just a few rock 'n' rollers of any description. These were the *dark ages*. Minnie's Can-Do Club, in the Fillmore," predominately a jazz club where countercultural literati like Ruth Weiss once hosted a poetry series, "was a cool scene, and we played there, but it was mostly oriented toward the black community, and our music seemed out of place there.

"But the future punk people were hiding out in different scenes around the town. The street scene around Polk Street centered around the Haven, an all-night restaurant that let people hang out," Case recalls. "This was where the glam scene met the gay street scene and the drug world. It was all happening, late, at the Haven. We rehearsed right up the street from there. I lived in a residence hotel around the corner. Alejandro Escovedo was hanging around this scene at the time, though I didn't meet him until 1977 at Mabuhay Gardens, when the Nerves and Nuns co-billed. A lot of people I'd see later in bands in audiences in San Francisco were from this scene" (Case 2014).

A major poetry movement jumpstarted in North Beach, too, "centered around the Coffee Gallery and City Lights books. These people were political and far out," Case continues. "Vale from *Search and Destroy* was part of this scene while working at City Lights. His magazine was a big influence on the direction of punk in San Francisco" due to "connecting it with the Beats. City Lights was basically my higher education when I was eighteen and nineteen. They'd let me hang out in there all day, and I basically read my way through the store, very rarely buying a book. I thanked Lawrence Ferlinghetti for that, in person, last year!

"Project Artaud, created in 1971, was a group of radical artists of all types that moved into an abandoned industrial building at 499 Alabama in San Francisco and set to living and working there," Case notes. "A certain surrealistic/Dadaistic high-level x-ray emanated from this place and zapped the whole city. It was an enormous, unsung influence" that later featured performance artists, such as Factrix, Z-EV, and NON, while the Mutants stemmed from the San Francisco Art Institute. "Art schools have always been a breeding ground for cutting-edge music scenes, but the street music scene is where I came from and where I hooked up with Jack Lee to start the Nerves. I went electric out there in 1974, using battery-powered amps, like the Matthews Freedom amp. Street music was a great training ground for the bands that followed: you could play as long as you wanted, say or do anything, get as outrageous as you wanted, and we'd invent all kinds of things to draw attention and provoke audiences. I was never shy on stage after that" (Case 2014).

"Another influence on the scene was the Times Theater at Stockton and Broadway in North Beach," Case argues. "They changed movies every two days, and for ninety-nine cents you could watch mind-blowing movies like *If* (about an insurrection at an English boys school, very radical and violent), *Performance*, Roman Polanski's *Repulsion*, or *Elevator Girls in Bondage*, and a thousand others. Going there was a chance to get a cheap education in cinema, and I'm sure this was a big influence on the punk scene." Meanwhile, "the psychedelic, outrageously dynamic theater group the Cockettes were still around San Francisco at this time, and though officially disbanded, they were an influence on punk, especially Tomata du Plenty, who founded the Screamers down in L.A. The Nerves wanted new music for our generation—fast, hard, loud, and minimal—just stripped of all the bullshit rock was loading onto everything. We hated guitar solos, the music business, radio, phony rock fans, standard rock clothes, long hair, and a lot of other things. And our music was very teenage oriented, though I didn't really realize how much at the time.

"For a spell, I wasn't overtly political, just angry at everything the culture offered and trying to make a noise," Case confers. "There were hidden scenes going on all over the place. It took the catalyst of the punk style and idea"—plus sites like Mabuhay Gardens, which held benefits for KPFA radio and striking Norfolk and Western railway workers, just as On Broadway would soon hold benefits for Casa El Salvador, Charles Briscoe Legal Center, Youth for Peace, and Hopi Indians)—"and the gravity/attraction of that to pull everyone together." Local punk seemed to combine "the newness of the look" with the music informed by "the anger and outrage of the Pistols heard about stateside" (Case 2014).

A decade later, the city was fomenting punk music of a different kind. The Beatnigs channeled the promise of the genre's experimentation and core political ethos with uncanny finesse and artful adventure. Signed to legendary Alternative Tentacles, home of the Dead Kennedys, the Dicks, and T.S.O.L., its smoldering tune, "Television: The Drug of Nation," released in 1988, stung with musical prowess and intelligence. It proved the group's ability to deconstruct media, attacked the powers that be in the Reagan–Bush era, and formed a trenchant groove, too. By melding industrialized punk hip-hop and atavistic performance art to sharpen its message, the Beatnigs seemed cutting edge but also avidly old school, too, partly due to the penetrating tone, wry wordplay, and pulsating elocution of singer Michael Franti, who would later front Disposable Heroes of Hiphoprisy and Spearhead. That side evoked the sociopolitical fervor and musical prowess of the Last Poets and Gil Scott-Heron. Nimble drummer Kevin Carnes, formerly of the Usuals, held down the pliant rhythm section with elastic aplomb.

"There was a lot of music shared between the members of the band, everything from Public Enemy to Bad Brains, the Art Ensemble of Chicago and Sun Ra," he says. "On the industrial side of things, there was a group called Test Department from England and another Bay Area crew called Survival Research Laboratories that were the biggest influences on us. West African music, particularly percussion-oriented stuff seemed to always be playing in the background. I was a DJ during that time. Some of us were really into fashion and visual arts and technology, while others were doing carpentry. Many of us rode bicycles as our main mode of transportation. We smoked and drank and talked into the wee hours like the bohemians we were. It's all there in the music" (Carnes 2015).

Though some tunes like "Burrito" seemed offered some levity, Carnes reminds me that "Global politics can't exist without personal politics, and I've never thought 'Burritos' was funny, though it is very clever. Everything we talked about on stage, we lived, and however many years later, class and race are still two of the biggest social problems in this country. It was very important to us to talk about what was right underfoot and what we were experiencing daily right here in the Bay, which many folks like to say is so 'free' and 'liberal,' but the reality for some? Not so much" (Carnes 2015).

And like so many bands, the Beatnigs reached out beyond the punk ghetto and also kept its eye on humanitarian aims. "We played with M.D.C., Fugazi, Living Colour, the Butthole Surfers, and Schooly D. We jammed with Genesis P. Orridge and Einsturzende Neubauten, as well as countless fans that were brought up on stage or had the stage dumped on them," says Carnes, who later formed the thriving acid-jazz unit Broun Fellinis and worked with Parliament-Funkadelic, Eric

McFadden Trio, and many others. "We did lots of benefits throughout our career. I feel like it's the duty of all artists and entertainers. I learned that from Adam Sherburne [the Usuals, Consolidated], and to this day, I continue to share my musical talents to help bring attention and funding to others" (Carnes 2015).

ABANDONING THE CITY OF THE EAR: PUNK AND DEAF CONVERGENCES

To fixate on the orality of a performance or subculture often eclipses other legacies of punk, including how the community fostered liminal social spaces, translocal community building, performative rituals such as distressing dances and rough-hewn dress, and the inventiveness of punk texts, which deaf punk participants can fully experience and appreciate. Since deaf punks have largely gone unnoticed in both academic and popular press, I explore a short history of punk orality; argue that deaf punks represent an unheard, invisible minority testing punk's sense of diversity; document the ways in which deaf punks navigate and make meaning from punk; and probe deaf/punk intersections, such as San Francisco's infamous Deaf Club.

For decades, describing the voice of iconic punk performers has constituted the normalized narrative of punk-rock critiques. The supposed raw power and authenticity of the genre link to such orality. Joe Strummer's "blast-furnace vocals," "singing in tongues" (Young 1989, 101), and "barbaric yawp" (Cibula 2002) shape perceptions of his inflammatory streetwise ideology even as his own "anger-choked" lyrics often remain "absolutely unintelligible" (Riegel 1978, 52). No matter, Dave Marsh reminds, given the band's charged music as "bitter and angry as the lyrics," for "the sound itself is a fundamental part of the politics" (1978, 53). Johnny Rotten's persona, in turn, is underscored by the filth, ugliness, and vitriol of his guttural growl, endlessly dissected by writers. Yet Calvert envisions this as a punk theater anti-aesthetic, which engenders a moral panic due to Rotten appropriating "moronic behavior" that combines "violence and destruction," "degeneration," and "degradation." These traits seem to "reference an existing mythology of learning" disabilities (Calvert 2010, 5–6).

The trope "gritty" often follows Stiff Little Fingers, too: Jake Burn's delivery was imagined as "gravel-throated," "harsh-throated," and "rabble-rousing" enough to stoke "the fire inherent in the group's music and ideals" (Chappe 1981, 29). Those voices, acting as memes emanating from the shabby urban milieu of London in the 1970s and 1980s, seem pushed to maximum effect by the charred voices of hardcore-era singers or icons like Wendy O. Williams, crossover punk-hardcore-metal singer with "excruciating hyena choke-hold vocals" (I-Rankin' 1986). Generally speaking, Rob Fatal argues that certain adjectives seemed to rise to the forefront as punk vocal descriptors: "shrieks, screams, off key, slurred, grotesque, casual, and predominately unsung" (2012, 165). Hence, punk vocals apparently fit a readymade index.

In particular, writers fetishize Strummer as a shrewd punk messiah figure and a late-twentieth-century soapbox orator radical subsumed by "passion as a fashion." Often strikingly glib and pithy, his tumultuous, breathless, bunched-up words still sprinkle punk's imagined collective memory. They become the fodder for folk-hero status, signal his clairvoyance, and define him as a "common Joe" in American parlance, on the brink of genius, like a poet of ardor and gut feeling. In death, his voice became paterfamilias.

Meanwhile, Poly Styrene's bristling howl, a codex for living in the age of commodity-hypnotized consumer culture, strips away the deodorized cruelties ensconced behind television's glow and continues to stir debates and delight writers. Karina Eileraas argues that punk women used such "impure" voices for "cathartic expression" to articulate their sense of self and "revolt against grammar and syntax" (1997). In songs like "Warrior in Woolworths" and "The Day the World Turned Dayglo," Styrene's teenage voice and assured lyrical phrasing interrogate the vacuumed corridors of the bourgeoisie, including the supermarket glares, "artificial" living and genetic engineering, and the pretexts of comfort without satisfaction. Others, like Mohawk-adorned and black-eyeliner-burnished singer Wendy O. Williams of the Plasmatics, were often considered to embody no more than "grunting" that was "totally indecipherable so she singlehandedly destroys any glimmer of hope for getting the group's message across to the public" (Finnegan 1981, 32). Such screams, Neil Nehring asserts, can be contextualized within a female's fragmented life, in which the scream is decidedly shunned at home for being too overtly emotional and shocking in public due to breaking the boundaries of ladylike behavior codes (1997, 155).

Only contemporary Debra Rae Cohen, covering Blondie for *Penthouse*, seem to understand that singers deliver much more than mere verbal fusillades: "Debbie, like David Bowie and Bob Dylan, sees herself as a canvas, chameleon like, registering the rapid changes of modern culture shock, the need to be a kind of human commercial, brilliantly nonverbal in the land of the self-erasing word" ("Punk's Dream," 1980, 72). Cohen also noted similar traits in ska-punk bands like Madness, "whose charm is visual," displaying rampant syncretic choreography that effortlessly fused together elements of commedia dell'arte, Three Stooges, Keystone Kops physicality, all while embodying "a youthful bar band's gusto, romping through their set [at Irving Plaza in NYC] with all the slapstick jollity of a music-hall troupe" (Cohen April 1980, 68). Such performances, splicing together sundry cultural pieces, are much greater than orality alone can transmit.

Another performer who often transfixed audiences during the same period was Ian Curtis of Joy Division (who played a Rock against Racism benefit in Leeds and City Fun Benefit in Manchester). His cryptic, forceful lyrics and moody, poetic, rueful baritone drew comparisons to Jim Morrison of the Doors and even Frank Sinatra with a frayed edge. Even more so, newsprint from his contemporaries are ripe with effusive commentary about his stage antics, which at times inherited or borrowed—perhaps entirely unconsciously—from the likes of proto-punks such as Iggy Pop. Curtis' idiosyncratic performances were fluid, unabashed, and hypnotic: he would break "off into a wild manic dance routine" unlike any other (Middlehurst 7); "Curtis often loses control. He'll suddenly jerk sideways and, head in hands, he'll transform into a twitching epileptic-type mass of flesh and bone" ("Joy Division: Manchester"); "pallid, hyperactive Ian Curtis, whose weird, wired meckanik dance routines are reminiscent of Lou Reed circa '74," ("Joy Division: Altrincham Inn"); "Curtis may project like an ambidextrous barman purging his physical hang-ups, but the 'gothic' dance music' he orchestrates is well-understood" (Moines), and could even leave crowds in a "goldfish-like trance" (Middlehurst n.d.). The notion of disability appears in the foreground, heightened by the fact that Curtis actually suffered from seizures.

More importantly, the audience-fan common consciousness—established during the key ebb and flow of performance, not with trite banter, which the band almost entirely avoided—seemed stoked by Curtis' unbridled physicality. In doing so, "hackneyed subjects—alienation, mental and social collapse," as well as "apocalypse, hopelessness and fragmentation," could actually rise above mere sonic ruckus and "act as an exorcism of passivity and neglect," revitalizing "the spirit of primeval rock'n'roll," wrote Steve Taylor after seeing them at the Prince of Wales Conference Centre in London. Instead of being enervated, meek, and passive, audiences often became enthralled (Taylor n.d.).

In punk, the voice is potent and invokes an oral terrain. Jello Biafra's (Dead Kennedys) trademark seismically shrill, warbly vocals—dubbed a "unique quiver" by *Trouser Press*—deliver sardonic axioms ranging from "Kill the Poor" to "Die for Oil, Sucker." Even when his utterances are garbled, rushed, indecipherable, and no more than caterwauling and mewling, they are deemed authentic, as if equated with a force meant to extinguish the last bits of disco, country, and pop conventions.

Punk voices are ground zero, even more so than the discordant, stripped-down, bare-boned guitar chords of punk. Everything seems staked on atavistic, aggressive, and defoliated vocals. The stressed syllables, battered rhyme schemes, and the subversion of symbols become lore. The Sex Pistols' snarling "we mean it, man," uttered on "God Save the Queen," does not merely evoke pop reflexivity; it amounts to a fiery declaration of punk's merciless power of wit.

Punk voices act as tropes: Voices erupt as teenage news and scavenge poetry from cities of ruins. Voices char the vocal chords of margin walkers. Voices scrape away the plastic of mass consumption. Voices give form to the psychological detritus of leisure society. Voices embody seismic shifts from the Me Generation to Blank Generation. Voices become soundtracks to doomsday vibes. Voices teach how to bully and how to survive being bullied. Voices calibrate dissent. Voices howl in art rage. Voices act as commodities in fractured free markets. Low-life voices project disobedience, dissidence, and dissonance. Voices catalog ramshackle rebellion and wanton sweat. Voices index angst, anxiety, and chemical imbalance.

Yet by the late 1980s and early 1990s, critics argue, punk and hardcore scenes often fossilized into a male monoculture disposed toward adrenalized aggression and sexist derision. During this era, Kathleen

Hannah from Bikini Kill felt a need to reclaim a "place/voice in punk rock—a voice we've always had that's been trampled on" (Hewitt 1997, 391). Riot Grrrl and female-led garage-rock subcultures seized back the microphones and fanzines, the spoken-word stages and practice pads. They resurrected punk's voice as a power broker, a leveler, and a feminist staging ground.

Years later, such movements and critiques appealed deeply to hard-of-hearing and deaf punks. "Punk rock and feminism inspired me to look into Riot Grrrls," recalls Muslim Deaf punk filmmaker Sabina England. "Then I became interested in women's rights and women's issues, and I discovered there was a disability rights movement within feminism!" (England 2010). "Riot grrrl has definitely been more radical and critical than other parts of punk," writes hard-of-hearing punk fan Christine Jensen. "Lots of feminist circles in the punk scene also tend to critique other privileges. I think once you get into the conversation of gender privilege, it's hard to overlook all of the other ones. . . . Many parts of feminist punk communities are openly critical of other -isms. After all, if you critique gender roles, then a whole bunch of problems unfold. It's hard to avoid" (Jensen 2010).

Still, even radical subcultures can fall short by failing to address "ableism," as well. "As for an example of sexism and racism being more important than tackling ableism," Jensen continues, "I would point to zines and workshops. There are tons of zines and workshops in the radical community here (which is a sister of punk) on racism and sexism, but none on ableism. The fact that workshops are oral presentations is also problematic" (Jensen 2010).

The punk community, despite its posturing and pronouncements, Jensen reports, is entangled in "old ideas about disabilities. It's not something people say out loud. Plus, there are very few people with visible disabilities in the scene. I recall that there was one guy in a wheelchair who played guitar for a band, but I was not close to him. . . . There is just the general ableist comments: saying things are retarded, Helen Keller jokes, and telling people with disabilities that they're not trying hard enough, et cetera. So, most punks carry on the master/normalized narrative—they really don't harbor different views than the average person, in terms of discussing and dealing with disabilities. In fact, may they be a little self-satisfied and smug—not realizing their shortcomings/biases?" Sometimes instead of solving problems, punk "is the problem," Jensen infers (2010).

Deaf culture has long been understood and examined as a subculture itself, Brewington argues, replete with "language, traditions, social values, etiquette, jokes and humor, and view of life" (2003, i–ii). Unfortunately, deaf citizens endure ostracism, neglect, disadvantage, rejection, and discrimination as they maintain and preserve their culture while vying for autonomy and self-control of institutions, including schools and social environments, sometimes managed by hearing communities, states Braden (1994, 49). Such tensions arise, Paddy Ladd argues, because even contemporary deaf citizens lack control over television programs devised in their name, deaf academic studies programs and research, and social welfare services, all of which constitute an effective form of neocolonialism (2003).

Simultaneously, as a subculture, the community is enriched with deeply embedded and distinctive practices, mutual customs and experiences, folklore and history, and other anthropological hallmarks as outlined by Padden and Humphries (1988). As Braden illuminates, through day-to-day interaction, deaf culture's outsider status is not necessarily evident, the "disability" largely unrecognized and invisible until person-to-person interaction occurs. Deaf citizens may fall prey to stereotypes or misinterpretation by a public weaned on inauthentic examples of deaf life; cultural glimpses gleaned from media; a gap in public knowledge about deaf figures as central to American lore as Thomas Edison; and years of denigrating epithets, such as "deaf and dumb." As a result, a master narrative has developed, relegating deaf life to subordinate, inferior status (Braden 1994).

"Teachers [made us] feel like we weren't capable of doing something simple like reading a classic book. That fucked up a lot of kids," England asserts. "She said that because we're deaf, we couldn't really grasp a good understanding of books such as *Moby Dick*" (2010). Other teachers discouraged sign language and stressed reading lips and speaking orally. "In one way, I am grateful for that, and in another way I feel resentful. . . . I had teachers who really cared about us and wanted to see us succeed as normal human beings in society. So they always stressed the importance of oral education, good writing and reading skills, and grammar skills. I've ignored the deaf part of my identity in the past before, and I've felt alone and unsure of my own abilities.

Sometimes I felt like I couldn't do something because of my deafness. I was worried how I'd get a job or volunteer due to communication problems. So it became important to me to start seeking out successful deaf people online. When I met Olin Fortney (deaf punk and American Sign Language instructor) and people from Deaf Women in Film, I felt so much more reassured, and then I became more confident" (England 2010).

Such mixed feelings of shared dissatisfaction and distress, identity-politic recovery, and subculture community building link punks and deaf citizens across class, race and ethnicity, gender, and abilities, sewing a sense of the translocal: "I met so many punks, feminists and deaf people online. They either found me through interviews and articles, or they've stumbled onto me through another friend. I've started talking to this blind anarchist from Australia who speaks about anarchism and disabilities. She fiercely speaks out against society institutionalizing blind people and making them feel incapable," England asserts. "I've read her essays and felt there was something very similar with deaf people. I've also met a lot of great feminists online who have opened my mind and taught me even more radical ideas. I've met many punks online who come from different parts of the world, like Lebanon and Indonesia. Deaf female filmmakers are always encouraging me, and I'm so grateful to them for their support" (England 2010).

Not all deaf or hard-of-hearing punks share the same course of actions. "I know that I haven't been super into finding others who are hard of hearing for some reason," posits Jensen. "It stems from me having a shame issue with my disability. I definitely can see how others would have a stronger sense of translocality than I would if they were really yearning to find other people to connect with (it's a lonely world as a young hard-of-hearing person; there aren't many others). There are lots of places on the Internet for people with specific interests and disabilities . . . [but] I am just not a part of them. But translocality definitely exists" (Jensen 2010).

Yet Jensen questions punk's end game: "I honestly don't see links between punk and deaf messages of empowerment. There are definitely many punks who are into anti-oppression tactics and empowering the marginalized, but it's not an overall punk thing. Empowerment of the marginalized definitely has an appeal for punks, for punk is about questioning authority, and authority tells us to oppress the marginalized. But punk is not about empowerment of the marginalized, even if it can lead to people wanting to do so" (Jensen 2010).

DEAF CLUBS/LIMINAL SPACES

Deaf clubs abounded in the United States until the 1960s because they offered "a piece of their own land in exile—an oasis in the world of sound" (Bragg and Bergman 1981, 421). For decades, the institutions supported "the deaf way." In doing so, spaces like deaf social clubs maintained "a sense of openness, free and relaxed communication, a cohesive spirit, and informal mentoring structure" (Hall 1991). The deaf clubs themselves, as some argue, belonged to an earlier era of deaf culture before the emergence of advocacy centers in the 1980s in metropolitan areas offering services ranging from job training to counseling services. The earlier deaf clubs were "places to congregate, to meet after work on weekends and weekend nights. Deaf clubs organized cultural entertainment: skits, beauty pageants, storytelling, and other forms of narratives. Advocacy organizations can have a cultural agenda, but it is planned and infrequent. Deaf clubs invited drop-ins from anywhere in the country, even the world, but advocacy organizations are professional spaces first and foremost, and social spaces secondarily. Instead of selling beer on weekend nights, these organizations have bookstores and sell educational materials" (Bauman 2008, 174).

In the late 1970s, the San Francisco Deaf Club, situated near the Tenderloin, became a space rented by non-deaf entrepreneurs for punk performances. As a result, it did not act strictly as deaf club leisure social milieu, nor was it purely a punk showcase where punks announced their portent to the world. It offered a betwixt and between space, invoking liminality. The space became unhinged, uprooted, and transformed beyond its common function, if only during the temporary anarchy and autonomy when punk promoters rented the venue and bands chased dissident dreams.

Across town, Mabuhay Gardens, considered "less DIY" due to its professional booker Dirk Dirksen, garnered more attention from the media and iconic musical acts, thus it remains more prominent in the annals of history. In contrast, the Deaf Club, an almost singular manifestation of punk-deaf interplay, slips out of focus. Many bands recall only the dimmest of memories, such as deaf patrons touching the stage or speakers to sense the music or speaking freely with their hands during raucous, noisy sets. "The Deaf Club was fun, and it was cool to see people enjoying the music in a way that was visceral—the vibrations through the floor, the visuals—and knowing the deaf people got punk and loved it, too," Exene Cervenka, co–lead singer of X, reminisced to me in April 2015.

In 1979, Terry Kolb, a fanzine writer, recounted her first Deaf Club visit in the zine *Cometbus*: "One of the deaf guys came over and stuck a rubber alligator in my face, making me laugh. I've since been told that deaf people like punk because they can feel the rhythm even though they can't hear it. I felt their presence significantly contributed to the ambience, which was light and cheerful. . . . I noticed a variety of sexual orientations in the audience, straight as well as gay" (Kolb 2002). As Bonnie Hayes from the Punts tells in an oral history of the club published in my book, *Left of the Dial*, "The club was utterly un-controlled, which was one of the best things about it. It was basically like a big, really messy party at someone's house. It seemed private, like an inside thing—you would meet everybody and be in the family" (Ensminger 2013).

"They let the people play there because they had no interest in music," suggests Winston Smith. "But they actually liked it because they could hear the vibrations. Everything else would go in one ear and out of the other, or it got over their heads. Or under their heads. It wouldn't go in their heads. But punk music would go in. And they did like that. And they also liked the fact that, in most good punk clubs, people were extremely polite. It wasn't like people were total assholes who would try and break each other's heads. That came later with suburbanites coming in trying to pretend they were TV punks" (Chick 1996).

"The San Francisco bands" that thronged the Deaf Club, like the Offs, Noh Mercy, Pink Section, and others, tried to "throw normal rock out a shut window," wrote fanzine editor Jack Johnston in 1979. "I quickly became tired, and continually railed against the audience members at the Mabuhay, whether they were more in the know or less. At the Deaf Club, the club members had no pretense to being pro-English, No New York or Yes Los Angeles; it was their club and they appreciated our loud music," more recently attested Johnston (2015).

"I couldn't find a reason to be divisive or dismissive. I learned the rudimentary ASL [American Sign Language] to spell out 'Bud,' the simplest signing needed to get a beer," Johnston tells. "The Deaf Club was special for not being in North Beach and for being a second-floor walk-up. The block on either side housed a dozen taquerias. It was around the corner from the crucial repertory cinema, Roxie Theatre: we all flocked like lemmings to David Lynch's *Eraserhead* at the Roxie. You climbed the stairs and faced the bar at the back, the stage behind you to the left, on the street side of Valencia. There were no frills, no seats. I had only one turntable; I'd have a forty-five poised to plop down after the needle had been lifted from the last seven-inch 45s" (Johnston 2015).

"I remember the club being a walk-up on the second floor," tells Klaus Flouride of Dead Kennedys in my "Oral History of the Deaf Club." "It wasn't a storefront, likely because they couldn't afford one, because it would have been twice the rent. . . . It was a small club, maybe the size of a storefront, from the front to back, which could cram 150 people in there. I remember the bathrooms being horrific, but bathrooms are always horrific at punk clubs. It could have been just the night of the punk shows that the bathrooms were horrific. I don't know why punk rockers cannot hit a fucking toilet. It drives me crazy" (Ensminger *Left of the Dial*, 2013).

To illuminate what the space represented to gig goers, Johnston's zine *20aMPC* printed the following exhortation under the headline "RIP Deaf Club": "*People who thrash must be regarded as enemies of punk rock*," especially those who "broke the sink, toilet, and kicked holes in the bathroom walls" of the club. This meant people "can't meet . . . can't hear the bands play and basically can just rot in our rooms." Instead of dismantling punk spaces, real rebels should redirect their anger, Johnston suggests, toward "the Bank of America buildings, IBM Headquarters, Bechtel Corporation Offices, or the Pacific Union or Bohemian Clubs," not their home turf, which had already drawn the attention of the police due to noise complaints, alcoholic beverages reported on the street, and patrons obstructing the sidewalk (Johnston 1979).

"This is the price of publicity," Johnston admitted at the time. "It is best to go upstairs or drift across the street. Just disperse. We are not the ones who should be put in jail" (1979). Such harassment of punk clubs was completely normalized in most communities, which often deemed such spaces a hostile affront to public taste and safety. Ironically, by enforcing such laws as dance code violations (lack of proper licensing), local authorities, the defenders of privilege, often wrestled continuously with the small-time anarchy epitomized by gigs by the Germs, Dead Kennedys, Zeros, Pearl Harbor and the Explosions, and many more, with their occasional valve effect of letting off the steam of the disenchanted, even as much greater, actual crimes occurred. Luckily, bands, promoters like Robert Hanrahan, and zinesters like Jack Johnston worked earnestly to create relatively safe, self-monitored spaces, despite police pressures to disband and discontinue.

Robert Hanrahan was fortunate to have earned the trust and developed a relationship with the membership of the San Francisco Club for the Deaf, which allowed him to run the Deaf Club, a venue within their own club. As Hanrahan attests, he became a member and continued to raise money for the club, integrate hearing and deaf people, and provide an open and welcoming venue radically different from the Mabuhay, where bands were ripped off, ignored, and abused. He found kindred spirits who shared his mission and his political and artistic vision to join together and cooperatively run the club and subsequent businesses. He and Peter Worral (who also designed all in-house graphics) booked the bands, and they also arranged tours. Hanrahan oversaw the club, the label, and the production company—Walking Dead—and, alongside Johnnie Walker, managed their music publishing company, Can You Hear Me Music.

Hanrahan insisted bands understand that their music was also their livelihood, and he encouraged them to develop business sense and to take the time to read the *Billboard* publication *This Business of Music.* Bands he managed, whether briefly or long term, like the Offs, Bags, and Dead Kennedys, benefited from the relationship. Established local and out-of-town bands like the Dils and Tuxedo Moon, the Pointed Sticks, Germs, X, and third-generation local bands like Pink Section, VS, Blowdryers, and Los Microwaves benefited because of the club and its community. As Hanrahan points out, he provided continuity, stability, and vision until Johnnie Walker pulled out of the partnership during the time the Offs were booked at Max's Kansas City and Hurrahs in New York City. Hanrahan finally left the Deaf Club to Bruce Conner, a close friend who used a university grant to host a final party that officially closed the club.

"It's disturbing for me to see that people are so committed to relive a singular moment in their lives that invokes 'the good old days,' even if it is about an honest dive like the Deaf Club," Hanrahan attests, "and they had an authentic and rewarding good time there. Better for me to honor the past, send the memories to a better place after learning from them, set them aside and not relive them or repeat any mistakes.

"Think of experience as a bottle of wine," he suggests, looking back. "You bought it, you drank it, you enjoyed it; it's empty and you can't ever refill it with the same stuff again. Hopefully it was good and the experience was rewarding. The Deaf Club was fun without restrictions; the people who went there are still special. Leave it like that" (Hanrahan 2014). As Brad Lapin wrote in *Damage* fanzine, "The Deaf Club . . . set amidst seedy transient hotels and tacky taco houses . . . was one of those venues which was less of a club than a focal point for a particular energy, for a special way of feeling and believing . . . a place where all the conflicting symbols and psyches that are both of and in the underground . . . suddenly merged" (1980). For a short while, the club seemed unbound by typical conventions, a place to explore the aesthetics of innovative music and unique setting rather than simply being a venue tied firmly to the maxims of money envy.

Years later, punks like Sabina England entered similar "unbound" punk spaces where she immersed in liminality, communitas, and shared practices: "Some places I've been to aren't padded very well, so I couldn't enjoy the vibrations. I'd just sit down and talk to some of my friends. At other shows, the vibrations were everywhere, and I would be dancing away and slamming with everyone. It's such a great rush. One of my friends who wasn't a punk always went to punk shows with me just to body slam with everyone because he had a lot of rage, and it was the only time he could physically unleash his aggression. Afterward, he'd be body bruised all over and sweaty. He'd be like, 'That was fucking awesome; I feel so much better now. Let's go home'" (2010). That physical indiscretion, constituting an embodied sense of vitality, is potent to deaf punk participants, too.

The history and interplay between deaf and hearing cultures is nuanced and complex. When deaf citizens are immersed in the oralist discourse of learning institutions—ones lacking deaf traditions, history, and pride—scholars like Ladd suggest the actions and discourse of those institutions can cause harmful results, such as feelings of inferiority, damage, or trauma (2003, 180–81). Punk situates that suffering and in turn acts as a counterweight—a stimulus to empowerment, too. As Dee Dee Ramone of the Ramones acknowledged in his biography, "if the Ramones were put into the position of representing something of learning value, it is that there is hope and that it is possible to rise above oppression" (2016, 262).

The Minutemen, Houston, 1984. ***Ben DeSoto***

Lisafer / Lisa M. Pifer, Houston, 2014. ***David Ensminger***

Bad Religion, Houston, 2011. ***David Ensminger***

Jello Biafra and the Guantanamo School of Medicine, Houston, 2014. *David Ensminger*

Cheetah Chrome, Houston, 2010. ***David Ensminger***

D.O.A., Houston, 2014. ***David Ensminger***

M.D.C., Houston, 2016. ***David Ensminger***

Gary Floyd, Houston, 2014. ***David Ensminger***

The Minutemen, Houston, 1984. ***Ben DeSoto***

The Ramones, Houston. ***Ben DeSoto***

X, Houston, 2015 ***David Ensminger***

Kevin Carnes (the Beatnigs), The Usuals, Houston. ***Ben DeSoto***

Plasmatics, Houston, 1981.

Raw Power, Houston, 2014. ***David Ensminger***

Scream, Tulsa, 2015. ***David Ensminger***

Really Red, Houston, circa 1979. ***Andy Abbott***

M.D.C., Houston, 1988. ***Ben DeSoto***

The Clash, Houston, 1979. *Andy Abbott*

Rock against Racism, "Divide and Rule? Never."

SUPRESS Benefit, Long Beach, CA. ***Victor Gastelum***

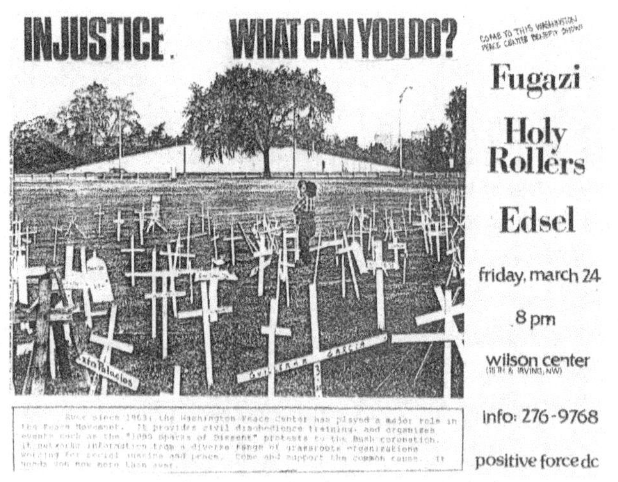

Washington Peace Center Benefit. ***Positive Force***

HARDCORE WEEKEND

Saturday 9th November & Sunday 10th November 1996

Saturday: First band on at 5pm. Sunday: First band on at 2pm

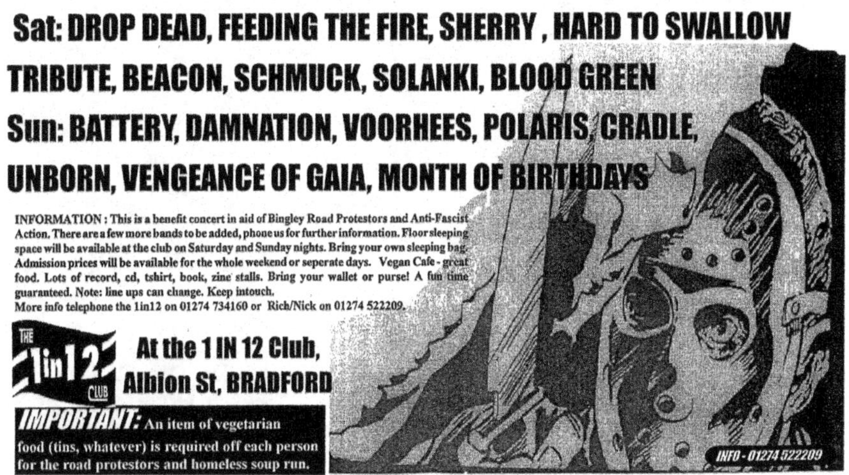

Anti-Fascist Benefit, 1 in 12 Club, Bradford, UK, 1996. *1 in 12 Club*

verbal assault fire party all white jury

BENEFIT FOR BIG MOUNTAIN LEGAL DEFENSE FUND

Benefit for Big Mountain Legal Defense Fund. ***Positive Force***

John Brown Anti-Klan Committee benefit, On Broadway, San Francisco.

4

SHOT FROM BOTH SIDES

M.D.C.

M.D.C. has remained steadfast and sturdy, like an emblem of undaunted, do-it-yourself (DIY), garage-born thrash punk whose veins run deep with humor ("My Family Is a Little Weird") and political conscience, including raising money for the John Brown Anti-Klan Committee and for groups like the Vancouver Five, No Business As Usual, Vandenberg Action Coalition (an antinuclear group), Nuclear Resister, Youth Action for Peace, and more via the *P.E.A.C.E* compilation. Chiseled from the input of three core members—David Dictor, Ron Posner, and Al Schvitz —the band has told uncomfortable truths and rattled innumerable orthodoxies since first seizing the subcultural night in Austin, Texas, during the seismic late 1970s.

Dictor's father, stationed in the Pacific Theater, fought in World War II, like the father of Gary Floyd, one of Dictor's punk heroes. Posner's father fought in the 1948 Arab–Israeli War, surviving with a metal plate in his leg and mental scars. Both families were hardscrabble folks who endured the sting of poverty but mustered courage and resilience, climbing the economic ladder, often on their own terms. "They didn't take shit from no one," Posner and Dictor agree. "Every cent earned and spent meant a tremendous sacrifice. One's word was final and good to the grave," says Dictor. "If family members were lucky enough to get a grant for college, they had to learn Latin and Greek, read all the classics, and memorize 'Locksley Hall'" (Dictor 2012). The parents worked endless overtime, slaved to a meager wage, and slept, barely, when they could squeeze in the time. During this era, "Saying 'God Bless America' and pledging allegiance to the flag actually got you somewhere . . . if you were lucky," tells Dictor.

Dictor grew up in Glen Cove, the far-flung tip of Long Island's north shore, during 1960s AM radio's bountiful pop fare, and he immersed himself in the Beatles, Otis Redding, Marvin Gaye, and the Jackson Five, which later came to be known as classic rock. "I loved the Beatles, big time," Dictor freely admits. "They nourished me and helped raise me. Life pre-Beatles was a very, very different world. Life in the 1950s was jarheads and *Father Knows Best* clones, Opie, Mayberry and Lawrence Welk—a really different world" (Dictor 2012).

Triggering episodes swept through Dictor's life. "One of my first conscious memories outside of family life was when JFK was shot. I was seven years old at the time the president was shot. I grew up Catholic in New York City, and it was a big deal. Right away, I knew things were not right. When I was in seventh grade, Martin Luther King was shot, then a month later Bobby Kennedy was shot. You just knew that things were terribly wrong. You'd turn on the TV . . . people were fighting with the police everywhere. You're brought up in this fairytale America where we won World War II, we saved the world from the Nazis, but it doesn't seem like everyone is all that happy. So I had that political bent, that curiousness, like, why aren't people happy? Why are we in Vietnam? Slowly but surely, you find out that this World War II hero, Ho Chi Minh, is fighting in his own country, to fight the French, then you realize American dominance is based on oil, power, this vague notion of stopping dominoes from falling and engulfing the world. You fill up with this cynical view of the world. That was me from early on. Bob Dylan's music supported that skepticism.

"I was brought up on rock concerts," says Dictor. "I saw Traffic, Edgar Winters, Johnny Winters, Mahavishnu Orchestra, Hot Tuna, and Billy Cobham. Some older friends were into Dizzy Gillespie and the jazz scene. Their whole thing was, 'You gotta see everyone at least once'" (Dictor 2012). Dictor headed to a Newport jazz festival, where he saw Ella Fitzgerald and Rahsaan Roland Kirk. At the time, popular music was often the focus of passion and humanitarianism, knowledge and heritage, not mere plastic jukebox novelty tunes for the Age of Aquarius.

Then came so-called prog, classic rock, and psychedelic rock, including Yes, an aging Who, and Pink Floyd. Eventually, these promising bands morphed into bloated, empty spectacle arena rock, losing rock 'n' roll's primal, boisterous intimacy. "I started going to concerts where there were forty thousand people, and I started to feel like a bug. Finally I saw the Who—and I love the Who, I mean we all love the Who, right? I didn't realize Peter Townsend had a cast on his arm 'til . . . someone told me" (Dictor 2012). Dictor soon dreaded being crammed into stadiums with ten to twenty thousand people. He chose to plop down outlaw country like Willie Nelson on his record player and eventually bluegrass, too, even as he soaked up the subversive rock 'n' roll fare of the Velvet Underground and the New York Dolls.

Schvitz, a trained drummer, and Dictor, who met in college in Florida, were genuine Grateful Dead fans. "I threw my clothes in the fire while watching the Dead in 1972 in Jersey City during my high school years. By 1974, I must have seen the Grateful Dead at least fifteen times. Al had seen them twenty-five to thirty times. In fact, he had collections of live show reel-to-reels" (Dictor 2012). Both of them headed back to Long Island after college. Schvitz gigged professionally, and sometimes Dictor tagged along. Within months, Dictor grew restless, grabbed a guitar, and began strumming jangly three-chord Dylan and the Band songs.

He also experienced the lewd lure of rock 'n' roll's potent power and symbolism. "I saw the Rolling Stones in New York City in 1973, and that's when they had the big penis floating in the crowd. It was Ron Wood's first tour" (Dictor 2012). That sexual, rock 'n' roll underworld felt magnetic. Dictor enjoyed the edgy street youth culture of Mott the Hoople and the sweaty romp and seductive ethos of glam rock. "I loved Lou Reed, 'Sweet Jane,' that heavy, sexual, ambiguous reality. I was very attracted to that. Then Roxy Music came along. I grew tired of the old regime. It was very fresh in contrast to the staid hippie rock era. Who needed Jefferson Starship after seeing Patti Smith?" (Dictor 2012).

By 1976, Dictor moved to Austin, Texas, hoping to run into Willie Nelson or Jerry Jeff Walker. "I was an acoustic-guitar-playin' stoner college boy with some gender issues," he quips. "*Like Fast Times at Ridgemont High* meets *Animal House* while looking to 'Take a Walk on the Wild Side'" (Dictor 2012). Trying to find Willie, though, proved daunting. A cold reality set in: he wasn't going to hang out with Willie, Waylon, and the boys at dingy, dusty bars. The outlaw idols didn't linger in the campus ghettos or fish taco stands. So Dictor went back to school at the University of Texas, enrolling in American studies and world history courses, but he didn't abandon songwriting.

"Everyone in that part of the world with a little freak headed to Austin," a bustling college town and state capital, says Dictor. As the punk and new wave scene kicked off everywhere, local weirdoes and movers and shakers immersed themselves in the Sex Pistols, Elvis Costello, Blondie, Patti Smith, the Ramones, Devo, and the Runaways. During this period, Dictor realized that the Ku Klux Klan and an army of antiunion vigilante groups in the south Texas valley were killing farm workers and labor leaders. Regarding race relations, the South sorely lagged behind much of the country. "I had a landlord that talked to me about field niggers all the time," Dictor tells. "When he talked about the football players at the University of Texas, he'd say, 'That one's a good boy. In the old days, he was a field nigger.' I had never heard that term" (Dictor 2012).

Deep racism still scarred the Texas heartland. Dictor had to make music to affect the conscience of people. Punk wasn't a facile, "look at me" fashion statement. Sporting a mohawk, spikes, colored hair, patches, and anything remotely weird and off-color was not acceptable. "The city was a local playground, a college town ripe with rich kids—privileged and entitled Frat Rats," says Dictor. "The police department was sleeping with the Klan and the city rife with redneck, bull riding, 'spare the rod, spoil the child' cowboys with thick Texan accents looking to lasso the next queer. For any minority, be it Mexican, black, woman, hippie, or gay . . . one moment, you're walking down the street minding your own business, and the next thing you know, a truckload of assholes jumps you out of the blue" (Dictor 2012). This happened to Dictor and countless others, for Austin became a territory mired in random acts of violence and bigotry.

Raul's Club, opened by Joseph Gonzalez and Roy "Raul" Gomez at 2610 Guadalupe Street between West Twenty-Sixth and Twenty-Seventh Streets, became an epicenter for local and touring underground music. Bands, such as the Violators, the Skunks, and the Huns, held court, and by 1980, punk graffiti accumulated there, too. Huge logos for the Dicks and Big Boys, as well as the slur "poser," lined the front wall, while the south wall was drenched in phrases like "Eat Out," "Go!" and "Freedom," as well as band logos for Action Toys, Offenders, INM8s, the Dicks ("Are Back"), The Ideals, M8, Standing Waves, and others. Interior murals on peeling walls featured large cavorting rats. Boxy speaker cabinets dangled from the ceiling, and the stage was high enough to bump knees. On any given night, patrons wearing *Roadie* tee shirts, scuffed sneakers, homemade shorts, or cowboy boots and suspenders danced while drinking Budweiser from sweaty cans, cigarettes dangling from alabaster fingers, and watching gaunt men with hairy legs wearing high heels and fishnet stockings sing as the makeup melted under their eyes. One generic flyer for the club featuring an inky illustration of a naked, duct-taped woman staring at viewers read: "Raul's: Keep Abreast of the Latest in Bizarre Experiences for Your Family." The club goers lived that creed at the club, which offered open mic night on Mondays. During one rather rambunctious session, some people playing simple, three-chord rock ended up breaking their guitars, while another night featured people throwing chairs at each other. "I loved how everybody really felt it," says Dictor, admiring the immediacy of the fan vibe and uncertainty of what might happen any given second. Plus, for Dictor, "the warmth of being in a room with one hundred to three hundred people really hits home" compared to the choreographed spectacles of self-obsessed dinosaur rock (Dictor 2012).

By this time, Dictor had already penned "My Family Is a Little Weird" but still felt like a hesitant kid. One night, after meeting Carl Sagan at a University of Texas event, Dictor was "coming home from it, feeling high as kite, and there was a crowd outside of Raul's, and I knew exactly what it was: it was Monday night open mic. I just went over there, and they were so inviting and so cool" (Dictor 2012). Dictor ran home, grabbed a guitar, and came running back to play a few songs. "I played it outside because I didn't dare get up on stage and play for punks, but they were like, 'That's a great song.' No one had ever said to me, 'Those songs are great' in my life. It took punk rockers saying it to me, not my Dylan and Deadhead buds from Long Island, not country-western people" (Dictor 2012).

After John Wayne died in the summer of 1979, Dictor penned the barbed "John Wayne Was a Nazi," a biting invective against the jingoist Hollywood icon. He tried to give it to renegade Ty Gavin of the Next, who responded, "Dave, that is your song. You should be playing it."

"That was a good kick in the behind," Dictor tells. "He reminded me, 'No one is going to do it like you mean it, like you feel it with the breadth of your experience'" (Dictor 2012). The song stemmed from heartfelt anger after watching countless Wayne films, whether he was charging up Porkchop Hill or killing Asians as a handsome Green Beret. "It was being shoved down our throat," says Dictor. "It was made to be popular culture, but it's not beautiful, it's not fabulous, and it's not what I think people should believe in" (Dictor 2012). Such hero worship was profound in the southwest. "In Texas, John Wayne's revered like a hero. If he could be alive and running for governor, he'd win in a snap," Dictor once insisted to *Ripper* fanzine (Bowles 1983). Dictor began pressing his pen to paper, configuring new songs, beginning to end, in as little as twenty minutes, catalyzed by the energy peppering the scene. He sketched "I Hate to Work" in the bathroom between hectic deliveries for Domino's Pizza. Other polemical lyrics soon followed.

The restless, eccentric underground figures of the ribald punk scene helped stir and encourage Dictor's slightly wonky urges. Though a loner of sorts, he started befriending more people. By sheer coincidence, he met Gary Floyd, future singer of the Dicks, after picking him up hitchhiking. "I had never met anyone who created his own version of the universe he was living in with as much conviction," Dictor intones. "He was the first real punk I had ever met. Gary really, really inspired me to get a band going, so I started writing about how I really felt" (Dictor 2012).

"They wanted him to just roll up and die," Dictor told *Ripper*, "because he's such a freak. Instead he got up and was strong enough to persevere against all the 'you fat queer,' et cetera, that he must have heard a million times coming from Palestine, Texas, the rural part of Ku Klux Klan country. He was a real influence spiritually and intelligently and emotionally" (Bowles 1983). At the time, Floyd had been creating posters for his punk band even though he lacked musicians. The Dicks, like the early Cramps, were merely a "poster band." Their cut-and-paste, "ugly beauty" flyers could be seen on poles throughout town.

After meeting in 1978, Posner and Dictor realized that they shared a common desire: each hungered to be in a band. Dictor discovered Posner's guitar prowess, which was indelibly shaped by a nimble background in flamenco. He could agilely pump out versions of the Who *and* Ramones with equal aplomb. Nothing happened easily or overnight, though. One project known as the Rejects included Kevin Bastion singing, both Posner and Dictor on guitars, Franco Mares on bass, and Colin Jones on drums. It evolved until Amy Mann sang for a bit. "We were a 'garage band' playing at home mostly," Dictor tells. "Occasionally we'd rock a party with maybe thirty people, where we'd get up and play three songs, but we would not even get up and say, 'We're the Rejects'" (Dictor 2012). The band was spontaneous and shifting and on any night might include someone on tambourine just because he or she happened to be standing nearby. Mann, a girlfriend of Posner, seemed to exude cutting-edge punk-meets-pop fashion trends, with a visual dollop culled from X Ray Spex.

Austin's 1979-era bands featured at events like the battle of the bands included the likes of Boy Problems, Re*Cords, and Invisibles. Yet, contrary to what Tim McKee argues, an ongoing rift between punk and new wave did gestate. Manager "Steve Hayden hedged his bets on the fluffy, 'fake band' new wave patrol as his major source of income and success," both Dictor and Posner agree, "whereas punk just wouldn't go away, which is what the establishment really wanted" (Dictor 2012). On the one side was the tamer blueprint of softcore: F-Systems, Standing Waves, the Judys, and Terminal Mind. On the other, the more raucous roster included the Dicks, Sharon Tate's Baby, the Offenders, us (as the Stains), and Perverted Popes. In terms of early Austin political events like the FDR benefit in solidarity with the people of El Salvador, the hardcore, or at least harder-edged, bands appeared en masse, with the Reactors, the Rejects, and the Inserts joining them.

One major band—the Big Boys, who also appeared at the benefit—seemed to straddle both genres and communities. "They were so accessible that they could have a foot in both camps," says Dictor. "The sentiment of in-your-face 'Frat Cars' or 'Brick Wall' would be followed by mind-boggling funk. Randy 'Biscuit' Turner would put XXX flyers all up and the down the drag where the students would see them on the way to class. One of them used an image from an S&M mag with a guy putting a nail up his penis" (Dictor 2012). As if responding to a challenge to disrupt good taste even further, Dictor made flyers with pages torn from magazines like *Enema Digest* and *Transvestite Transformed*. The poles of Austin became a raw, unpolished, irreverent gallery, a visual analog to their lyrical fare.

Although few might suspect it now, funk music played a huge role in the early Austin punk scene. Mikey Donaldson's (The Offenders, MDC) early record collection featured well-worn albums from Funkadelic, Bootsy's Rubber Band, Cameo, and Chic. Such music continually played on M.D.C.'s "ghetto blaster," which also rippled with early rap like Grandmaster Flash, Melle Mel, and Fat Boys. When James Brown came to Austin, the first four rows on the dance floor were made up entirely of punks, attests Dictor. The link was also robustly evidenced by Big Boys' fun, fun, fun style grooves, including their sets sizzling with Chubby Checker covers and stabs at go-go music, like "What's the Word?" and "Common Beat."

In 1980, Steve Hayden bought Raul's and continued the more new wave–geared style of music, much disliked by up-and-coming hardcore bands. Bouncer Tuck was the venue's muscle. Posner actually spray-painted "Steve Hayden sucks ass, Fuck Tuck" above the marquee. It was soon blotted out by black paint, but Posner returned, in revenge mode, repeating the spurious effort. Dictor, in turn, was blacklisted for life after pogoing at the first Black Flag show in Austin, featuring the frenetic outpourings of wiry Dez Cadena on vocals. "No slam dancing" was one of Steve Hayden's restrictions decried by younger fans.

The Stains headed to Los Angeles in the summer of 1981, where the huge rough-and-tumble crowds and the police brutality, especially toward punks and minorities, became notorious. A hostile divide existed between intractable, overzealous, baton-wielding police and restless, feral, hardcore youth in ripped jeans, combat boots, bandanas, and spiked bracelets. Incidents at the Elks Lodge and Cuckoo's Nest, where the Austin-based Stains gigged with the Los Angeles–based Stains, became part of the memory, lore, and emblems of the West Coast punk underground. "We started saying 'fuck those dead cops,'" says Dictor, haunted both by the deplorable police riots at the Cuckoo's Nest and by the death of Tate Bryant, a college cohort of both Dictor and Schvitz, killed in 1975 by police in a drugstore break-in. "We always had issues with the cops. I was a little kid watching the 1968 Democratic Convention, where the cops were beating everyone, including Dan Rather. Cops hassling people were an everyday occurrence. If you are of a certain age, you experienced it" (Dictor 2012). After returning from the gig at Cuckoo's Nest, the band briefly discussed changing its name to Texas Stains, Tex Stains, or even Fatal Stains, but Buxf Parrot of the

Dicks suggested the much more intense moniker "Millions of Dead Cops" (M.D.C.), which stuck but also raised the band's visibility as "troublemakers" as well as its status. M.D.C. explained to *Maximum Rocknroll* that the name was "an emotional response to police repression and the abuse of authority. . . . The name shows an empathy with the feelings of the victims of extreme police abuse," though the band certainly did not advocate "killing cops or . . . merciless killing" ("Rock against Reagan" 1983). Partly to cope with such heated debate, as well as with the violence suggested by the name, they later experimented with other variations, like Multi-Death Corporation, Missile Destroyed Civilization, Millions of Dead Children, Millions of Damned Christians, and Metal Devil Cokes. Posner even jokingly suggested Misguided Devout Christians and Male Dominated Culture to *Flipside*. "M.D.C. is more like the block and that block stands for a number of different things," Dictor explained to the same fanzine in 1983.

California buzzed with the hard-edged, vociferous, buzz-saw music of youthful dissent stemming from Black Flag, Youth Brigade, Social Distortion, and T.S.O.L. from SoCal. San Francisco, home to fanzines like *Maximum Rocknroll* and bands like the Dead Kennedys, was rupturing and ricocheting with second-wave, emergent hardcore punk, too, and offered accessible soup kitchens to feed the poor youth. "San Francisco was really a 'Wild in the Streets' kind of town, and we were the farm boys that couldn't go home after seeing Paris. The *All's Quiet on the Western Front* compilation really captured these golden years of American hardcore," remembers Dictor (2012).

By 1981, M.D.C. started meeting touring bands like Black Flag, Fear, and D.O.A. and realized that DIY—"doing it yourself"—was the real deal of the hardcore modus operandi. "Before DIY, the deal was to play locally, work on a demo, wait for the word to get out, and pray some big label hears about you and backs you," Dictor says (2012). Early American hardcore punk bands realized that no label was going to finance and produce them like the more marketable Clash or Devo. Hardcore punk was simply too brash and brusque, too choleric and cantankerous, too indignant and irate. Like Black Flag, the Nerves, X, and Alley Cats before them, M.D.C. had to network and write friends, send freshly recorded vinyl singles to other cities, procure a hearty van, and get on the road by tapping into the approximately twenty places on the dog-eared map where underground, independent bands could even hope to get gigs. In doing so, the band would eventually gig with Minor Threat, Reagan Youth, and others on the East Coast.

According to Posner, M.D.C. desired to test itself, not just to gig to safe, hometown crowds where the same people clustered. He wanted to know whether its brand of blitzkrieg hardcore and its unapologetic, agitprop messages would be accepted or tossed aside. He was keen to leave Austin. Schvitz was, too, telling *Ripper*, "Logistically, Texas is not a good place for a hardcore band to be because Austin and Houston are the only viable cities to play in. And it's a thousand miles in any direction. The media support for hardcore is *nil*. . . . There's fanzines and stuff, but radio isn't interested" (Bowles 1983). The time arrived to jettison the safety of Raul's and zoom a thousand nervous miles away from the seeming black hole of the South.

M.D.C. first toured the states in 1982, organizing a hundred gigs in 120 days, then headed to Europe for eighteen shows with the Dead Kennedys. In New York City, it helped the Rock against Racism efforts alongside the Bad Brains, which eventually congealed into the Rock against Reagan tour, with D.R.I., the DKs, Reagan Youth, the Dicks, and so on. The Rock against Reagan tour in 1983 featured approximately thirty-nine shows sponsored by the Yippies from April through July. The events were free, politically centered shows, often held on state capital steps and public spaces, which fused punks with regular agitators, activists, and various progressive people. Fun and furious, sometimes poorly organized and chaotic, many of the participants felt punk could conquer the world. As Dictor explained to *Suburban Punk*, "Woodstock was, 'everyone get their ya-ya's out, taking their shirt off, putting up tents, let's go ball in the woods,' [while] this is directly involved with Ronald Reagan and the United States foreign policy" (Quint 1983). In *Maximum Rocknroll* in May/June 1983, M.D.C. published an open letter describing the tour as a response to that odious side of America: "The U.S. government encourages 3rd world fascists, appropriates billions for them, uses the C.I.A. to cause psychological and physical terror to students groups, peasants, unions, and the intelligentsia—all in the name of freedom" (M.D.C. 1983). From Madison, Wisconsin, to Buffalo, New York, and Washington, D.C., the tour intended to counteract that tide with information, spirit, unity, and calls for justice.

From 1982 to 1983, after releasing its eponymous first album on its own label, R Radical Records, the band crisscrossed the country, staying with friends in New York City, including members of Cause for Alarm and Reagan Youth. While in the teeming metropolis, they recorded the "Multi-Death Corporation" single with Papa Jerry, who's featured in the *American Hardcore* documentary film. "We'd stay until the point we were quasi-considered a New York band. We weren't really a New York band, but we just hung there so much," Dictor recalls. "One year we stayed there three months. The next year we went back and stayed there about four months. That's how we got this part-time New York City–band reputation at the time" (Dictor 2012). Before hardcore punk started its descent into divisions, subgenres, and identity politics, places like New York boiled with people "going crazy, declaring independence, being part of the hardcore music revolution, and then it broke down. We started realizing [that] we don't have that much in common with others," explains Dictor. "We liked the Bad Brains politically, but what they said about gay people didn't rub us right; then the scene started breaking apart" (Dictor 2012).

From their very first chords onward, M.D.C. touted political agitation and aggression. "We weren't singing about straight edge and we weren't singing about, 'If I could only have a Pepsi [a reference to a line from "Institutionalized," a song by Suicidal Tendencies] or I am about to explode.' Not to put anyone down, but that just wasn't our thing. Right away our songs were 'John Wayne Was a Nazi,' 'Corporate Deathburger,' 'I Hate Work,' and 'Church and State,'" explains Dictor. "We were older. We were twenty-four by the time 1981 came around. So, we weren't like sixteen and seventeen. We kind of had been on our own for six or seven years. Nobody was living at home with their parents. We had a certain amount of political sophistication. When the shit went down with the Bad Brains, the Bad Brains, who were also about our age, were used to dealing with Teen Idles and the like in the D.C. scene—people like five to seven years younger than them. So, due to a certain amount of respect for their age, just social maturity, they could get away with saying some outrageous homophobic things, and nobody would challenge them on it" (Dictor 2012).

Those attitudes made M.D.C. bristle. "But when they did it with us, I'm looking H.R. of Bad Brains in the eye and going, 'We're the same age, and your homophobia is creepy and doesn't ring a bell at all'"

(Dictor 2012). Dictor was not willing to shrug off the Bad Brains and its demeaning stigmatization of homosexuals. "I'm not going sit there and go, 'Wow, you're a great musician and you write some great songs, so everything that comes out of your mouth is so cool or plausible.' I will call you on what I find not plausible" (Dictor 2012). Ironically, the Bad Brains were older, as was Randy "Biscuit" Turner from the Big Boys and the Dicks. Therefore M.D.C. chose not to offer the Bad Brains any slack or to accept the prejudice as the misdeeds of misinformed youth.

"I always wanted to perceive punk as political. Or at least art as political statement," Dictor informs. "By 1982, we were elevated to being a political band. First we thought of ourselves as that, but *Maximum Rocknroll*, the California punk zine, elevated us to that, and by 1982 we were doing Rock against Racism/Reagan tours. It was something that really was meant to be. Soon enough there were splits within the political and nonpolitical American punk scenes. Many bands and fans found it easy to slide into and out of these factions. We still played with all sorts of apolitical bands. Just not with ones that were hostile to our politics. It was always on our mind to be deliberately political. From 'John Wayne Was a Nazi,' 'Multi-Death Corporation,' 'Millions of Damn Christians' to our last singles 'Patriot Asshole' and 'Maryjane for President.'

"The hardcore thing just exploded," tells Dictor. "Thousands of people were at these L.A. shows at the Olympic Auditorium. It was just an incredible feeling. We played this Rock against Racism event in New York City and San Francisco in 1983, free events put on by the Yippies. There were ten thousand people showing up. It was so special, it's hard to put into words. But it became a rock business, a rock commodity, and arena rock—like if we can get twenty thousand people to pay fifteen bucks each, we start dividing up the money, like when Madonna sells out Madison Square Garden" (Dictor 2012).

Yet punk rock was not one big happy family. M.D.C. made huge sacrifices to live together, and sometimes those pressures were volatile and bruising. They moved to San Francisco and ended up living for about a year and a half in a room in a warehouse that was about fifteen feet wide by about thirty feet long, a notorious hideout known as the Vats, an actual old beer vat covered in rubber. The band members entered by crawling through a hole like a submarine hatch door. Dictor slept in an air shaft, bass player Franco and Schvitz slumped down on foam mattresses, and Posner lived in the van. They survived on food stamps and by eating at soup kitchens. "We were in our mid-twenties," Dictor says, "And we were living like we were sixteen, seventeen, eighteen. Like we were the Pinocchio kids that ran away from home to live in Candyland or wherever" (Dictor 2012). Still, that gnarly space, which hosted bands from DRI to Verbal Abuse, retains a dingy, down-and-out glory of its own. "It's very spartan, but I'm having more fun and more good feelings about my life than I ever did than when I was seventeen living in mommy's house with mommy's car and daddy bringing home the paycheck," Dictor told *Ripper*. "Those days were okay, and were part of my growing up, but don't get caught in the bourgeois trip of supporting your new car to support your expensive apartment to support fuckin' big business who support whatever" (Bowles 1983).

Dogged touring bands tried to steer American hardcore through growing pains, but often the workload and visions became tedious and wearisome. "After a few years, it started taking its toll on everybody, not just M.D.C. Other people said, 'I want to start making it financially,'" Dictor bemoans. "People started busting their moves to try and move up a notch. Bob Mould left Husker Du, sold out to a big label. Little by little, that whole snowball happened. When you are young, it is very fresh and exciting; later, it becomes less so. Ron Posner left the band in 1984, though he came back to us years ago. At the time, he just said, 'I don't want to do this anymore. I'm just burnt out on it.' That happened to a lot of people" (Dictor 2012).

People like Dictor clung to a sense of renewal and resurgence. "You start trying to recapture the magic of those first four people you were doing the music with, and in the case of M.D.C., in the course of ten years, we had . . . five to six guitar players between 1984 and 1994. There was Gordon Frasier, Eric Calhoun, Ron came back, and there was Bill from Fang who joined us, then there was Chris Wilder from Sticky who joined us, so there were five different guitar payers. With us, we'd have people join us, do a tour or two, and then just . . . well, a lot of people figured out it's tough to be in a band. It's like you're married to these people, and you've got to get along with them, and everyone's got their drug habits, everyone's got their weird personalities, everyone at certain points wants to be with their girlfriend and have a baby, and a lot of that different stuff happens. It became watered down and less special for us. It was still special for me to perform, but it wasn't the exciting feeling of 1981, when we drove out in two little cars to play with the Dead Kennedys at Mabuhay Gardens and then with Black Flag at the Cuckoo's Nest on a two-city tour. I thought punk rock musically was gonna conquer the world, and it did somewhat as a fashion and then later as a music thing, but by 1990 it was all so watered down, commercialized, and trivialized. In 1984, though, I thought we would defeat Ronald Reagan and the military industrial, multi-death corporation/complex. I was young and idealistic" (Dictor 2012).

AT WAR IN AMERICA: POLICE BRUTALITY

"One more huge factor, possibly the biggest leading to the creation of California hardcore," points out Peter Case, "was the passing of Proposition 13, a law that lowered taxes on wealthy land owners, and by doing so, defunded the school systems in California, depriving kids of nearly *all* organized extracurricular activities" (Case 2014). The law, decreed the end of the New Deal's progressive redistribution by urban theorist Mike Davis, was the result of suburban homeowners, whose antipathy toward taxation for the purpose of social programs peaked as they reaped the benefits of an inflated housing market, joining right-wingers equally interested in anti-busing campaigns. Both groups desired to stop the flow of money to county services (Moore 1998). However, the proposition did not impact police budgets, which increased slightly. "As a result, a million disenfranchised youth were on the streets starting 1978, with nothing to do and nowhere to go . . . *boom*!" exclaims Case (2014).

Soon thereafter, the authorities were ready and willing to monitor, control, and even eradicate youth activities. On St. Patrick's Day 1979, sixty riot police supported by helicopters were dispatched to the Elks Lodge Auditorium in Los Angeles during an all-ages Go-Go's/Plugz/X/Alley Cats/Zeros gig with six hundred attendees, causing a melee and resulting in eight arrests. Even years later, gig goers decried the use of force on the Go-Go's blog. An eyewitness described a phalanx of officers rapidly ascending the stairs, fanning across the gig space, and taking up circular positions with batons wielded, then brutally engaging the crowd, a behavior that one fan described as more frightening than the antiwar rally breakups he witnessed during the 1960s (KS2 2010).

Similar instances occurred for years, instigated by what Keith Morris of the Circle Jerks called the "special SS branch of the LAPD" (Spitz and Mullen 2001).

"I was at that show," Lisa Fancher recalls, "and the police went berserk on the crowd for no reason! I'm far from a conspiracy freak, but it genuinely seemed like the LAPD was trying to eradicate punk rock. They showed up at the most obscure venues and always used excessive force on the crowd, not to mention threats and intimidation on the club owners and promoters. I remember the night that *The Decline of Western Civilization* opened on Hollywood Boulevard. We were standing in a long line, and dozens of police showed up in SWAT gear! They closed the boulevard and lined up across the street in formation, waiting for some action. When nothing happened, they goose-stepped up to the line and started shoving us. Still no action. . . . I was close to the end of the line, and there's nothing quite as panic inducing as an L.A. police officer with a riot shield shoving his baton into your back, let me tell you! I guess I should count my blessings that they didn't shoot me" (Fancher 2013).

Meanwhile, SST Records, a Los Angeles label of Black Flag, Minutemen, and others, was placed under police surveillance, including tapping their phones, notes writer Michael Azerrad (Spitz and Mullen 2001). Mike Watt recalls the Torrance, California, police department raiding SST headquarters on suspicion of "moving drugs" (Spitz and Mullen 2001). This serves to confirm the feelings of Greg Ginn, who noted, "We feel we're political by playing the music we play, doing the shows we do, and releasing our records. Sloganeering is insulting . . . purely ignorant. . . . You end up as relevant as the Bay City Rollers" (Fritz n.d., 22). Simply being Black Flag seemed a resilient political act, at least in the group's hometown, where the police were conniving.

Such occurrences happened well into the 1980s, including at a November 1984 gig with the Ramones and Black Flag, which drew riot police to the Palladium, attended by Adam Pfahler, later drummer for Red Harvest and Jawbreaker, as well as Blake Schwarzenbach, singer and guitarist of the same bands. And the police were not the only worrisome side of violence. In 1979, when the Clash played the club, "boys showed up sporting swastikas, then jumped the stage, forcing Paul Simonon to fend them off with his bass guitar in a nightmare Alamo scenario" (Hogan 1981, 31). As if predicting impending violence, the gig poster for the event features a sword-wielding half-naked Asian slicing the chest of a victim whose hands are tied.

"What were the real political actions? Outside of 'visceral expression' and the self-proclaimed '100 percent honesty' in public and personal matters we hear about from Danny Furious? Activist and gay community leader Harvey Milk was elected to the San Francisco Board of Supervisors in 1977. He was assassinated in 1978, and there were riots in the streets," exclaims Peter Case (2014). The *San Francisco Examiner*'s haunting image of a police car engulfed by flames at one such melee, the White Night Riot, appears on the album cover for *Fresh Fruit for Rotting Vegetables*, the first album by the Dead Kennedys. "Both his election and his death were political milestones in San Francisco and California. Punks participated in the election and the riots," tells Case (2014).

"In San Francisco and L.A., just having punk shows at all was a political act," Case continues, for "shows were often shut down by the police and fire departments" (2014). Punk-rock riots were a weekly occurrence at places like the Elks building in MacArthur's Park, Blackies in Hollywood, and Baces Hall in East Los Angeles (where members of the bands John Q. Public and Kingbees were arrested). Even the legendary Whisky A Go Go was not immune: after a handful of the eight hundred punks in attendance threw bottles at a police patrol following the first round of a double-bill Black Flag and D.O.A. gig, a police helicopter descended while droves of police—apparently led by one officer who walked to the middle of a blocked intersection and lifted a shotgun above his head—brandished billy clubs and rushed the concert goers, capturing the next day's headlines as the first riot on Sunset Boulevard since the Doors played there (Keithley 2011, 52).

Police conflict occurred throughout the South Bay at places like the Fleetwood, as well as in Costa Mesa in Orange County, where the Cuckoo's Nest—host to Case's band the Plimsouls and others like the Damned, Ramones, 999, Middle Class, and Social Distortion—was deemed unruly (due to unlawful drinking, loitering, and incidents of nearby property damage) by local authorities, who compelled a police task force to monitor the locale. "The Minutemen played there a couple of times, but I don't know that much about that pad," says Mike Watt. "One conflict was with an owner *after* Jerry Roach (I think he originally booked punk there) and this new guy fucking threw us out after one forty-five-second sound check tune! He asked if that's what we sounded like and started laughing. . . . I heard about the profiling in Orange County. SST was harassed big time by both LAPD and small forces like Hermosa Beach and Torrance [police] departments. The early 1980s were nightmare for punk rockers in some way in Southern California" (Watt 2014).

The police began surveillance of punks in outlying communities, as well, where the profiling of punk youth became standard procedure. "In about 1981 or 1982, the cops in Newport Beach ('Surf City') were stopping everyone that looked like a punk, usually on our bikes, as we couldn't drive yet," informs photographer Greg Jacobs. "But the cops were stopping us and taking our photographs and taking 'field identification cards' on us. I think they thought they were creating a punk rock database or something" (2014). One of his peers, fifteen-year-old Thomas Wilcox, and his mother filed a lawsuit in the Orange County Superior Court against police for cracking down on undesirable, problematic youth—set apart by jagged haircuts and punk gear—which led to systematic harassment without probable cause based on appearance alone.

In 1985, the police unleashed its force in San Diego after the conclusion of a peaceful punk anarchy picnic and concert, which included the Insolents, celebrating a newly pressed single on Mystic Records; Diatribe; the Front; Ministry of Truth; and others. Though no police had patrolled the area and the punks had been issued valid permits, "At 4:30 cops filled the parking lots. Minutes before 5:00 everyone was leaving," tells Vince Udo, singer of Diatribe. "I remember the crowd was cool punks united from a positive day. When the first group of people reached the parking lot, the cops made moves toward us. . . . A young girl with a baby was pushed by a cop. What the hell? That's all it took. My friend went and pulled the cop from the young mom. Well, that made the crowd react, and a riot ensued. Chaos was in full tilt. Punks either ran to leave or joined in the battle. It happened so fast, then it was over" (qtd. in McWhorter 2015). Eleven arrests were made.

Greg McWhorter, accompanied by his mother, was there, as well, relaxing before a gig later that night featuring the Exploited, U.K. Subs, and Dr. Know. As he remembers, "Many squad cars started entering the parking lot and police poured out and gathered along the edge of the grassy picnic area. My mom noticed what was happening and called to me and my friends to follow her to her car. As the show was wrapping up anyway, we followed her to her car and heard a lot of commotion behind us. We turned and saw the police starting to rush into the picnic area. They were pushing punks and swinging their nightsticks in threatening ways, yelling at the punks to disperse. We saw a few kids get hit by nightsticks from afar. Several police rushed up to us and yelled at us, but we were already at my mom's car and she started yelling at the police to leave us kids alone. I think an adult being present rattled them, so they just yelled at us to get in the car and get out of the park" (McWhorter 2015). In this case, parent culture stood on the side of punks dealing with vociferous local authorities.

Punk is more than a single lonely conversation. It's about thousands of ordinary people challenging their own storylines—at times poetic, flippant, and tongue-in-cheek, furious and often furiously moral—and undergoing often-unplanned conversions under the Sisyphean weight of popular media, morality, and business models nakedly in need of retrofitting, revolution, and regeneration. Punk is a model of "dangerous" imagination at play, armed desire, steering its adherents to feel more alive and in control of the wheel of destiny, not ludicrous and helpless, immobilized by their social roles.

5

LITPUNK FUROR

The Wit of Jennifer Blowdryer

One woman who sprang from punk's year zero in Berkeley, California, is the incomparable Jennifer Blowdryer, a satirist whose writing has appeared in publications ranging from adult magazines like *Chic* and punk bible *Maximum Rocknroll* to literary anthologies. "The first things I read were what my parents had lying around—*Last Exit to Brooklyn* by Hugh Selby, *Last Picture Show* by Larry McMurtry, and copies of *National Lampoon* and *The New Yorker*. There was a local library I could walk to [though] it didn't have many books—there was a writer called Peter DeVries who dealt in humor and puns, this writer Erma Bombeck who was writing in a witty way about being a mom. When I read a Vonnegut or a George Saunders, it's the truth cutting across my brain, just like the violent world of Selby's Bay Ridge, Queens. Because I was isolated; I didn't have a way to differentiate what was supposed to be light humor, a burlesque of society, or deadly serious. Satire is a more truthful portrayal of people and society. There are writers like Muriel Spark, Barbara Pym, [Charles] Bukowski—it's like somebody talking right into my ear.

"The first I ran across punk, it was my big sister's magazines, *Creem* and *Rolling Stone*, and then the music. One can intellectualize in hindsight, but I operated in a feral manner, and what I gleaned about Sid Vicious, Johnny Rotten, Lester Bangs writing about the Ramones—and I do think he was deadly serious about his writing and that or the booze sent him packing a few years earlier than some others—was funny. Devo's song 'Mongoloid' was a good song" (Blowdryer 2014).

In the hands of writers like Kathy Acker and Blowdryer, punk-imbued satire became pregnant with pithy possibilities, a finely honed tool that spared no one, especially those cloaked in the garb of culture. "There's violence attached to such a young recognition and love of satire—a feeling that nobody's telling the truth, an anger that's too fucked up and throbbing to spew out social niceties, and that was definitely first-wave punk," says Blowdryer. "The New York Dolls I'd include, just a gander at that album cover—and those songs. People who are invested, pleased, sated, or rewarded by their culture norms feel violated by satire. Things are going all right for them, and it's an affront to give away the game. The game wasn't going so well for me, and I don't court the affection or approval of strangers, so what the fuck.

"Kathy Acker never hit home with me; I didn't put much energy into reading her," argues Blowdryer, "I appeared with her once, in San Francisco at Slim's, and my sister was there. 'Jeez, why don't you lighten up?' was my sister's reaction to Acker. As Albert Murray said, you can't put an entire career into being avant-garde, because in military terms, you're the shock troop, the first into battle, and wind up dead or badly wounded. Or [the first to] snap out of it, I suppose. Acker was lucky or unlucky enough to have 'yes-men' surrounding her, I suspect, and lost the thread. The thread of literature, entertainment, communication. I liked one thing I heard her say in a doc, that after [age] thirty women are 'past the age of beauty,' and it resonated with me. So, she told some truths but life got on top of her" (Blowdryer 2014).

Blowdryer once told a writer that punk catalyzed her sense of voice—not the air-conditioned, cushioned craft of fine-edge, academic-approved poetic lines, but living-in-America "screams"—wickedly trenchant, observational Polaroids—that made her realize she need not impress or be liked by "jokers." "I must have liked that term 'joker.' It's such a weird putdown. Inauthentic is what they'd say now, as 'authentic' is the advertising word of the day. Almost said du jour but not sure how to spell that.

"I'll tell you the truth: my parents are failed artists. My father is a terrible lifelong poet; he's eighty-seven and still sending out fifty submissions at once for possible publication. My mother has talent and was a pretty honest person before she suffered an attempted murder about nine years ago at the age of eighty; she's regressed a bit. So you can see why I don't think a nice poetic line is any kind of relief. Living in close quarters with my father was hell, not being urban made it worse as there was absolutely no way to leave until I was fourteen and [I] did so. I think that calls for a scream. If somebody crawls out from under the thumb of a sociopath—oh, I love Jon Ronson's recent work on the subject! And the way Gary Indiana mind melds with them in his crime trilogy, or Jake Arnott when he evokes the Kray Twins—anyway, if and when one does, you'd better not be working the nice guy angle. That is not a nice place to be from, Evil. Evil was misused for awhile; it's still a dangerous word as it was used way too lightly for a couple of decades. . . . I had a stalker and have encountered a couple of con men way too close, and at some point the best thing is to pull away completely, but also, for safety, to make it public. 'I know you, I know what you are,' I've had to say—and oh, they kick and scream. Simone Weil, in *Gravity and Grace*, describes the phenom of the afflicted soul or half-dead soul being touched by love, concern, or truth. They'll claw at you. There ain't nothing sweet about any of that—it is nasty, nasty, nasty. I don't wish a shitty life or experience on anyone, if they haven't encountered operators, killers, and the like, and they've never had to resort to screaming to survive, well—god bless 'em" (Blowdryer 2014).

Part of Blowdryer's legacy is her deeply burrowed do-it-yourself (DIY) creed, whether making her own clothes while attending Berkeley High in the late 1970s or setting up the notorious Smut Fests with the likes of Annie Sprinkle in the late 1980s. "I understand the kids that do DIY now—it makes sense—you've handed me this mutated environment and this premade crap, and I'm going to break it down with a Xeroxed zine, a silk-screened patch I'm gonna sew on my own damned self, and what's more, I'll give you the same goddamn patch for a dollar, because I don't even take your profit schemes to heart. A lot of the Crusties or Gypsy Kids, whatever you want to call them, are indeed on the outs with society. Somebody fucked with them. Or they're just beautiful kids, and I can think of a couple, and the first Occupy, their own march to their own drummer parents, something clued them in to making their own gear.

"I had to make an Anarchy shirt because nobody had heard of punk. I had to get pants made into peg legs because you just couldn't find them anywhere. I couldn't afford Doc Martens so I wore cheap shoes.

Leopardette and rhinestones were mostly flaunted by some prior bunch of floozies or overly flashy members of the demimonde such as the Gabor sisters, who were really raised to be mistresses and what used to be called hookers and strippers. You had to take a bus to some godforsaken town to even find that unfortunate pattern on a Salvation Army clothing rack. Oh, I would have been happy if I'd been able to go to an affordable clothing chain, during the now-dying era of the Chinese sweatshop, and buy a flashy outfit for dead cheap. Bangladesh will not be able to do the equivalent—they don't have the tools or the know-how" (Blowdryer 2014).

After playing with her band the Blowdryers (who gigged to support the 1979 Gay Freedom Day Parade and the White Night Riot Defense Fund) at venues like the Deaf Club, where she joined the likes of the Zeros, Negative Dils, No Sisters, and Ivy and the Eaters, Blowdryer began dating Peter Belsito, the man responsible for the tiny, claustrophobic Tool and Die on Valencia Street, a regular haunt for the hardcore brethren like M.D.C. and Social Unrest. "I really fell for that boyfriend. I suggested he start to book bands—he had a rehearsal studio anyway. I remember lying in bed and hearing this band the Black Dolls sing 'I'm *not* your little girl!' over and over. Living in a rehearsal space is not joke. It'll make you meaner than a snake.

"Social Distortion played a gig with me," recalls Blowdryer. "I had my keyboard player on a Farfisa [organ, wearing] a chiffon dress, silver hair, and singing a song called 'I want to take these herpes and give them give them give them back to *you*.' And I had this Cuban guy whose job was to basically drug-sit and take the fall during a raid, so it was Jennifer Blowdryer and the Cuban Next Door. He came out of things OK; he was actually getting ice cream when the cops came and ended up in New York City doing hair at a franchise called Dramatics. Social Distortion . . . [were] edging me off stage, doing their organized thing, and that type of pop is very almost military in the synchronicity that's required; it's a young man's game by definition except they're in a show arena rather than acting as cannon fodder. . . . They are definitely show people because to this day more than a quarter of a century later, you can bet they will run through an identical set with skill and panache. A different animal than I. That space is now the site of spoken word, I believe. It was a Santería shop for a while, Mexican style dishwater-scented candle witchcraft, and that was a good use for it. I like

Voodoo. . . . Queen bees have to retreat and do a little magic now and then" (Blowdryer 2014).

By the mid-1980s, Blowdryer was living in New York City and working at Harmony Burlesque, one of the first clubs to feature XXX stars like Tina Russell and Tempest Storm. When she returned to read at Gilman [an all-ages Berkeley punk club], the culture gap was apparent. "Berkeley was never a gritty place as far as the Caucasian culture went, Gilman Street developed after I moved to New York, which I think was 1985. I was really clueless about the redefinition of punk and these quiet people who had a philosophy—words change, labels change. I was pretty hard, in my reading, because I'd cashiered at this swamp-like lap dancing parlor in New York, working for a woman thug, and then written about it for an artist friendly editor, Allan McDonnell, who was at *Hustler* (Larry Flynt Publications) for a long time and then wrote this hysterical mean book *Prisoner of X* that Feral House put out. I wrote it noir style, which is a tough style, and felt it might go over well. I had no idea how very out of place I was [at Gilman]. There was dead silence. I felt like some, well, blowsy Eugene O'Neill type floozy who'd wandered into *The Nutcracker.* I had no fucking idea what time it was. Didn't sell too many books at that one. I was just weird, old, and scary.

"I liked a book I bought, though—Kurt from the band D.R.I. had a chapbook about basically living in Golden Gate Park in a tree and going to soup kitchens for lunch. My British grandmother was a soup kitchen lady, and living in a tree and having the wits to describe it is pretty good. I think that book was also merch at D.R.I. shows, so he indeed knew what time it was and was in that time and seemed very sweet. The guy who booked me may have been telling his own kind of joke. He had to know that I in fact did not know the current situation of what was and wasn't called punk. His name was Mark Sterry, but he was like a Henry Rollins borg, the aliens from *Star Trek: The Next Generation*, whose motto is 'we must assimilate.' I bet Sterry's married, works, raised a few kids, his youthful trend just happened to be as a Henry Rollins replicant, and I'm sure he snapped right out of it" (Blowdryer 2014).

Blowdryer's stint as a free-agent, nonsectarian voice in *Maximum Rocknroll* also fell prey to pitfalls, despite her affection for Tim Yohannon, its longtime ideological and production chief. "*Maximum Rocknroll* got started because I always cracked up Timmy Yohannon. He loved the Blowdryers, and he loved me and my lame jokes. I was on that radio show, and he'd seen Modern English and asked if I wanted to write a column. I started to write it while living in an eight-by-ten room at International House [in New York City], completely isolated, and had no idea that anybody was reading it. Once a year I got a check for $100 or $200, and that actually seemed like a lot, as I was living on a pretty thin margin and scarfing down vending machine food" (Blowdryer 2014).

Blowdryer also reveals a side to Yohannon underexplored in punk histories. "Timmy was a man who quietly patronized sex workers—it's not uncommon or a lesser thing to do. It's actually quite fair and honest to have an ongoing relationship with a hooker for sex when you are not in a situation or frame of mind to get sex any other way. He was supportive of all this dialogue of hookers; I was onto it for a whole other reason than Katy Odell," who was a contributing writer to Yohannon's *Maximum Rocknroll* and a self-declared sex worker who edited the zine *Working Girl*, as well (Blowdryer 2014). In 1991, Odell declared in her column, "I am compelled to speak up and make myself heard in the din of voices going back and forth about pornography, censorship, and the sex-industry. . . . As a feminist, I am outraged by the laws and restrictions on my privacy and sexuality. The ban on prostitution is not about sex or morality—there are no laws against promiscuity. It is a fight for control, for financial independence" (Odell 1991). That struggle for volition and choice, as well as autonomy and sexual freedom, soon spiraled throughout the punk community's discourse.

One reader from Seattle, a sales clerk at a magazine shop, felt moved by such pieces, including the views of Lily Braindrop, a dominatrix who also penned columns for *Maximum Rocknroll* at the time: "it is refreshing to hear Lily and Katy talk about self empowerment in the individual," he says, "especially since the public is surrounded by a marketplace that exists as an 'orgy of gratification.'" To provide context, the writer sketches a brief biography of growing up in commodity-saturated, buy-and-sell America in which an orgasm means much more than a simple biological pleasure: "I grew up in the 70s and 80s when the media had perfected its control stratagem. Millions and millions of manipulated images from our breakfast cereals to our bedsheets." In the writer's view, reality itself "is too hectic so people search for the 'little death' [orgasm], a moment of eternity. All addictions (which are intrinsic to capitalism and control) seek solace in these brief deaths." Hence, sexual objectification in the media is just another facet, no better or worse, of an omnipresent materialism, from cars and sports to *Time* magazine (Zicari 1992). Therefore, orgasms become a way to cope, or find relief from, that relentless and disempowering deluge.

Blowdryer quit writing for *Maximum Rocknroll* after she and Odell swapped columns and impersonated each other for a single issue, but overall Blowdryer feels the whole experience fostered audience bonds, perhaps even a learning environment. "I'm so glad people read those columns and I think they did help some folk. Thank you, magazines! Thank God for men like Timmy Yohannon" (Blowdryer 2014).

6

SLAM DANCE IN THE NO TIME ZONE

Punk as Repertoire for Liminality

I try to speak, but words collapse.—Siouxsie Sioux, "Halloween"

[Stage diving is] like diving into a human carpet . . . something like the old kids' trust game. Just my way of getting into it. Gospel people got their thing, I got mine.—Alexa (Blauner 1986)

In 1997, Kim Hewitt published the penetrating study *Mutilating the Body: Identity in Blood and Ink*, in which she likens punk rockers to performance artists. She notes how punk audiences morphed from passively witnessing pioneering performers like Iggy Pop to performative agents in the era of the Sex Pistols. This period embodied new phenomena, such as audience members offering up body fluids like "blood, spit, and vomit . . . [which were an] antithesis to the integrity and hygiene of the Western humanist body"; hence, such performativity blurred boundaries between artists and fans forever (110). In that ongoing revolt of signs and seepage, punks carved out a "subterranean society . . . to rebuff and drive away normal people" and "reserve . . . allurement for those who override normality" (110).

Inside punk squats, art co-ops, all-ages clubs, shoddy bars, rental units, and house parties, punks could carve out their own societies and immerse in *becoming*—the process of morphing and transforming. To make it plain: when fueled by noise, commotions, musculature, body heat, chemicals, and the rhythm of thronging participants, normative routines melt away in disorderly, sometimes grotesque punk pleasure in which the power relations between performer and fan or the modes of power between them ripple with both frisson and friction—dynamism. Peter Jones, in his cogent examination of punk as Bakhtinian carnival, thoroughly recognized this shift in fan-performer discourse, interaction, and positionality, including shifting subjectivities. "With its alcohol and amphetamine-fueled cathartic frenzy, almost 'oceanic' crush, stage invasions, irreverence for performers and audience alike, 'pogoing' and 'gobbing,' the punk concert is an example of collective *jouissance.* A display of excess and disorder where rational control is relinquished and differences between subjects and the distinctions between audience and performers, stage and street, are blurred" (2002).

This has long been evident, even in the United States as far back as 1978, when Tomata du Plenty from the Screamers electrified audiences at places like the Elks building in Los Angeles. He "raced around like a man in nightmare . . . suddenly leaped from the four-foot stage onto the dance floor to join in the frantic, up-and-down pogoing that is integral to English punk," breathlessly wrote Robert Hilburn in the *Los Angeles Times*. "Friday's crowd darted about, bouncing off each other. It was like bumper cars without the cars. For the uninitiated, the dance floor looked like a combination gang fight and Demolition Derby" (1978).

Such sense of sheer disorder was rampantly apparent at a Vandals gig in 1983 at the KPFK radio studios in Hollywood. A *Flipside* gig reviewer who admitted his own breathless joy "of screaming and writhing on the floor like a possessed spasmodic" cataloged the sundry disarray, including a dance pit filled with such debris as "couches, cushions, sound padding, reels of magnetic tape, ripped curtains, and tin foil" as well as "empty envelopes . . . beer . . . and fire extinguisher fluid" (Gary 1983). All such planned punk gigs were canceled after that mayhem, whose audio was broadcast live. When the Sex Pistols played Winterland in San Francisco, "Lydon danced—waded, actually—through a mounting pile of debris: everything from shoes, coins, books, and umbrellas, all heaved his way by a tense, adulatory crowd" (Gilmore 1980, 20). Others, like the Minutemen's D. Boon, also became a symbolic target of an audience's hurtling debris, though this time a group of punks was offended by the Americans' shaggy hair length; unfussy clothes; and, in the case of D. Boon, the singer's girth, which quickly became a target for "condoms, trashcans, packets of sausages, whatever was at hand" (Parker 2000, 110). During such times, the communitarian idea was unthreaded, even balkanized.

Outsiders unaccustomed to the habits and traditions of punk express shock and dismay at the physical mayhem. One teen, who signed her letter "Bruised and Confused," wrote to the "Ask Beth" column of the *Boston Globe* in 1983, claiming that her peers, who were "skanking" to a new wave band at the high school, seemed intoxicated on drugs. Beth (Elizabeth Winship) responded firmly, "There's no place for violence of this kind on the dance floor." On the other hand, punks see an evolved form of dance that "maintained both its simplicity and savage intensity," David Cuatt vividly pictures, as it shifted from pogoing, slamming, and thrashing to stage diving, in which "partners or complicated dance steps are unnecessary" (Cuatt 1984, 28). Punk whittled down dance norms to an inchoate, if alarming, "cathartic release of energy. It erupts, rather than starts—always close to the musicians—and ends as suddenly" (Cuatt 1984, 28). The physical wrangling, sometimes construed as rivalry, often relates to prejudices, events, and issues brought to the floor by aggravated and aggrieved participants. The outside world seeps in. Still, however precariously, the slam dance, mosh, and pogo dance forms help stir a temporary communal space, in which malodorous, writhing, sweat-tainted bodies attempt to maintain a kind of ecosystem.

Phillipov, visiting the ideas of writer Jude Davies, argues punk's "construction of communality is based on communication—the first step in a truly democratic engagement with progressive politics . . . since the singer [has] no special status, no mandate to be spokesperson, songs [can] only succeed by an act of agreement, rather than identification" (2006, 28).

In concert settings, through the barrage of music, a participant's entire body is potentially transmogrified by the shimmering electric field of the band's wattage and voltage of amplifiers, which can trigger a chemical and physiological response in listeners, including intensely felt sensations during dance: mosh, pogo, crowd surge, skank, slam, or variations therein such as "cowboy stomp, slam, chicken slam, beach bugaloo . . . and the worm" (Gary 1983). As Greta Fine from the Chicago-based neopunk band Bang! Bang! told me in 2009, "Punk brought me out of my head and into my body. Nothing was emotional anymore: it was physical. The music was rough and immediate. It was raw and ugly." The body, not the mind, becomes a sizzling transmitter turning the body from a passive piece of inert, stiff-as-a-statue mass into a seizure-riddled, gesticulating, dramatically thrusting and contorting vessel intent on shattering its own prescribed, controlled behavior. That undoubtedly comes with danger, too; hence *Maximum Rocknroll* published "Punk 1st Aid" by Jerod Poor in issue 2, which described how to cope with bruises, broken bones, concussions, and shock.

Punk seems to offer a two-way liminal door, allowing practitioners and listeners to slip away from normative habits and roles into their own surging physicality. As neuroscientist Daniel J. Levitin declares, dancing triggers a person's action system, including "motor sequences and . . . [the] sympathetic nervous system . . . in a sort of neurochemical dance." Music increases "alertness through modulation of norepinephrine and epinephrine and taps into . . . motor response system[s] through cortisol production" while also modulating other chemicals such as serotonin, melatonin, dopamine, and more (2008, 101). Hence, although outsiders may consider punk dancing a kind of anarchic bombardment—total flux and disjunction—it may actually stimulate and shape shared neurochemical states of being, even resynchronizing and resocializing youth long suffering under antidance patriarchies, especially in the Western world (2008, 101).

Music, as Levitin argues, is part of a common evolutionary and biological past that diffuses tense social situations while conveying intense emotional states (2008, 86). Instead of experiencing real combat, death, and distress, punks marshal their energies and inner chemicals (sometimes amplified by drugs and alcohol), often dressed in combat boots, in staged, mock-battle situations on the dance floor, which feel metaphorically akin to combat rock as collective ritual. That synchrony with the band and with each other, especially in sing-along rapture, stimulates "cognitive operations of memory in the hippocampus and prediction in the frontal lobes" while also creating a "motor action plan—a specific set of instructions sent to the motor cortex." If the band and audience pursue call-and-response patterns, another common ritual in punk music (and throughout global music), this may symbolize "democratic participation in music" and inspire "cooperative activities" (2008, 58–59).

Robin Sylvan has avidly correlated music subculture practices—including body language, lingo, mannerisms, and a core set of musical tastes and ritual expressions—to groups affiliated and intertwined with religious organizations. These "highly valued" shared practices seem to culminate at the "live concert or dance hall," where participants "experience a sense of ecstatic communion" (2002, 4). These tendencies and traits, Sylvan makes explicit, provide spaces for gig goers to experience community bonding while also translating the subculture "into a code for living one's day-to-day life" (2002, 4). Gigs do not simply embody a music-marketing means to an end—a convenient conduit for disempowered fans to passively view a musical commodity—instead, gig spaces blend secular and spiritual territories while providing space for epiphanies.

Additionally, punk audience performance often hinges not on "mindfulness"—seemingly steeped in Western modes of thought—but rather a release from Cartesian dualism. Ensconced in frenetic musical dissonance and dissidence, audiences actually yearn for "no mind" or for the sudden collapse of the discrete boundaries between the body and mind. "When I am at a concert, there is an increase in enthalpy [the internal energy]. At one show, people were throwing bottles and objects in the air, and a bottle hit me in the forehead," admits student Eric Hernandez, an avid concert goer. "I was knocked out, but I got up and shrugged it off because I wanted to get back into the music. My brain was releasing dopamine and serotonin, and I was feeling the *transcendence* of the sound" (2012). By no means is Hernandez alone in expressing these sentiments.

No wonder crowds scream at bands to quickly proceed to the next tune, for their bodies desire no stasis after such riveting and ricocheting flux. "No mind"—or body-mind reunification—is far preferred to mindfulness. The ritual of dancing forms the fluid architecture of the participants' atavistic purging—not unlike a reenactment of bodily trauma—controlled by local customs, inherited norms, styles, and rules. In his cautionary tale about slam dancing, Bradford Scott Simon surmises, "The slam-pit contain[s] several diadic oppositions, including order/chaos, absorption of self in mass/centrality of individual asserting self, and violence/physicality (1997, 149). However, he neglects temporalities—how the dance operates within a no time zone, meaning the sense of suspended or collapsed time found within a liminal punk space.

Punk dance—crowd swelling, scrambling, pogoing, crowd surfing, and sudden surges of acrobatic stage diving—embody a kind of sacrificial rite of self-transformation. As a crowd throbs, heaves, squirms, and skirmishes, akin to mimicking hordes of swarming insects, a hive mentality often seems to take effect as chemical communication occurs between members embracing the dance language. Those embedded in the rituals can abandon their former roles for brief periods of time (in which time itself seems void, as if collapsed, as if there was no time at all) and undergo a moment of interrelatedness and interpenetration with others. This co-intentional space fosters communitas, oneness, and "antistructure," which anthropologist Victor Turner identifies with liminal spaces. Those inside the ritual, which he refers to as "threshold people" and "liminars" experiencing "neither here nor there," feel suspended between positions assigned and arrayed by "law, custom, convention, and ceremony." Such communitas is spontaneous and unpredictable, as he attests, and, in the case of punk, pell-mell. Those stepping into the space from a high position in the social, cultural, or economic hierarchy experience the rowdy "low" sense of punk melee and riffraff.

Although the rapport between punk fans and performers has long been considered theatrical with its inherent call-and-response patterns, shtick, chides, wisecracks, sarcasm, and mock threats, little attention has been paid to the ongoing disposition of audiences to negate and rupture discrete audience boundaries. In footage from locations across the globe, punk fans can be seen hurling themselves from stages, grabbing mics from performers mid-sentence, commanding the stage in temporary abandonment of their positions as mere listeners, singing along in mimicry and mime, throwing their bodies into tumultuous piles, heaving to and fro like bird flocks chasing zigzagging insects, and sometimes fighting each over often-invisible infractions.

However, a crowd's volatile presence on stage wasn't always welcomed with open arms by the bands. In the column "Memos from the Mouse Trap," members of Angry Samoans, Youth Brigade, and Dr. Know decry fans unplugging guitar cords, stepping on guitar pedals, and densely packing the stages to the point of frustration (1986). Meanwhile, Youth Brigade penned songs questioning crowd mentalities and rituals, including senseless violence ("The Circle," *Sound and Fury*, 1982). In turn, 7 Seconds took aim at sexist patterns ("Not Just Boys Fun," *The Crew*, 1984) and even what frontman Kevin Seconds calls "fascist tendencies" on the bootleg live recording *1984: Live at the VFW #18*, which documents their performance in Kansas City. "We're against the whole idea of a pit," he can be heard uttering before beginning the song "Bottomless Pit." "It's a dance floor. It's a place to have fun, not a fucking war," he continues. Violence, sometimes unintentional yet often inherent in the routines, did lurk. In Houston, Texas, during the mid-1980s, Dianna Ray, bass player of the female-led Mydolls, had two teeth knocked out on the Island's dance floor by two male gig goers. In this case, the club later held a benefit (advertised literally as "Two Teeth Benefit") to aid her medical expenses, but most victims of gig violence were not so lucky.

For many fans contributing to a performance, rational mind becomes far less tangible than gut feelings, second-by-second intuition, and disorderly action. A 1986 article in *New York* magazine pictured the tumultuous milieu of hardcore punk venues this way: "the dance floor begins to look like a giant pinball machine. . . . Dozens of boys and girls seem to be caught in a sudden whirlwind, flinging themselves hard into one another and then careening away, only to be jolted back by more oncoming bodies" (Blauner 1986, 40).

As Stacy Thompson notes in *Punk Productions: Unfinished Business*, a club like iconic CBGB allowed for interchangeable roles between audience and performer—"any audience member could also be a performer and vice versa. This desire finds its expression in the literal proximity between band member and audience member" (2004, 11). Spatial dynamics are not all that matter.

Given CBGB's heritage, identity, and performance rituals, the audience *is* the performance, in part. No liminality exists if a band plays to an empty house surrounded by decades of graffiti, hasty paint jobs, dingy tables, and dog-eared posters. That relationship between fans and musicians, each dependent on each other for music-making myth and mystery, is a fluid friction. Or, as Paul Marko succinctly notes in *The Roxy London WC2: A Punk History*, "Punk was as much about the audience as about the bands, the club goers were also required to play their part" (2008, 214). This is bolstered by a March 1980 article in *Trouser Press*, which describes a gig by the Slits at Hurrah's in New York City. Near the end of the performance, lead singer Ari Up "extended an open invite for anyone who wanted to do anything on any instrument to come up and join in" (Sommer 1980, 13).

For bands like the Slits and hybrid musical misfits the Big Boys, a late-1970s-to-early-1980s American punk band from Austin, Texas, which melded lean art rock, bombastic funk, melodic hardcore, and early rap scratching and go-go music grooves into ever-morphing, unstable formats, such cross-hatched practices in which the vigor of the audience and musicians seem to reach uninhibited, Dionysian vortex levels were essential to core performance rituals. Whereas singer Randy "Biscuit" Turner might exhort an audience to avoid cables, cords, and equipment as fans joined them onstage, he nonetheless relished the tumult and urged them to "go start your own band!" ("The Big Boys" n.d.). Of course, a semblance of pandemonium was the norm: "It was insane—like a riot," guitarist Tim Kerr told the *Daily Texan* (which dubbed the event a "big disturbance" in the headline) about one gig, describing "piles" of dancers jumping on tables, breaking glass, and getting into scuffles as beer pooled throughout the venue (Selby n.d.). However, this was not distinct or abnormal: "everybody has a good time. . . . Our shows are always wild," he continued (Selby n.d.). A *Flipside* gig review reported one 1982 Bad Religion gig at Florentine Gardens in California featured "a mass dive by about 75 kids simultaneously off the stage" (Helen 1982). To outsiders, the lack of hierarchy and structure—the maelstrom that disrupts and frays inherited norms—may shock, anger, and dismay.

In fact, the abovementioned Texas incident prompted the club to institute background checks for future lineups scheduled to play the site. And the antics of the Big Boys were not welcomed or heralded by all Austin music fans. One, Hank Vick, writing a letter to the *Austin American-Statesman*, decried their musical "outpouring" as "self-indulgent, childish nonsense 'music'" that appealed to "bored third semester [University of Texas] freshman with strange hair" and often overshadowed more "discernable music" in the city (Vick n.d.). Hence, the music of the Big Boys represents deviant noise "mobilizing bodies" in the contested space of the city environs or splinters in a "conflict soundscape"—terms evoked by sound ecology/auralities researcher Steve Goodman, who attempts to deconstruct "a whole cartography of sonic force" (2009, 9). But the Big Boys perceived such actions as a way to upend the norms of inherited rock 'n' roll culture in which the rigid spatial relationships are maintained by a series of rules, protocols, bouncers, and barricades. In an interview with *Zone V*, Kerr further explained, "Because we don't perceive much of a line between where we stop and everybody else starts. We've always invited people up on the stage, whether they're dancing singing, or thrashing" ("Interview with the Big Boys" 1983).

Punk gig performances often exhibit and evidence, even in offhand, unconscious forms, both consistency and change (or conservative and dynamic portions) in regard to practices. For instance, although the genres of punk continue to mutate, evolve, and transform, much of the allure is still directly tied to physicality. Student Christine Jensen explained to me the allure of screamo—a derivation of hardcore in which vocalists sing in a gruff, noisy, truculent, and choleric style—even to those hard of hearing: "Music is more about the movement of the music. Screamo's movement is amazing. It slows and wavers and then shakes and then explodes. It pounds. It moves all up and down your body" (2010). Though disconnected from the zero hour of punk (1976) by decades, her valid experience reinforces punk's potential to disable Cartesian bodily gridlock, for it is a wild thing.

Thus, punk edges close to Artaud's sense of shocking, incendiary, passionate, and convulsive art forms outlined in *Theatre of Cruelty*—a brutal, invigorating, and terrible beauty. As Lee Jamieson asserts, "Artaud sought to remove aesthetic distance, bringing the audience into direct contact with the dangers of life. By turning theatre into a place where the spectator is exposed rather than protected" (2007, 23). To that end, punk has also employed, fostered, or hosted a similar series of sensibilities, illustrated in comments by Chris Thomson (Soul Side, Circus Lupus): "I remember going to these shows that were very life or death. You traveled to these shitty, sketchy neighborhoods, you saw bands like Black Flag on the *My War* tour, and it was just a big fistfight, and there would be people on acid and drunk and the weirdo art people were there too. . . . That's what I really got off on was this whole feeling you never knew what was going to happen next. You got punched, the singer threw the mic stand in the audience, and then it seemed overnight things got so damn neighborly" (Thomson 2004). Thomson seemed to yearn for the risk factor, not the creature comforts of punk becoming mass marketed, expanding into proper, manicured, and homogenized venues and communities.

Newer generations don't simply regurgitate and resuscitate practices disseminated and culled from punk lore, media ecology, and received forms. Instead, they sound their own "barbaric yawps"—to steal a quote from Walt Whitman—and imagine their own bodies made electric.

They sift through forty years of gestures, texts, habits, memes, practices, and values, all while infusing and merging with their own aspirations. They see themselves, urgent and restless, with old wounds made anew. In some places, venues and gig goers gestate new practices, hyperlocal folk practices unknown to outsiders. At the Factory in Lufkin, Texas, which hosted a gig on the last Friday of every month from 2013 through 2014, eager all-age fans ages five to sixty-five gathered round the local band Social Bliss to pound, lift, and shake plastic and metal folding chairs, fostering an inclusive, performative, and democratic spectacle. It was jolting, synchronized, and percussive, an accompaniment to the band's sing-along choruses and refrains. This can be understood as "both a substitution and an homage; individuals simultaneously honor the past—including its ideas, traditions, and mores—by recreating it, and transform that same past, by inventing and revising it" (Maskell 2009).

As Jim Ellis sums up punk's promise and premise, the body is much more than a masquerade; it's a "site of history, signification, and revolt" seen on clipped and cut clothes, found in overripe guitar chords and tumbledown percussion, present in myopic stares, and rage in the seemingly out-of-joint body disarticulations of slam dance routines, even after four decades of corporate "defanging" of punk's content and style (2009, 57). If one enters a riotous gig tonight, the dances will continue to demarcate a liminal space—body tumult will become much greater than a mere sweat-smeared sum of gestures and movements. These spaces still suddenly erupt, both literally and allegorically, for the feverish rituals never quite abate: punk timelessness tramps on.

7

THROUGH THE LURID LOOKING GLASS

> To disgust us a little more with ourselves
> for being this useless body
> made of meat and wild sperm
> —Antonin Artaud

> We are dreaming of sex,
> . . . of huge thighs opening
> to us like this night. . . .
> All I want is a taste of your lips."
> —Kathy Acker

Punk has never been a monolithic, consensus-minded community. Its underpinnings are loose knit and often contradictory. For decades, punks have struggled to balance "cooked" and raw identities. On one side of the continuum, bands maintained rather strict and staunch codes of political righteousness, while on the other side, bands stoked a stubborn Dionysian impulse by reveling in the rank, grotesque, and filthy, like GG Allin, Bloody Mess, Turbonegro, the Dwarves, and El Duce of the Mentors, who seemingly sought to epitomize the debauched squalor, sexual licentiousness, and self-destruction bred into punk's charged mythos. "Oh I loved him so much. We did get grief from the feminists for loving him/the Mentors! We played a show with the Mentors and called ourselves the Tormentors," tells Deanna Mitchell of Frightwig (2015). "It was epic. We went to Tijuana and bought wrestling masks and Mezcal. At the show, we drank the Mezcal on stage in the masks and played 'Dreams' by Fleetwood Mac really slow for twenty minutes. Oh, El Duce was running around the club trying to kick us off stage. Turn our sound off, etcetera. It was so fun to torture Eldon [El Duce]! . . . I talked to Eldon on the phone for two months before our gig about how excited we were to play with them and how we thought they were hot, etcetera. I set him up so hard. It was so very fun to watch him freak out at our show. . . . Sigh. . . . Good times! After the Tormentors show at a party, he passed out standing up. Someone (we) drew 'Frightwig loves you' on his big belly and face with a Sharpie. He played such a pig, but we saw his art. I mean their songs, 'I'm Going thru Your Purse,' 'My Woman from Sodom.' . . . Dude, they were funny. We weren't stupid about the Mentors. We just turned their sexist game around and had a good time doing it. I saw Eldon the day after the gig at a barbeque and his face was red from scrubbing. So funny. He was like 'God damn it, someone wrote on my face last night.' I'm smiling in glee, like, 'Oh, who would do that?'" (Mitchell 2015).

Punk's response to sex culture and workers has been mixed, too, sometimes bristling and contentious and often contradictory. One thing remains central, though: the body itself is invariably cast as a site of political discourse, freedom anchored in flesh brought to bear in cases like the arrest of Marian Anderson (also known as Seaweed and Swamp Thing), the subject of the documentary *Punk Goddess* and singer of the band Insaints and later the Thrill Killers. She was arrested at Gilman Street in Berkeley in 1993 for offending the "heterosexual rights" of religious-minded Carlos Cadona, known as 6025, former member of the Dead Kennedys and Mailman. Anderson was a counterculture icon in her community: she appeared in *Sadobabies: Runaways in San Francisco* (named after the dolls that serve as abused avatars for the traumatized teens) in 1988 and on the cover of the *Spectator* ("California's Weekly Sex News and Review"); gigged alongside the likes of the Offspring and Rancid; released a vinyl 45 with the Insaints; and overcame family sexual abuse, self-cutting, bipolar disorder, suicide attempts, group homes, juvenile hall, squats like the Polytech High School, and more to revel on stage in the manner of anything-goes GG Allin. During gigs, Anderson, who dated Tim Yohannon of *Maximum Rocknroll* for a short time, regularly pushed the borders of "good taste," even within punk territories. "We'd invite other girls that she worked with [as a dominatrix] to do sexual acts onstage with her. Fist fucking and pissing, we had shows where dildos were involved. Bananas were going all weird different places," recalls guitarist Daniel DeLeon (Boulware and Tudor 2009). Due to Gilman Street's "private club" status—people attending shows needed to have a membership card—Anderson beat the charges against her, which the district attorney dropped, helped by Ann Brick of the American Civil Liberties Union and civil rights attorney George Walker. Sadly, Anderson died from a heroin overdose in 2001.

"I grew up in a small Midwestern town. I grew up surrounded by religion, and what I felt was a stifling atmosphere where I felt enormous pressure to 'fit in,'" tells Miss Eva von Slut of Thee Merry Widows/White Barons, who was invited by guitarist Daniel DeLeon, Insaints guitarist and now a psychobilly fellow traveler of hers, to front the tribute version of the Insaints. "I just was not able to do so; I was a weird kid who liked strange stuff like horror movies. Later on, I got into punk rock and threw myself wholeheartedly into underground music. I was a regular reader of *Maximum Rocknroll* in my teen years, and I ached to be in a place like the Bay Area, where freedom of expression was not only allowed but encouraged. So, reading about women like Marian Anderson and Wendy O. Williams was nothing short of a miracle. I remember reading about Marian and being struck by the fact that she was creating music and art on her own terms and was willing to accept the consequences for where her art took her.

"In the pre-YouTube days, I was never able to see any footage of the Insaints, but I did order their split 7-inch record with the Diesel Queens and was blown away by both the music and the words. When Marian sang 'I Am a Whore' in her fabulously spiteful voice, I got shivers down my spine. . . . Although the onstage sex shenanigans are what people talked most about, the music stands up on its own as great punk rock. Her voice was powerful but feminine. I think she is a very underrated punk rock frontwoman" (von Slut 2015).

Above all, Miss Eva still finds power and perseverance in Marian's candid clamor. "Obviously, Marian was enjoying finding ways to assert her sexuality onstage. She was a woman showing she was beautiful and sexual and could not be pushed around. That was one of the biggest things that attracted me to the Insaints—the obvious enjoyment of being 'in your face' about sex and the control that shines through in Marian's vocals and lyrics. I don't ever re-create what Marian did onstage, as that isn't my thing, and I feel as though that would be almost disrespectful of what Marian was doing as an artist. We do usually incorporate some kind of nod to her onstage performances. For instance, I had some friends from the Lusty Lady perform some striptease onstage with us a few shows back. The most recent Insaints show had a burlesque performance with a banana incorporated into the show. I think you can't separate Marian's sexuality from her music, and although her story ends tragically, her strength and resilience in the face of a terrible upbringing are something many women can identify with. She remains one of the true icons of underground punk rock in my mind" (von Slut 2015).

What one does to his or her body obviously has deep repercussions. In 1996, Mykel Board declared Women against Pornography "one of the most detestable organizations in America" and described a member of Riot Grrrls secretly slipping "This Exploits Women" notes into records by his band Artless, then scurrying "away begging for the comfort of her fellow grrrls, unwilling to verbally put up her dukes" (Board 1996). A decade earlier, in 1985, Eugene Chadbourne of Shockabilly and Ruth Schwartz of *Maximum Rocknroll* debated pornography. Schwartz insisted, "Pornography by definition is of a violent nature," while Chadbourne countered that nuance does exist in both storylines and content (Schwartz 1985). The more troubling aspects of the porn, he felt, is that "it suddenly connects these feminists supposedly of the Left with people who are really on the Right" (Schwartz 1985). Hence, the Moral Majority and mainstream feminists, unlikely partners, took up a common cause, desiring censorship and bans. Yet as Chadbourne delineates, the violence of horror movies, from *Texas Chainsaw Massacre* to *The Tool Box Killers*, some of which feature former porn actresses, seemed less sadistic than the actual violence of the era, such as the potential threat of annihilation by nuclear weapons, which "is what people should be trying to get rid of, not magazines." Banning weapons made much more sense than keeping sex workers sidelined by banning filmed sex.

The late 1980s and early 1990s was a dizzying era for convergence between punk and sex worker communities: Miss Koko Puff (Leaving Trains, Sluts for Hire) worked for Ed Powers porn productions; Kurt Brecht, singer for D.R.I., published his book of fiction *Whore Stories*; porn star Aja and Killing Joke both appeared in such magazines as *Skin Trade*; actress Jenna Jameson was interviewed in *See That? Magazine*, which also featured Social Distortion and Mighty Mighty Bosstones; *Taste of Latex*, which promoted itself as a "polysexual/female edited," "wacky, all-inclusive pornzine for punx of all persuasions" and "a sexzine with brains," advertised in *Maximum Rocknroll* and *Flipside*; guitarist Rune Gronn described an encounter with a Midwest prostitute in graphic detail in a Turbonegro diary published by *Maximum Rocknroll*, which also featured Mykel Board's column showcasing his sex with a Thai prostitute; and Leather Tongue Video ("rare porn . . . foreign . . . gay") advertised in *Flipside*. In the same zine, Shane Williams interviewed fetish, tattoo, and pinup photographer (and former nude model) Justice Howard; meanwhile, *Money Talks* profiled Matt Zane Pictures, emblematic of crossover punk and punk worlds, replete with a photo of Ron Jeremy as well as a nude actress. Porn star Janine (former wife of Jesse James) appeared on the cover to Blink 182's *Enema of the State* album; a full-page advertisement memorializing porn star Savannah (Shannon Michelle Wilsey) appeared in the fanzine *Under the Volcano* in an issue with Jello Biafra and Ian MacKaye; and adult stars Taija Rae and Jeanna Fine appeared on the covers of Chemical People albums (*Ten-Fold Hate* and *So Sexist*), a band that contributed music to pornographic films as well.

Some bands simply named themselves after pornographic stars, like the group John Holmes: "dark, twisted and nasty devil rock" one show flyer from the Indian Queen pub in Brighton, England, read. Others commemorated the porn star. Poison Idea played a "John Holmes Memorial Tour" in 1988, the flyer depicting a caricature of the star with an elongated penis tracing the tour route across the western states of America. Some bands, like Midget Albanian Porno Wrestler, simply referenced the genre in an absurd manner. Zines like *In the State of Nature*, whose flyer portrays a nudist female punk, seemed aimed at a crossover audience of punks, naturalists, free thinkers, do-it-yourselfers, and environmentalists, too.

Fanzine writers weighed in on pornography at regular intervals. Perturbed by the systemic, problematic nature of porn at large, Anita Lawson insisted, "I am so fucking sick of *porn*!" She bemoans women giving away their "beauty like it's a piece of garbage. . . . There is nothing wrong with looking beautiful, but society has raped the meaning of beautiful" (Lawson 1999). She encourages women to stop making porn, which is akin to "being a puppeteer's puppet" and to fully realize that men are "at our mercy" (Lawson 1999). Meanwhile, writers like Queenie covered National Masturbation Month and the sex shop Good Vibrations, filled to the brim with clitoral stimulators and silicone dildos, in her July 1996 column in *Maximum Rocknroll*, as well as tackling *The GV Guide to the G-Spot* and *The GV Guide to Adult Videos* in September 1998. Furthermore, the 1999 compilation *Porn to Rock* featured noted actress Ginger Lynn and punk icons like producer Geza X (as composer) and Paul Roessler (as composer) as well as Vinnie Spit, who later worked with Jello Biafra. Such charged criticism and blatant support for porn coexisted uneasily in the punk public sphere.

Some fanzines addressed the sex worker subculture, like *Teen Punks in Heat* (1989), which featured an interview with a call girl, while Anarchist Sex Workers provided advocacy and workshops, including such events as the 1989 Anarchist Conference and Festival in Berkeley, California. More recently, Aaron Lakoff discussed the issue openly in *Fifth Estate* by exploring how anarcho-syndicalist and gender-queer theories can converge when addressing the topic of sex as work: "If we want to be consistent with core anarchist values of freedom, self-determination, and the elimination of capitalism and patriarchy, it is crucial that we stand firmly in support of sex workers' struggles for better working conditions, and by extension, better lives" (2014).

However, he thoroughly recognizes the lack of agreement on the sensitive issue by acknowledging feminist-based, materialist, abolitionist, and insurrectionist-leaning anarchist collectives, such as Les Sorcieres, which prefer dismantling of the sex worker system, or at least shaming the men involved: "we should point the finger at clients. We need to discourage men from consuming women's bodies" (Lakoff 2014). Doing so, Lakoff notes, may be considered the centerpiece of a desire to abolish wage/slave labor of all types, but it also draws lines between types of workers: rather than recognizing sex workers' rights to self-organize—their own essential self-determination—it condemns the industry. Furthermore, authors like Carol Queen placed the whore stigma in high relief. Arguing that female sexual emancipation—women seeking sexual agency on their own terms—is both "threatening and despised"; the best way to decrease sex workers is not through prosecution, zoning, and withering cultural attacks, she attests, but by fostering sex-positive communities in which the exchange of sex services is unneeded (1998, 132).

Others punks attempted to disable sex and military-industrial complexes with a form of sabotage, such as the "urban guerrilla" organization Direct Action, also known as Vancouver Five, which included Gerry Hannah (also known as Gerry Useless and Nature Punk) of the Subhumans, who attacked a hydroelectric substation in British Columbia and dynamited the outside gates of Litton Industries, provider of cruise missile guidance systems, injuring seven workers and causing $4 million in damage. Though the group took precautions—providing a warning and instructions—and also later apologized for the bodily harm, its members remained adamant about the choice to act: "remaining passive in the face of today's global human and environmental destruction will create deeper scars than those resulting from the mistakes we will inevitably make by taking action" (Hansen 2014, 7).

Meanwhile, the Wimmin's Fire Brigade (a group sharing members with Direct Action), firebombed three Red Hot Video stores, a Canadian chain of thirteen stores that were known to distribute violent pornography, including depictions of rape and forced enemas, imported from the United States. This took place only after activists had spent much time pressuring the local attorney general's office to take action under the Motion Pictures Act. After the legal authorities refused to do so, and "demonstrations, petitions, and [a] letter-writing campaign" (Hansen 2014, 8) failed to prompt enforcement action, three groups of three women, including Direct Action members Ann Hansen and Juliet Belmas, launched the attack against Red Hot Video, successfully destroying one building entirely, damaging another one badly, and aborting an offensive against a third when a police vehicle was seen in the vicinity (Hansen 2014, 8). Ironically, the same day that members of Direct Action were detained by police for the incidents, authorities fined and prosecuted the video company on three counts of distributing obscene material.

Members of both guerrilla groups received prison terms, including Hannah, who was only one of two to plead guilty. The official bulletin of the band D.O.A. (adamant supporters of their "friends on trial for their lives and freedom") announced, "Free the Five—jail the real terrorists: the people who promote violence against women and children, environmental collapse and ultimately, the destruction of the entire planet" (Keithley 2011, 80). In such sentiments, the destruction of war and degradation of women intersected.

Looking back, historians note Direct Action was inspired by both local and global concerns, including Vancouver's own radical traditions. The city featured vigorous, long-running feminist and environmental movements (Greenpeace); a radical working-class history; student-thronged movements from Students for a Democratic University; and the local Industrial Workers of the World branch to the Youth International Party. The city also housed queer activism, such as the Vancouver Gay Liberation Front. By the mid-1970s, diverse anarchist activism took root and blossoms to this day. So the sociopolitical microclimate of the city did gestate such activism, as the global guerrilla movements of the day likely did, although those operating during the 1970s and 1980s, like Red Army Faction, tended to embrace Marxism-Leninism, not the anarchist aims of Direct Action. Those outliers often engaged in armed attacks on citizenry, which Direct Action attempted to avoid.

In her biography, Hansen acknowledges working passionately to distribute leaflets and aid "RAF fugitives" while living in Paris in the late 1970s, but she felt their tactics seemed self-defeating, a model she would not aspire to. Instead, she felt more inclined toward "autonomists," which she calls the "political version of punks," which organized squats, dressed outside the norms, and shoplifted, living a kind of pungent outlaw code on the margins of liberal democracies (Hansen 2014, 25–26). Ultimately, she was sentenced to life in prison for planning to rob an armored bank vehicle and for bombing Litton Industries and Red Hot Video, though by 1990 she was freed. Her fellow activist Julie Belmas, who worked with handicapped children, enjoyed the outdoors, and attended Douglas College, had been depicted as "an urban guerrilla soldier" that "laid down her guitar, picked up a gun, and started reading books with titles such as *How Terrorists Kill*. She practiced shooting at targets with human figures drawn on them, . . . rehearsed robbing an armored car guard," and dreamed of blowing up an icebreaker, too (Odam and Glavin 1984). After spending fifteen years in prison, she returned to college to study film and now produces media.

Writing to *Maximum Rocknroll* from prison in August 1984, Gerry Hannah continued to advocate on behalf of urban guerrilla groups, such as Red Brigades, Direct Action, Revolutionary United Freedom Front, the Irish Republican Army, African National Congress, and the Farabundo Marti National Liberation Movement. He criticized the pacifist agenda ("non-violent civil disobedience") at length, especially the antinuclear moment as a "meaningless 'cop out,'" which not only perpetuates "an age-old state-inspired myth" but also isolates "the guerrillas from the popular support they need to succeed in their struggle" and strengthens the absolute power of the state (Hannah 1984). In all, he served five years in prison and played with the Subhumans sporadically afterward, making such albums as *New Dark Age Parade* in 2006.

The diatribes of such punks did not exist in a vacuum: the August 1984 issue also contained reports from several 1984 riots, revolts, and marches in San Francisco relating to the Democratic National Convention, an anti–Moral Majority Family Forum led by Jerry Falwell, and pro-marijuana legalization, which led to ongoing scuffles, intimidation, and arrests by riot squad police. Swaying across three stories of a vintage building, one banner read, "Do we fear our enemies more than we love our children," while another posted behind a stage read "No Fuckin' War!" Live bands performing during the ruckus, such as the Dead Kennedys, featuring lead singer Jello Biafra in a Ronald Reagan mask; the Dicks; and M.D.C., provided the pummeling soundtrack. Hannah's words reverberated—the state power he condemned was very real, unleashed, and physically coercive during the era.

Punk and porn communities, both formerly marginalized and shunned, have converged since the mid-1970s. Together, they fissure notions of discreet bodies that repress primal, shameful, improper, and "grotesque" biologic urges. In early punk, "filthy" spit became normal form at gigs, a way for attendees to authenticate the subterranean experience by revolting against previous routines and condoned customs of audience boredom, passivity, and adulation toward performers. In certain pornographic genres, especially the gonzo and fetish films of Mike Adriano and Belladonna, spit—a plentiful and fetishized exchange of bodily fluids—reveals boundless "filth" tied to an indecent pleasure frowned upon in marriage practices.

Canadian director, actor, photographer, and writer Bruce LaBruce began "making underground fanzines and experimental Super 8 mm movies" with "aesthetic," "political," and "revolutionary" undertones in the 1980s, which helped inaugurate the homocore and queercore scenes (2007). His contemporary work spanning the 1990s through the 2000s, like *Skin Flick* and *The Raspberry Reich*, which often toured film festival circuits, skirt transgressively between hardcore pornography and art films. LaBruce reminded a novice journalist, "I think a lot of gay kids did identify with punk and not just find solace in it. It was a very active and political movement and very much based on style as well, something which a lot of gay kids in particular would find stimulating and important. . . . Gay culture had gotten very boring and bourgeois, so they needed an alternative. Punk came from a very gay-identified place to begin with (punk was the prison slang for a passive homosexual, and then later became associated with juvenile delinquents), and the early days of punk in the seventies were very much about sexual revolution and difference" (Thibault 2000).

Just as the multiple piercings, tattoos, and body modification of punks are unwelcome by moral conservatives—even within a secular society—as forms of immoral and unhygienic debauchery, pornography issues challenges, too. Even more so, the subculture sites of such transgressions—run-down punk clubs and seedy sex cabarets, peephole bookstores, bathhouses, and midnight theaters—are in fact equally marginalized in terms of geography and social expulsion. The sites, most now closed, often cohabited the same neglected city blocks or buildings in a metropolis.

Under pressure from zoning and political clout, such commercialized sexual spaces have increasingly vanished from cityscapes. Instead, the Internet has become the epicenter of uninhibited leisure and sexual avenues, where hedonism offered by the ever-flowing content of fringe industries can be explored without end. Due to the Internet, a series of prurient dreams are mere clicks away and rendered invisible by cleared search histories, though potential viruses loom in the form of malware/malvertising. Hence, the psychogeography of the city, with its derelict, fecund side-street marketplaces of dirty books and looks, has been increasingly erased. "All those who stand in the middle of a transaction, whether financial or intellectual: gone! . . . Small retailers and store clerks, salespeople of every kind—a hindrance, idiots, not to be trusted," avowed Ellen Ullman. "No one, no professional interloper, is supposed to come between you and your desires, which, according to this idea, are nuanced, difficult to communicate, irreducible, unique" (Ullman 2000). Netporn opened the gates and crushed portions of the city of Sodom—record stores and porn shops simultaneously—except in cities vowing to stem the closures by marketing to exclusive subgroups that still believe in the cultural capital of stand-alone shops, like curated "black metal" record stores or gay book stalls.

Whereas staid, sexist, and standardized mainstream beauty norms deem that women models should be sizes 00 to 0, symbolizing a body of condoned depravation and disorder (undereating, anorexia, etc.), pornography tends to document and promulgate physical diversity (mother/grandmother taboos, amputees, little people, BBW—big beautiful women). Pornography also appears to test—even to melt or shred—the fluid boundaries between everyday life and ambiguously performed authenticity (Is it real or simulated aggro and orgasm, or perhaps both?). Semantically, the association between punk and porn is "hardly accidental. In presentation and performance, hardcore music and hardcore films aspire to identical ends—'going all the way,' 'nothing left to the imagination,' 'in your face,' (or 'in your eye')," according to James Ward (1996, 163). Both sought to blur borders dichotomizing the lawful and unlawful, tasteful and tastelessness, proper and profane, sensible and senseless. Both punk rock and pornography were coded and branded as outlandish and outrageous, sick and intolerable, and they act as avatars of messy, tainted, smeared bodies in revolt against the inherited sense of discretion and shame operating within Judeo-Christian traditions.

Punk not only acted as bold and reckless as pornography, but punk also hijacked elements of pornography, like bondage pants, rubber masks, and hardcore gay illustrations, wrapping them into an aesthetic assault on the senses. In the hardcore era of the 1980s and beyond, the backs of Yeastie Girlz tee shirts featured an enlarged medical illustration of a vagina. Album covers or advertising for garage bands, including the Nomads, Hagfish, Bulemics, Dwarves, Turnedown, Easy Action, Buckra, Phoenix Thunderstone, the Cruel and Unusual, Monomen, Mummies, the Gimmicks, Mad Daddys, Oblivions, Dirtys, Elvis Hitler, Raggity Anne, the Daxls, Hellacopters, Lustorama, Hi Pro Glo, and Detroit Cobras, routinely employed striptease, scantily clad, S&M, nude, exotica, bikini, hook 'n' grind, fetish, and burlesque images often favored by designers like Art Chantry. In a reversal or parody of such norms, the female pop-punk band Binge featured a male stripper on stage—skimpy G-string dotted with crumpled dollar bills—on the cover of their album.

Such irreverent mingling of imagery and content helps illustrate notions of the carnivalesque—the ritual rejection, liberation, and deviance from orderly society and "normal" practices, as Bakhtin asserts. However, even subversive and ironic products may benefit exploitative economic systems. Laissez-faire economics that benefit punk-sex filmmaker Rob Rotten—whose film *Fuck the System* contained a soundtrack and CD sampler with Rancid, Smut Peddlers, Complete Control, Blacks 77, Antiseen, and more—and director Joanna Angel, a longtime fan of Rancid who uses actresses like Kleio (once photographed sporting a Reagan Youth tee shirt), also benefits the exploitative music industry.

Still, the transgressions of punk and sex—now easily globalized by the click of a button—*are* about dismantling behavioral codes induced and policed mostly by an interwoven apparatus of laws, customs, surveillance, and local values. Perhaps considered superficial and sexist or anchored to patriarchal dictates, both punk and porn can allow for a sense of maximum agency. In such cases, the body and the voice, the lifestyle admired or attacked, is a vehicle for semiotic shifts of expression, as Lauren Langman illustrates in "Punk, Porn, and Resistance." These industries have sometimes appropriated and incorporated motifs, personas, and production values from each other; meanwhile, a significant portion of each community remains underground, restless, procreative, and defiant. Misogyny and liberation may coexist in the communities, just as Shawn Kerri, illustrator for the Circle Jerks, Germs, and D.O.A., also penned cartoons for *Hustler*.

Jennifer Blowdryer, punk writer and singer for the Blowdryers, regular fixtures on the San Francisco first-wave scene, also wrote for similar publications about "cashiering/playing music at a lapdancing parlor in New York City" for *Penthouse* subsidiaries. "I think one was called *Hot Talk*. I wrote an account of 'My Very First Porn Movie,' which was true, but I sexied it up by dwelling on my hot outfits and making the sex sound, well, good. For *Penthouse Forum*, I interviewed Lydia Lunch and introduced her to Annie Sprinkle, who did a photo session with her, and they continued their whatever the show version of a friendship/alliance is. Annie used to be an amazing six degrees of separation person in the field of the arts/punk/outsider/whatever meets hack erotica, and now she's an eco academic and has kept a lot of those friendships" (Blowdryer 2014).

Annie Sprinkle left the lurid world of blue movies in the mid-1980s and entered the provocative world of performance art, where she broke audience participation barriers. By inviting members of her audience to explore her vagina with the use of a speculum, Sprinkle's work has been linked to predecessors, such as Courbet (*L'origine de monde*, 1886) and Duchamp (*Étant donnés*, 1968). Disarming the "lewd gaze" while acting as an "agent of both sexual education and enlightenment exorcises both the taboo and the sexual mystery" (Cramer 2005). Sprinkle's work heralded a whole new era of peep shows for the postmodern world.

"I wrote a piece on having sex with a thrash metal bf [boyfriend], which was like the punk of the late 80s, for *Penthouse Hot Talk*," Blowdryer continues, "and one combining boxing match/sex piece. It was all based on very true things, and I have my own peculiar selethics (my own word for selected ethics). Writing porn is okay, but exploiting other people's experiences for cash is not. Once I'd burned through my own material, I couldn't do any more work in that genre, according to me. There were some proto-typical and great things about the confluence of punk mind and porn mind.

"There's long been a connection between sex mags and rough writers—Bukowski was often published in them. Allen McDonnell of Larry Flynt Publications bought a lot of original art by artists like Robert Williams, published it, got them some green, and kept it. Lydia Lunch also wrote for him. Lily Barana"—who started as a punk fan and editor for *Taste of Latex*—"wrote a really important book called *Strip City* about her last year on the road as a stripper. I'm a bit fearless, and go by my own mores. I made a porn movie because I was broke. Allen tracked me down because he loved my first book, *Modern English*, and he was trying to think of a way to possibly meet me but definitely get me to write for *Hustler*, which was so subversive you couldn't really prank it. Anything goes in what I call hack erotica. There's a freedom I call Anarchy through Indifference. Most buyers just wanted to jerk off and look at the pictures. You could write or say any damn thing, and that is a good opportunity for ballers like us to step in. I still look at the titles of porn movies, and it's impossible not to laugh—they're wonderfully camp and absurd" (Blowdryer 2014).

Blowdryer desired her work to embody a distinct style and narrative thrust. "My story lines were kinky, the jerk off factor involves some violence, some degradation. In turn, on the part of the sex worker, there's disdain. They're two really different mindsets, and when Johns confuse themselves with Sex Workers, they are way wrong. Straight men don't always know when they're actually trolls. I noticed that Lydia's piece for *Hustler* did have one woman violating another—with a beer bottle no less!—which was sexy, I just don't roll that way. Porn is for the customer. They want girl on girl, they got it" (Blowdryer 2014).

Still, Blowdryer has little taste for punk porn. "I've never seen [it], outside of this one Bruce LaBruce movie that was supposed to be a real movie or transgressive or artistic or something, but it was just this hot guy wearing those goth contact lens who was supposed to be a zombie, and he was fucking other guys a lot. Yawn. When you compromise porn you get no art, no porn. It's like when they kept trying to sell the American public on different flavors and colors of ketchup, but we just wanted red Heinz ketchup.

"There is an exception: queer transmen and femmes. I've seem some good stuff, and Carol Queen I'd say would be an expert on the who, what, and where's. What gay guys want doesn't change too much over the decades, from where I sit," she argues. "What men who need to be women do had such an economic determinant for so long. I find it hard to think there are 'chick with a dick' support groups, so I'm assuming that is not a genre chosen by its leading actors, but in the case of transmen and queer women, here were these new people with new things they got off to, and really the people in those movies have kind of a thrilled look more than a 'when do I get paid' look, and these communities, oh how I've come to hate that word, they fight and splinter group a lot, so I wouldn't even venture to guess who did it first or best or whatnot, but that is some good new type of porn that steps out of the normatives and is still sexy" (Blowdryer 2014).

She also describes the gap between academics and sex communities. "There's a huge, huge movement of erotic hypnosis that for some reason intellectuals have no knowledge of, which is crazy because there are millions of followers—it's all over YouTube, and the basis is often Bimbo-ization, a degrading feminization for men, and the men self-hypnotizing are taking mushrooms, mind-bending drugs, smearing on lipstick, kissing the floor. I don't know where it's going and maybe it went there, but if I was a student of porn/transgression I'd look into it, and I bet a lot of men who joined the U.S. military and came back burned and betrayed and a lot of software/programmer men, the only ones who really count economically, are very, very into it. They mostly would listen to punk, thrash metal, speed metal, hip-hop not so much" (Blowdryer 2014).

For many, Blowdryer's counterculture haven Smut Fest is her definitive contribution. "I started Smut Fest because this woman owned a lap dancing parlor and had a panel of artists, including Penny Arcade, come meet with her to see about running shows. I was running shows with bands, street performers, spoken word, at ABC No Rio, and [I was] used to figuring out the PA, the door, the flyers, pretty much operating on my own, so I was the only one who followed through, and this woman thug let me run about thirty shows in her space. I got to make performance art fans walk through a metered turnstile, which is what you'd use to clock how many perverts attended and make sure the staff didn't cheat you out of their entry fee. I got a laugh out of that" (Blowdryer 2014).

Still, tensions existed. "When I ran Smut Fest, it was a real battle to keep it actually sexy. Erotic meant lame. Exhibitionists run toward the unattractive. There was this likable numbskull who let my friend call her Tracy Love. She was doing the 970-PEEE (the extra E is for Extra Pee!) ads on the former sex channel, which I was also on in a different way, and I egged her on to tromp naked up and down the runway because I wanted my show to work. I was The Man. It wasn't a side of myself I liked. At the U.K. Anarchy Smut Fest, I made out with this woman on stage. I couldn't tell if it was because my guard was down, and I just wanted to go for it, or because it might make the go better. Again, not cool in my own selethics. Same reason I stopped writing hack erotica, same reason I walked away from years of freelance writing, same reason I only turned about ten tricks in my life, same reason I fucked up writing a general interest book. I cannot afford to become The Man because I will be A Creep and I will lie. I'll lose the only thing I have—my mind and thinking will bend and never snap back to Blowdryer Mind. All you got's yourself" (Blowdryer 2014).

Blowdryer also adamantly refuses to relinquish control of her enterprise. "For Smut Fest, my goal was to have the strippers, hustlers, hookers, speak and perform for themselves—I have a lot of footage, and I will not put it on YouTube; propagating other people's images and acts without permission violates my selethics. I did get the footage digitized, and I'd like to donate it to the Center for Sex and Culture, but they're not ready to handle an archive from what I can tell. No space, no structure, and I'd like it to be viewed only by a visiting sex worker or curious person, so there's no Bradley Manning episodes. This idiot couldn't believe that I didn't want him to just post myself doing a reading about making a porn movie on YouTube, that I might be a person with a freaking half-brother or what have you, and I had to tell him about a million times not to do it. It was like talking to a child. True Outsiders don't want to be known at any price, which is usually no price, for every damn thing they do" (Blowdryer 2014).

BEFORE WE UNDRESS: LET'S TALK THEORY

Mirroring the sentiment of feminists like Catharine MacKinnon, some punks insist porn will always be misogynist and hetero-patriarchal, representing the actual rape and abuse of women like Linda "Lovelace" (Linda Marchiano), the actress discussed in *Are Women Human?* (MacKinnon 2007). In contrast, Lauren Langman stresses that porn exposes tension between social control and agency and empowerment, offering "a critique of patriarchal codes of morality and adornment in which the body becomes a basis of empowerment and authenticity" (2008, 1). This is also likely the case with Courtney Trouble's Reel Queer Productions, which advertises itself as "authentic, queer, smoldering, and diverse." This "authenticity" is countered by hetero alt-porn, including the new version of *New Wave Hookers*, in which alt-porn girls use "performative mechanisms to denaturalize gender"—such as acting out "clichés," according to Katrien Jacobs, which "make viewers aware of the constructed nature of the sex" (2005, 224).

By 2005, the conference "The Art of Netporn" convened, which, according to news releases, attempted to pave the way to "awaken media activism and intellectual sharing" and "immersion in pornographic networks" while averting "hysteria" and a "climate of narrow-mindedness." For these participants, Netporn is a nexus where "major political tensions and gender wars come to light" amid a progressive desire for a "post-utopian quest for pleasure and media awareness." As such, porn is neither a "beckoning commodity" nor "queer counterculture" but sheer "data that can be modified by social actions, communications and relationships . . . in DIY online eroticism" with literary and cultural roots reaching back to Bataille, Rabelais, and de Sade. Overall, the activists fostered certain tenets:

1. Porn culture is a breeding ground for alternative body tolerance and queer sexuality—or gender morphing and a willingness to experiment with a subculture, like being butch.
2. Porn fosters "gender-fluid modeling" and the denaturalization of "binary gender codes," such as Buck Angel, a female "bear" (DeGenevieve 2005, 228).
3. Porn provides a series of interesting, nuanced, and layered works of art and writing.
4. Porn is an evolving, democratizing zone housing autonomous sex communities or places for self-activated sex workers to decode, subvert, and re-encode signifiers and produce workers who are "creative, dynamic, and unexploited" and who may undo the "colonial gaze" (Miller-Young 2005).
5. Porn is an evocation of grotesque sex and punk activism.
6. Porn is a space to "execute . . . project[s] of ownership, design and control of images . . . the cultural labor of self-authorship against, or in friction with, hegemonic real and virtual views" (Miller-Young 2005).
7. Porn is a transformer of queer identities and an active contributor to minority (sexual, ethnic, etc.) social networks.
8. Cyberporn is a network of cultural codes and cybertypes—"transcripts of fetishized Otherness" (Miller-Young 2005).

CUM2CUT cofounder Tatiana Bazzichelli further notes that pornography becomes an experimental realm, especially in alt-porn, Netporn, queer porn, and amateur porn settings, for it breaks "the dynamics of crystallized power, self-governing one's own sexuality. The conscious role of women (and men) in this vision is to personally enter inside the mechanisms of bodily expression and the production of desire, to subvert them from within, in favour of a fluid dimension" (2006, 3–4). Hence, pornography is not about viewers' passivity but about their willingness to play, experiment, explore, and widen the capacity and shape of their desires.

On the ground, sex politics is still tied to a sense of place, infrastructure, and social landscapes. Author Timothy J. Gilfoyle described the rise and fall of a boisterous New York City sex worker infrastructure from 1790 to 1920, which served as an alternative economy with customs often challenging the norms of the day. In doing so, he also recognized its inherent flaws and limits. "The Milieu of the underground economy offered a variety of alternative subcultures, some of which countered the dominant, sexually prescriptive mores of the age. But discrimination rooted in gender, class, race, and other types of difference ensured that the benefit of these subcultures were never equally shared" (1992, 315). Therefore, if Netporn and punk porn do not rectify or at least recognize such challenges, they may not truly act as a vital, empowering, and fulfilling countercultural zone erecting a brave new sexualized world within the old.

WHERE THE SEX INDUSTRY AND PUNK MEET IN THE NIGHT

Hustler's punk memes and motifs stem from at least the 1980s, when Lois Ayres/Sondra Stillman with her proto-mohawk and nose piercing appeared routinely, including a 1985 issue featuring the third nude appearance of Dale Bozzio of Missing Persons. In a lesbian-themed layout, "Bam-Bee and Shredder," in which Ayres' teased hair glows in chemical blue and shock white, the text sets the scene: "The band has left the stage at Screaming Skull Club, and just about all the slam-dance punks who filled the dance floor have gone home. That's when Bam-Bee notices another late-night straggler" ("Bam-Bee and Shredder," 1985, 87). Carnal love ensues as handcuffs and studded belts sway.

The "underground" sex economy produced Traci Lords, a supposedly drugged-out sixteen-year-old porn problem and "overlooked Jewish cultural hero" who much later inspired the late-1980s scum-rock band Traci Lords' Ex-Lovers, who appear on the compilation (as does Traci herself) *New York Scum Rock Live at CBGB*, produced by Mykel Board, a member of the band Artless and a writer for *Maximum Rocknroll* (Rogovoy 2000, 133). Her story, soon splashed across major newspaper headlines, uncovered a modern 1980s teenage wasteland in all of its reckless grit, not unlike film noir or a dimestore novel, before mainstream movies like *Less Than Zero*. Hollywood was the epicenter of both punk and porn, of the film *Desperate Teenage Lovedolls* and angry "Kids of the Black Hole," as the Adolescents once sung.

Lords, who pursued a dance-pop genre and fitness career, guest-sang on a Ramones record ("Somebody to Love," *Acid Eaters*), had a cameo on the sitcom *Will and Grace*, was thanked in the liner notes of *Mother's Milk* by Red Hot Chili Peppers (in flagrante sex sound clips of Lords are inserted into their mix of "Stone Cold Bush"), and sang the duet "Little Baby Nothing" with Manic Street Preachers on their debut album. She's never quite escaped her early skin-flick infamy, though she has appeared in the Steven King miniseries *The Tommyknockers* and the reality TV show *Celebrity Wife Swap*. In 2013, she appeared on talk shows discussing her single "Stupidville," a solid slice of modern-rock fare that protests rampant sexual violence against women past and present in places like her hometown of Steubenville, Ohio. That same year, she appeared with the cast of *Cry-Baby* at a tribute to Johnny Ramone at Hollywood Forever Cemetery, which also attracted Steve Jones of the Sex Pistols, Slim Jim Phantom of the Stray Cats, and Billy Zoom of X.

Mavericks like outsider/art house film director John Waters, a "punk before punk existed," tried to resurrect Lords for a new audience in *Cry-Baby* (Sargeant 1999, 11–12). Waters' punk status is self-evident, for his early films "look and sound terrible," like a crude music set catapulting from dead city nights (Rombes 2005, 60). Tommy Ramone even likened the 1970s audiences at CBGB to people in *Pink Flamingos* (Rombes 2005, 59). Furthermore, Gina Schock of the Go-Go's was also a member of Edie and the Eggs, a short-lived promotional band that made a handful of appearances at CBGB, Max's Kansas City, and the Nuart Theater, backing Edith Massey, who played the "egg lady" in *Pink Flamingos* (Gimarc 2005, 326). On Labor Day 1976, Massey appeared at the "World Sleaze Convention" in Delaware, featuring the founders of *Punk* magazine as guests. She eventually released the single "Punks, Get off the Grass" in 1982, a few years before her death, though she lives on, gracing the cover of a John Cougar Mellencamp album and as a sound sample in the song "The Days of Swine and Roses" by proto-industrial dance band My Life with the Thrill Kill Kult. Its singer, Frankie Nardiello, founded Special Affect with Al Jourgensen of Ministry, self-releasing the cult single "Mood Music" in 1979, a sly new-wave outing with well-placed rhythmic jolts, treated vocals, tribal drums, snaky guitar lines, and taut post-punk vision.

In *Carsick*, published in summer 2014, Waters admits to being picked up by the indie rock band Here We Go Magic, which he describes as open-minded, while hitchhiking across America for nine days and taking members of Hell's Angels to a Baltimore punk rock club called Ottobar, where he enjoyed the "faces of the tattooed new-wavers and their goth girlfriends" (2014, 178). For his midnight movie *Polyester*, he hired Stiv Bators from the Dead Boys, stirring some rancor among punks. "I play a punk delinquent gang leader and they wanted my hair this length [longish] for the role," Bators mentioned to *Swank* magazine during the course of a discussion of poolside oral sex and his band the Wanderers. "Now, all the skinheads look at me like they're going kill me or something when I'm hanging out at clubs. In England that shit is really bad. They take it all much more seriously there" (Mora 1982, 86).

Meanwhile, Bator's own hero, Iggy Pop, appears in *Cry-Baby*, also featuring Traci Lords and infamous Symbionese Liberation Army kidnap victim Patty Hearst. Film critic Edmond Grant considered the film "offbeat," "smirky teen level," and "colorfully campy" but lacking the "delectably subversive quality of [Waters'] lower-budgeted work" in which "anything society considers gross, depraved, and abnormal is . . . worth reveling in" (1990). This description—filth and subversion—echoes the content, perspective, and modus operandi of first-generation punk bands aplenty. In fact, the character Cry-Baby, played by Johnny Depp, is the "delinquent" face of the "teenage mutant rock 'n' rollers," as writer Paul Baumann describes the "drapes," the delinquents in the storyline (1990). He found the same film to be like a "lurid and absurd dream" replete with "leering, grotesque, and seemingly deformed bodies" that use the spoof genre to explore race, class, music, and sex (1990).

Just as punk riotously reveled in grotesque avatars (see chapter 6), Waters exposed the undercurrents of the American psyche in tumult, on the brink of change, in which emotional aspirations and anarchy seemed like twin engines of juvenile life. "I'm proud that I've invited you into a world where'd you'd be uptight and I make you feel safe and I can be your guide and you can laugh . . . then people don't judge people," Waters himself attested on the *Colbert Report* in June 2014. Insight into generational zeitgeist is the vital byproduct of Waters' films. The storylines and mannerisms, the clothes and slang, the attitudes and vices, provide a kind of witnessing, although Waters frames it almost entirely in a campy, winking style.

Mudhoney, still-running Seattle proto-grunge garage heroes, lifted its name from the title of a 1965 Russ Meyer film; the notorious director was dubbed the "Einstein of sex films" by John Waters. Meyer is recognized for his voluptuous starlets and highly profitable, do-it-yourself, C-movie, sexploitation cinema, which he staged "like military operations" (Ebert 1985). His work, offering an amalgam of cultural traits, was partially indebted to lurid stag films, grindhouse cinema, *Playboy*, and even Al Capp's "Li'l Abner" (Ebert 1985). Rising from the underground, his genre-spanning films range from wide-eyed comedic fare to supposed high melodrama and parody stitched together with "art-house aesthetics" that found its way into first-class theaters (Hatch 2004, 143–44). This is important because Meyer wanted little to do with the porno circuit, which would require sharing his profits with the mob (Ebert 1985). In fact, his profit margins were second only to *Gone with the Wind*.

His pantheon has been praised by lesbians, who extol his lionization of aggressive, rule-breaking women (Hatch 2004, 144), while Ebert has noted that the real sex objects in his catalog are "invariably men" who are "tantalized, tempted, dominated, thrown around, tortured, used, abused, cast aside or simply smothered by strong, powerful women" (Ebert 1985). Upon first viewing, leading New Queer Cinema film critic B. Ruby Rich felt "outraged that I'd been forced to watch this misogynist film that objectified women and that was really just short of soft-core porn. I was *really* annoyed and so were all my feminist friends" (Myers 2014). Yet a new generation recognizes how his work evokes nuanced "ambivalence, dissatisfaction with existing social structures combined with anxiety over the loss of a stable social order" (Hatch 2004, 148). Far from being one-dimensional throwaways, some of his films act as the epitome of a cultural crisis regarding unbound female sexuality, reconstructed notions of femininity and feminism, and outdated male control of morality, social hegemony, political power, and sexuality in the wake of seminal mid-1960s books like *Valley of the Dolls* and the *Human Sexual Response*. Female sexuality was the new *now*, partly reshaped in the age of increased immigration, technology seized by women (ultra-fast cars), lesbianism, and the insatiable self-pursuit of unfettered, sometimes even brutal, desire (Hatch 2004, 149–150, 152).

Malcolm McLaren and Julien Temple reimagined Meyer's work in *The Great Rock'n'Roll Swindle*. The project actually began as a script called *Who Stole Bambi?* cowritten by director Rene Daalder (*Massacre at Central High*) and movie critic Roger Ebert, who also penned the script for *Valley of the Dolls*, which became lyrical fodder for a Generation X song. The film experienced a stillbirth during preproduction when funding plummeted and the "chasm" between the two camps became testy: "there was no way to avert the clash between Malcolm's anarchistic art-school earnestness and the camp sensibility of the King of the Nudies," declared Daalder. "It all ended in bitter tears of rage and lawsuits" and with McLaren firing an irate Meyer (Spitz and Mullen 2001, 154). The aborted scheme might have been a wise move, since the "100 Club with big tits" leanings of Ebert and McLaren could have sidetracked and dimmed the credibility of the Sex Pistols, journalist John Shearlaw concludes: "The idea of the Pistols disappearing into a film studio like Elvis Presley was strongly dismissed by the music press," who desperately wanted the band to be gigging frequently, active and alive (Colegrave and Sullivan 2013, 268).

On the queer side of history, The Dicks "Saturday Night at the Bookstore" is an unflinching ode to glory holes. The hole's presence is no simple passing reference or metaphor but part and parcel of naked homoerotic candor, not unlike later queercore bands like Pansy Division, which would write singles like "For Those about to Suck Cock," "Nine Inch Males," and "Touch My Joe Camel." One Big Boys poster with a naked cowboy on the front nearly got Raul's shut down in Austin; on the West Coast, H. R. Giger's *Penis Landscape* art found on the Dead Kennedys' *Frankenchrist* album insert caused a massive No More Censorship campaign after Mary Sierra, whose children were in possession of it, notified the state attorney general's office, which felt such indecency violated California Penal Code 313.1. Yet singer Jello Biafra adamantly declared that it embodied "literary, scientific, political, *and* artistic value" and symbolized "consumer culture on parade" (Eddy 1986, 24).

By mid-1988, the debts from the Alternative Tentacles trial regarding Code 313.1 violations were paid off, in part by fundraisers by, among many, Lee Joseph of Dionysus Records and Paul Grant of Bomp! Records, who jointly set up a gig at Raji's in Los Angeles with the Fiends, the Long Ryders, fIREHOSE, Dave Alvin, Thee Fourgiven, and the Untold Fables, which netted $1,180.30 for the cause. Meanwhile, in Washington, D.C., Positive Force sponsored a defense fund concert at the Complex featuring the Freeze, Soul Side, Carpe Diem, and more. No More Censorship remained intact as a "low-profile political and information organization" that derided such groups as the Ed Meese Pornography Commission, Parents Music Resource Center, Missouri Project Rock, and National Federation for Decency (which attacked Madonna's "Like a Prayer" video), while aligning itself with such groups as the Illinois Coalition against Censorship, Music in Action, Australian Independent Music Association, and Fundamentalists Anonymous, a group exposing the tactics, worldviews, and methods of Christian extremists. Other punk artists caught in the crossfire of censorship often go unnoticed in the history of this tumultuous era, like the Dayglo Abortions, whose album *Here Today, Guano Tomorrow* caused both the record company (Fringe Records) and distributor (Record Peddler) to be harassed by Canadian authorities. No More Censorship's fact sheet kept these issues afloat in the punk and underground media.

Undoubtedly, punk and porn threaten good taste and overturn the rules of the body politic, in which mainstream culture tries to reign in the body or at least keep it suppressed. Perhaps that's why, in the terrible comedy *Armed and Dangerous*, the director chose rockers and punks to hang inside and outside the porn store where John Candy and Eugene Levy seek shelter and don the gear of transvestites and leatherboys. Obviously, he wanted to show these two "normals" or "squares" masquerading in sin city, not unlike Italian film director Federico Fellini using an all-girl punk band to stir his surreal, some say plotless, 1980 work *City of Women*, which ended up inspiring a *Playboy* pictorial that highlighted the film and spurred Gang of Four to write the song "Woman Town."

Other early punk bands contributed music to films. The song "Electrify Me" by East Los Angeles punk innovators the Plugz was used as the opening song in the infamous film *New Wave Hookers* (a number-one rental in its time, starring Traci Lords), which was a film "about women being enslaved by the voodoo powers of punk and rap music," made by Greg Dark of the Dark Brothers, later a director of a hit Britney Spears video (Wright 2000). The music of the Plugz can also be heard in *The Devil in Miss Jones 3 and 4*; meanwhile, San Francisco acid-punk band Chrome was commissioned by 1970s porn producers the Mitchell Brothers to create music for their blue-tinged, mural-covered (some painted by Lou Silva) O'Farrell Theater in the Uptown Tenderloin, opened in 1969 and regarded by countercultural writer Hunter S. Thompson as "the Carnegie Hall of public sex in America."

It was far more than a simple venue for films like *Resurrection of Eve* and *Behind the Green Door*; it was a "sex emporium" featuring themed rooms "rooted in the world of burlesque and stripping as a legitimate cultural phenomena," which churned out money for the "merry Pranksters of Porn, lovable rogues whose reputation as pornographers was softened by the fact they were businessmen who brought a sense of familial camaraderie to the craft of smut mongering" and lured both "vibrant bohemian[s]" and the "liberal elite" (English 2013).

In the 1990s, punk stripper, activist, and writer Lily Burana successfully sued the iconic club, after four difficult years of litigation, for missed wages and backstage fees that amounted to more than $3 million paid out to 600 former and working dancers. But in the mid-1970s, the band Chrome, which rehearsed in a building owned by the brothers, created a reel-to-reel tape to be used by the dancers at the theater, which the managers declined for being too avant-garde. Known as *Ultra Soundtrack* (after the Ultra Room at the sex club), it formed the basis of their first album *Alien Soundtracks*, a punk cornerstone.

Former Sex Pistols and New York Dolls manager Malcolm McLaren briefly worked for a soft-core French porn company in Paris before managing Adam and the Ants and Bow Wow Wow (whose fifteen-year-old Burmese singer Myant Myant Aye, rechristened Annabella Lwin, was coaxed by McLaren into posing scantily for several 45 single and LP sleeves). Lydia Lunch from Teenage Jesus and the Jerks had a pistol inserted into her vagina in Richard Kern's transgressive cinema verité black-and-white short film *Fingered*. Genesis P-Orridge, one of the founders of the noise-wave band Throbbing Gristle, staged the exhibition "Prostitution" at the Institute for Contemporary Art in 1976. With partner Cosey Fanni Tutti (later of Chris and Cosey industrial music fame), he displayed used tampons and porn magazines featuring forty layouts of Tutti herself (she appeared in *Playbirds* in 1974, *Park Lane* in 1975, and other skin mags). Scottish member of Parliament Nicholas Fairbairn, whose comments were featured in the *Daily Mail* next to the picture of Siouxsie Sioux, attacked the two artists as "wreckers of civilization"; ironically, he was later arrested for indecent exposure (Hodgkinson 2004).

Furthermore, *Hustler* layouts featured Dale Bozzio from Missing Persons; Blondie graced the cover of a *Penthouse* issue that also featured poet-rocker Jim Carroll. At *Penthouse*, Cherry Vanilla ("poet laureate of groupiedom, bard of the hard") wrote "Rock Sex: A Supergroupie Spills All" in 1975. Later, the subject was revisited in a 1982 issue of *Oui*, also featuring the Go-Go's, in which she was honored as "Our Lady of the Dressing Room" in the self-interview article "Cherry Vanilla: Supergroupie's Saga." Her punk-rock jaunt with the Police earned her coverage in *Penthouse* in the article "The Naked Punk: Cherry Vanilla Bears All" in 1978. Lastly, the Dead Kennedys were the focus of a 1980s *Playboy* article. The magazine also featured artwork by the band's iconic designer Winston Smith for "Global Shock," an October 1999 foreign affairs article.

Simon Reynolds' book *Rip It Up and Start Again* does not shy away from revealing the warts of bands like Devo, most noted for its "Whip It" video and timeless images of half-clothed new-wave ranch-life mockery. Reynolds, a former editor at *Spin*, quotes singer Mark Mothersbaugh as saying, "Porn is important to the lower economic levels, simply because they can't afford real sex" (Ensminger 2011). A Devo spread, "Spuds in Duds: Step into Nerd New Wave's Clothes Culture—and the Punky Pleasures of Potato Power," appeared in a 1983 issue of *Penthouse*, along with photojournalism by S. Duroy/Black Star documenting second-wave U.K. punk. Titled "The Empire Strikes Back," it depicted "aimless young punks" wandering "through the streets of London, thousands of urban eyesores wearing Day-Glo Mohawk haircuts, safety pins in their ears and noses and ungrateful dead expressions on their faces" who "rejected their working-class backgrounds and . . . regrouped into shiftless punk tribes who spend their time warring against each other" ("The Empire Strikes Back" 1983, 64). Delivered by a publication that features some degree of hard-hitting journalism, such coverage only heightened the public's suspicion of punk's supposed nihilistic, aimless ethos.

As a keen and eagle-eyed writer trying to unfold the crinkles of post-punk, Reynolds doesn't gloss over the "plain misogynistic" edge of Devo, which loved "pornography, whether it was Bataille's avant-garde version or *Hustler*'s mass-marketed hardcore"; Reynolds even decides that much of *Duty Now for the Future* "sounds like a robotic version of the Knack's sexually pent-up 'My Sharona,' all choppy New Wave guitar and frantically pelvic jack-off rhythms" (Ensminger 2011). Or perhaps it mines and mimics the Vapors' "Turning Japanese," with its supposedly not-so-veiled homage to masturbation, strapped musically to an equally quirky, lean beat. Punk devotees also can point to songs like "Whip in My Valise" by Adam and the Ants and "O Bondage Up Yours" by X Ray Spex and draw their own conclusions about punk and new wave's ties to S&M, bondage, and underground sex culture, where fetish, irony, and punk merge.

"There are a number of things going on here," Reynolds argues. "Obviously, there was this avant-garde tradition of pornography (Susan Sontag wrote a famous essay about this, differentiating between "the pornographies"), going back to de Sade, and taking in Jean Genet, Georges Bataille, and—most crucially for the post-punkers like Cabaret Voltaire and Throbbing Gristle—William S. Burroughs and J. G. Ballard. This wasn't porn as titillation, porn for prurient stimulation, porn as wank-fodder, but as a mode of perception perhaps, or a route to certain kinds of avant-garde literary effects. And obviously transgression. There's also a sense that would have been around that modern world had a pornographic aspect—things like that famous image of the Vietnamese girl screaming and naked because she's torn her napalm-soaked clothes off, or the equally horrible one of the Vietnamese man being executed with a revolver to the head. Groups like Throbbing Gristle would have plugged into that aspect: the pornography of the Final Solution, the gruesome accounts that were being published of serial killers' exploits, or the book *Beyond Belief*. Porn would also relate to . . . the anti-liberal backlash of people like Legs McNeil. Feminists, by the mid-Seventies, were anti-porn, and so if being anti-liberal was your shtick (or genuine creed) then being pro-porn would fit. And as it happens Legs McNeil followed up his punk oral history *Please Kill Me* with an . . . oral history of the porn movie industry!" (Ensminger 2011).

Margaret Doll, singer and guitarist for Demolition Doll Rods, was one of many young rebels who migrated to New York City, in her case from Detroit, and befriended women who introduced her to the fetish media underground. "I thought, sure, I'll have my picture taken," she admits. "I was in a fourteen-hour photo shoot. It was all fucking day and half the night, in these pointed shoes, and I took ballet my whole life, so it was nothing. And every fucking contraption, all day, pent-up Catholic girl, I was just fresh off the school bus you know, and I remember having this red rubber suit on that had a zipper on the crotch, and him [the photographer] unzipping it, and him going, 'but your pussy doesn't even pop out,' and I'm like, 'why would it?' He's like, do you have sex,' and I'm like, 'no, not really.' And people think of me as this big sexual creature, but sex is in here [points to head]. I don't have that much sex, and he was just like click, click, click, it was just non-stop. I had no idea what I was even doing, but I loved it. I'm like, I love the rubber, I love these skirts, I . . . pee'd in the sink. . . . I'm like, ooo, I love peeing in the sink and having my picture taken!" (Ensminger *Left of the Dial*, 2003).

As Reynolds relates, "It's complicated, because there would have been a Sixties impulse towards libidinal liberation, breaking taboos, building a culture of Eros vs. Thanatos, and the feminists at that point would have been right in the thick of that (as would the gay liberation movement—porn, I think, has a much less negative status in gay culture than straight). That late Sixties, early Seventies stage of women's liberation was called 'radical feminism,' it was much more like women claiming the freedoms of men and attacking things like Miss World for their sanitized view of what women were like. You look at a figure like Germaine Greer, she was into female wildness and female libertinism, sleeping with whoever you liked, she was into the whole Sixties rock 'n' roll dope and fucking in the street trip, etc. So, while that generation of feminists might have criticized a magazine like *Screw* for chauvinist attitudes, there's an extent I think that they'd have regarded it as a fellow-traveler in cultural liberation" (Ensminger 2011).

When porn home video had overtaken the cliché era of sleazy men in raincoats looking for seedy succor in Times Square back alleys and bookstores, the "new" Clash toured America and hit places like Detroit, where Joe Strummer was apt to say, "Pornography is rape," partly to offset the endless hedonism of rockers like Motley Crue, who relished teenage girls loaded up on speed and beer. Bill Holdship interviewed Strummer for *Creem* magazine in October 1984, where the writer admits, "I'd rather hear Joe Strummer telling a crowd of Detroit teenagers that 'Sex Mad War' is dedicated to 'a time when a woman can walk alone in the park at midnight without being afraid—which is her divine right' anytime over Motley Crue's 'We love fucking girls in Detroit because their pussies taste so good!'" (Holdship 1984).

The walls separating punk, fetish, porn, and stripping amount to thin membranes, especially with a generation of women including Nancy Spungen and Connie Gripp, a girlfriend of Dee Dee Ramone and Arthur Kane of the New York Dolls. Gripp was a former roommate of Jobriath, the openly gay stage actor from *Hair* and underground rock 'n' roll figure, and as lore illustrates, she chopped off a bit of Kane's thumb, inspired the Ramones' tune "Glad to See You Go," and danced at the infamous three-story topless go-go Metropole jazz club in New York City managed by a tough-skinned Gerri Siner. The place has been credited with fostering the Brazilian dancarina scene, where women danced on a catwalk behind the bar, and it became a setting for one scene in Neil Simon's *The Odd Couple* and a reference in *Kennedy's Children* by playright Robert Patrick. It also served as iconic drummer Gene Krupa's home territory and Kiss legend Peter Criss' first gig after he briefly joined the Barracudas. Even the rather austere Paul Auster took note of the club's downward spiral: "The Metropole had been a quality jazz club, but now it was a topless go-go bar, complete with wall-to-wall mirrors, strobe lights, and half a dozen girls in glittering G-strings dancing on an elevated platform" (2003). It became a haunt of the novelist H. L. Holmes, one of the founders of the *Paris Review*, who offered Auster a "rattling . . . rambling . . . monologue . . . the rant of a hipster-visionary-neoprophet" after leaving the premise (2003, 287–88). Hence, the club might be understood as a haven, not for sex tourists and gawkers alone, but for a wider web of personalities, musicians, and literary recluses, a nexus germane to the New York of the past, which had waned by the late 1980s, except in places like Harmony Burlesque, which became home to strippers, performance artists, underground literati, and activists like Sex Panic! cofounder Eva Pendleton.

Later, as the Giuliani administration implemented new zoning meant to crush the sex trade, such dancers as Pendleton—who admitted in the late-1990s, "Some of the best sex I ever had was on stage at the Harmony Burlesque"—and Melissa Hope began to realize that they could tap into the proprietor's libertarian sense as well. The duo had a "politics of pleasure ideal. . . . For some, it was 'the state should stay out of my underwear'" (Shepard 2010, 205, 206). As workers, they were vulnerable: "transient and really replaceable," according to Cindra Feuer, but the impending laws catalyzed a change of perspective. Owners began to understand the role of dancers—once demeaned and taken for granted—as pubic sex advocates and organizers defending freedom, jobs, and their turf from creeping—and creepy—"urban neoliberalism." These efforts exposed the antisex agendas of "suits" infringing upon "sluts" (Shepard 2010, 206). Such tensions eventually led to the 1998 march on Show World (one of the remaining old-school sex theaters) by a sex-positive activist brigade, including dancers and the Lesbian Avengers, who chanted, "More Booty, Less Rudy, Keep New York Sexy!" and "No strippers, no peace!" (Shepard 2010, 208).

In some cases, stripping is inverted, as with Frightwig, in which a male member of "the audience was inspired to climb on-stage and perform a striptease to the pulsating beat. The other men in the audience were dumbstruck. Needless to say, they were unable to make the connection between the striptease and the strip-act modern man has to go through everyday of his exploitive existence" (Cadeaux n.d., 9). Bands whose performances transmorphed into nude appearances, dance, displays, or stripping included both females from such bands as Diesel Queens, Woodpussy, Tribe 8, Demolition Doll Rods, Texas Terri, and the Voluptuous Horror of Karen Black and males from the Cramps and GG Allin to Fuckemos, the Dwarves, and Demolition Doll Rods, whose singer and guitarist Danny Kroha (also known as Danny Doll Rod) partially imploded gender boundaries by using a neo-drag persona.

"I don't wear makeup any more, but I've always been into the feminine side of myself," Danny Doll Rod told me in the early 2000s. "When I was a kid, I used to pretend that I was a girl sometimes. For some reason, that has always been attractive to me. I've wanted to know what it is like to be female, wanting to know about the female side of things. But you know, when we first started out, we could barely play, and we would love to get dressed up. Margaret and I lived at a house together at that time where we had one room that was all clothes and wigs and dog collars and a vanity and everything, and we would just love to get all dressed up, but that was the fun we had.

"Still, it's really fun to do that. So she was like, 'I want to do this band, and I want it to be an all-girl band, and I want you to be a girl in my band,' and I was like, 'Yeah,' because I had already done that," he said. "When I was a kid, I had already pretended I was a girl. I was already into that. She knew that, she saw that in me, and she wanted to help bring that out and use that side of me that I hadn't really explored since I was a kid. So we got on stage not knowing how to play at all . . . and people who saw us at the beginning did think we sucked, but we always had something, we were always balls out, and people couldn't take it then. We have changed a lot, and we have grown a lot. So once we started getting better, then we played better and moved around more; all of a sudden, the wings started falling off, the makeup was getting so sweaty . . . so, we really couldn't do that anymore. We started to evolve and say, 'okay, I love being a drag queen,' but then when you meet somebody like Jane County, you're like, 'I'm not really a drag queen. I'm not really that intense about it, and I am not really representing people like Jane County, because Jane County is really doing it.'

"So after awhile the wig just started falling off and the makeup started coming off," he recalled. "I feel sexy being able to have both sides going together, to have the male side and the female side . . . integrated and . . . [to] have one come out at one time and the other come out another time. I think it's really healthy to be able to in touch with both sides, because everyone has both sides within them" (Demolition Doll Rods 2003).

WENDY O. WILLIAMS: BEYOND THE VALLEY OF GENDER NORMS

Adult film *Candy Goes to Hollywood* featured Wendy O. Williams, a former gypsy troupe dancer known for shooting ping-pong balls out of her vagina. She also cavorted with animalistic, exotically adorned women, never having sex but acting as a kind of peripheral, otherworldly, indiscreet, and untamed creature in *800 Fantasy Lane*. As "singer-demolitionist" for the band Plasmatics, she became an avatar of porn-rock, covered avidly by the likes of *Rolling Stone*, just as singer Gen Vincent from the 1990s industrial-metal-punk act Genitorturers—featured in both *Flipside* and *Hustler*—became one for the S&M and dominatrix subculture ("Random Notes" 1980, 33). Williams also appeared in B-movies *Reform School Girls*, *Hell Camp of the Gland Robbers*, and *Pucker Up and Bark Like a Dog*.

As singer in the Plasmatics, though, she achieved a perversely iconic status. Often adorned with innocence-lost bobby socks pulled up to her skinny knees or donning dizzyingly tall S&M boots, she topped her unkempt aggro look with peroxide-wounded blond hair and fierce, eyeliner-caked lids. She aggressively blew up cars and attacked guitars and televisions with sledge hammers and chainsaws on shows such as *Tomorrow with Tom Snyder*, confounding the staid, buttoned-up host; ABC's variety comedy program *Fridays*; and the mainstream bellwether *Solid Gold*. She even appeared in a low-key role on an *SCTV* skit, too. In 1980, she appeared in a layout for *Punks Not Dead* fanzine wearing a bra lowered to expose one nipple, hiked-up shorts, and with a chainsaw nestled between her legs.

"I was intrigued by the Plasmatics from the first moment I laid eyes on the 'Butcher Baby' single," says Ronnie Barnett, bass player for the Muffs. "The cover showed this was no ordinary live act! I really became a major fan after witnessing the first interview appearance Wendy did on Snyder's show. This woman who performed with shaving cream and electrical tape on her exposed breasts, who savagely used sledgehammers and chainsaws, was actually smart, funny, and down to earth. While I was a fan of their actual music through the first two albums, I must admit that by the time I got the chance to see them on their first, and maybe only, appearance in Houston in late 1981, a little career confusion and desperation had already set in. The *Metal Priestess* outfits with the rhino horns and shit were pretty horrid, as was the new metal-based musical direction. Dan Hartman (Tina Turner, Joe Cocker) produced that record for Chrissakes! For some reason, I continued to buy all of Wendy's solo albums through the following years, even though I really couldn't tell you what they sound like. I must admit I was shocked and saddened that she took her own life. We sadly don't know truly what all of the thoughts were that led to the most brutal of decisions, but I wish she had somehow found the strength. In this day and age, a reformed Plasmatics could tour forever. Though it might be getting harder to find suitable television sets!" (Barnett 2015).

This gruff, chiseled, sandpaper-voiced, "tornado-proof" Mohawk-sporting woman, the "Evil Knievelette of shock rock," first entered stage life as a child dancer on the *Howdy Doody Show* and became every bit as volcanic and seditious as Iggy Pop slicing himself with broken beer bottles on albums like *Metallic KO*, upsetting the norms of proper pop music (Wallace 1983). "What I do is conceptual art," Williams argued. "If a lot of what I do seems excessive to the 'real world,' then I find the real world excessive and offensive to me" (Stackel 1984, 22). She felt indignant about consumeristic habits, nutrient-decimating factory farming, government suppression of diet-related information, broad and blind conformism to hegemony, repressive decency laws, unrepentant materialism, and state violence. In Italy, she noted, police carried machine guns, a true sign of impending coercion and control. In contrast to her role as curator of chaos, Williams herself was intrigued by union activists and corporate whistleblowers like Karen Silkwood. Williams, a former health restaurant cook who lived in Florida for a stint, grew her own macrobiotic food for a "live food" diet, actively composted, worked out obsessively with free weights and swam, and asked concert promoters to provide peppermint tea at gigs (Stackel 1984, 22–23).

Williams' performances, described by one reporter as "a series of brutal experiments in high-speed rhythmic noise . . . raising the art of pure spectacle to heights of abstract depravity not witnessed since the decline of the Roman Empire," seem to recognize the body as ground zero for the revolt against the Christian, Judaic, and Islamic notions of the body as God's unmarred, discreet temple (Stackel 1984, 23). Even within the counterculture, not everyone saw the worth of her riotous performances. Writers like Dave Marsh dismissed her talent, or lack thereof, though Gene Simmons of Kiss was quick to defend her off-key, imperfect voice. To other writers, she was a blunt wedge used to fight "ennui and banality and the torpor of common life," akin to Flaubert, albeit with costly pyrotechnics (Williams 2006, 134). According to this perspective, Williams evoked a simulated but howling late-industrial primitivism—the epitome of filth spat out in rogue theatrics with a soundtrack as raw and "dis-chordant" as Detroit factories married to cantankerous sounds with an uncanny dose of noise musique thrown in, all tethered to blitzkrieging, fiery punk-metal guitar.

In 1976, Wendy O. Williams began working at Rod Swenson's strip club, Captain Kink's Sex Fantasy Theater, housed in an off-Broadway burlesque building. It offered comedy and erotic-themed skits five times daily, seven days a week during an era in which the vector still remained seedy, especially at night, and "loaded with energy, character, and grit . . . now . . . eliminated in favor of corporate, mass produced vacuity," tells Swenson (Webber 2013). A graduate of Yale and marketer of Good Shepherd granola who actively produced videos for major local players like Blondie and Dead Boys, Swenson, also known as

Butch Star, brainstormed the idea of the Plasmatics and became Williams' decades-long partner (Williams 2006, 137). Though the former Brownies member and Dunkin' Donuts employee soon gigged at splattered CBGB, wore nurses' uniforms, brandished whirring chainsaws on stage as whipped cream dropped from her sinewy limbs, and provoked police from Milwaukee to London, Williams was an avowed raw foods proponent who was interviewed in *Vegetarian Times* and posed in a nude pictorial for Hefner's *Playboy*, replete with shots of her posing thousands of feet in the air on a trick airplane.

When she appeared alongside Jello Biafra of the Dead Kennedys and Mike Muir of Suicidal Tendencies on the *Donahue* show in 1990, she explained that she spent two years defending herself against trumped-up charges of lewd behavior in Milwaukee, where police battered her a day after watching her band "made up of niggers and queers" on *Fridays*. Hence, her staunch anticensorship stance was not a trite, convenient pose of liberalism and guile but something she paid for, sometimes brutally. Punk writers like Jennifer Blowdryer recognized the complexity of her situation as a woman caught between lurid limelight, a deep conscience, and sycophants, even as others, such as Clinton Heylin, crowed, "the Plasmatic's music was totally devoid of substance" (1993, 322). "It looks like Wendy O. Williams knew how to reflect a dream version of the hard-edge heavy metal tropes of a vixen who could also fix a car. [She was] a terrific performer and heaven-sent for a lot of folk who no doubt gave her free blow and then health food," Blowdryer posits, "but I suspect she paid a heavy, heavy price for it. I've had talented gigolos, and they will kill you if you let them" (Blowdryer 2014).

For her detractors, Williams was a Johnny-come-lately purveyor of show-business stunts and schlock, as well as an emblem of outright media blitz gimmicks, and thus was omitted in oral history books like *Please Kill Me*. For others like me, who stared wide-eyed at her television performances, which interrupted and distressed my notions of gendered performances, she became a fluid avatar of sound and fury. Though in her later years—and likely in her internal life for years—she was a Henry David Thoreau type, preferring secluded walks in the woods mixed with a steadfast hippie diet fare totally unlike the junk food cornucopia evoked by the Ramones. She was much more: a recombinant being who basked in the visual lexicon of the post-apocalypse à la *Road Warrior*; a hawker of industrial mayhem using people instead of robots à la Survival Research Laboratories; a punk-as-hell Carrie Nation smashing the swaggering male accoutrements of the late-twentieth century, their penis-envy vehicles, televisions, and guitars; and a dominatrix whipping the leisure society itself using metallic riffs, Mohawks, and blistering speed to savage the commodities lulling people into passivity and boredom. In fact, she was a satire of the politics of boredom, presenting the television set on *Friday*'s stage as if she was hosting *The Price Is Right* as her guitarist—the hollow-eyed, pasty-faced Richie Stotts wearing a tutu—whirls in a postindustrial dervish frenzy. On *Solid Gold*, she entered like a pro-wrestler, tossing flowers in the air, wearing what seems to be either a strap-on dildo or a fake rhino horn on her face, then proceeded to chainsaw an obligatory guitar in half, like a magician tired of faking the trick. This was the black leather empress emasculating rock 'n' roll.

Consequently, the Plasmatics seemed to engulf a self-parody of warrior chic dreamed by John Carpenter as a clusterfuck gender, ethnic, and class skirmish with Orwellian forces of control and groupthink, offending, quite miraculously, the cultural monitors of both the left and right wings. Williams' visual hyperbole, bombastic sensationalism, and emergent guerrilla media allowed her to act as a slash, bash, crash, and burn priestess in a doomsday post-disco terrain. The critics deride her for being devoid of authenticity, inferring she is no more than a white trash biker chick performing mock metal and punk cabaret at the behest of a Svengali-like smut peddler. But she was more complex, offering desexualized kink like a choreographed, supercharged, end-of-the-Cold-War-era gender terrorist torn from the cut-up pages of 1960s and 1970s William Burroughs text, the switchblade prose of Kathy Acker, and the combined worlds of *Blade Runner* and *Faster Pussycat Kill Kill.* (Note: a still from the movie was used as an advertising graphic for Judgementil Music, the music label for Gag Order and Queen Mab.)

"The first and second (including Wendy and the Plasmatics) generations of punk were a complex mixture of hard, hard victims. They were tough, and used their sex to survive and hustle," argues lauded artist Michael David, bass player for Mary and the Immaculates, as well as for Numbers, the band that became the nucleus of the first Plasmatics lineup. "Therein lies a complicated brew of empowerment by any means necessary, with an ultimate cost of victimization to the beat of fame and fortune. Wendy attenuated those polarities more than anyone. She was Rod's creation—a punk rock Frankenstein, a punk rock golem. Her creation ended up destroying the band" (David 2015).

Yet this relationship was not simply a copycat version of British counterparts. "Wendy and Rod were much different than Malcolm McLaren [Sex Pistols] or Bernie Rhodes [The Clash], for lots of reasons. Johnny Lydon and Joe Strummer were brilliant in a way that Wendy never was. Strummer for years was ambitious and ruthless on his own and never really was a punk," posits David. "He just saw the traction that the Pistols had, dumped his existing band for what he figured would be the next big thing, but because of his intelligence, the original concept could sustain, grow, and develop. Strummer was already an ambitious musician and poet, while Wendy was shooting ping-pong balls out of her pussy on Forty-Second Street for tips.

"Lydon and the Pistols were closer to Wendy and the Plasmatics in terms of being a golem, for they self-destructed and could not sustain, but McLaren was far more creative and intelligent than Rod, and Lydon's intellect and talent as a singer were exponentially at a different level then Wendy, who was closer to Sid Vicious (who I encountered a couple of times and replaced in the Music Industry Casualties playing with Cheetah Chrome and Jerry Nolan for a couple of gigs, before that group self-destructed), but the fact that she was a woman makes this a much more complicated and complex narrative.

"In spite of her being some crazed silicon-injected Punch and Judy puppet," David continues, "the gender fuck in her persona gave her a gravitas and credibility that Rod and she never intended or could envision at the beginning of the band. The very thing that gave her credibility—this repulsive inversion of being a female sex toy, all hard and male with her 1950s Cadillac fake torpedo boobs, and aggressiveness here to fore—was the domain of just a sacred few male performers, like Iggy and Stiv, which made us rethink gender roles and the laws of attraction" (David 2015).

Yet Williams was not the sole genderqueer performer, for Stotts looked like a psychotic femme. "Richie got the concept for the Mohawk after watching *Taxi Driver*. Meanwhile, the tutus and the Playboy bunny outfit and the French maid costumes all came from us watching the Damned's (with Captain Sensible) first U.S. concert at CBGB after the Dead Boys opened for them wearing Damned masks. Richie was the soul and the natural leader of the band. Wendy and Rod fed off of Richie's energy, as Richie had fed off of mine" (David 2015).

The origins of the band are important to note as well, since the core of the band predated Williams' involvement. "The band's sound and the first songs came from a band Richie, me, and Roy Stuart, the first Plasmatics drummer who was involved somehow with Rod and the Forty-Second street sex business and then became a very successful erotic art photographer in France. Remember, everyone on the scene (not the art half, like the Talking Heads, etc.) sold drugs, sucked cock, stripped, or did porn. We had a band called Numbers, but little did we know at the time *Numbers* was the biggest gay mag on the market. I came up with the name after the Who (all punks loved Iggy and the Who), whose first name was the High Numbers, and we played loft gigs with the NY Niggers and the Communists, early bands that never made it, in this great underground punk loft scene on Greenwich Street and Canal and in Richie and my loft on Bond Street.

"Rod knew Roy and told him he had idea about doing an art-project punk band and was looking for a band to put behind Wendy, so Roy invited him to see one of our shows at one of these loft parties. Voilà, the Plasmatics were born," David recalls. "Half the first Plasmatics record, and the first single ("Butcher Baby" b/w "Tight Black Pants"), are Numbers songs with changed lyrics, simplified form, and tempos sped up. Richie was the band: it was his sound on guitar, his feel that was the sound, period. I was gone, Roy was a decent drummer at best, Richie created the sound that people came to listen and see, and provided the tone, the violence, for Wendy to do her thing. I am not 100 percent sure where the chainsaw concept came from (I wasn't there), but I know Richie was a big fan of the film *Texas Chainsaw Massacre*, and the sound matched the speed and attack of Richie's playing. I believe Richie once told me the whole chainsaw thing came out of a conversation he initiated. Wendy [as rock 'n' roll performer] stemmed from the collaboration with Richie and Rod, which came out of the stillborn collaboration between Richie and me. Half the theatrics were Rod's via Forty-Second Street and Russ Meyer, the other half Richie's from Captain Sensible and the movies *Freaks, Texas Chainsaw Massacre*, and *Friday the 13th*" (David 2015).

In the end, the band mutated far beyond the loft parties and art-project domain. Success and money became paramount to Williams and

Swenson. "Gene Simmons became personally involved with her and tried to turn the band from punk to metal, for commercial reasons, and to focus everything on Wendy, forcing Richie out the band (half of the concepts for that band came from Richie, not Rod, not Wendy), and the band turned to stone, grumbling and destroying itself, like the golem of Prague," David argues, "turning Wendy to dust, a victim of empowerment by any means necessary, never really having any say or control in her destiny or the outcome of her life, which in the end, only makes the story, the legend, more poignant, deeper, and more important" (David 2015).

"I always wanted Wendy O. to give me a Germs' burn, just like in *Reform School Girls*. She was awesome, and it makes me really sad to think about the way she ended her life," says Lisafer (Lisa Pifer) of 45 Grave, Lisafer, Snap-Her, and Screech of Death. "She seemed to feel, so I am told, awkward in her older self and not useful to the world, even though she was so rad, and such a hardcore animal rights activist. I just love her for that. I learned most of the Plasmatics' songs on bass because that's how much I love them and used to jam them out with friends. We were going to do a Plasmatics cover band a long time ago. It never came to fruition, but I learned most of those songs. She is huge to me. Wendy was fierce, fierce, fierce" (Pifer 2014).

Kembra Pfahler, known for her shock troop the Voluptuous Horror of Karen Black, is another performer who dared to blur the lines between transgressive performance art and cinema, Artaud-like theater of cruelty antics, explosive pop-culture terrorism, and punk antagonism toward idols and static forms. Sister of Adam Pfahler of Jawbreaker, she also coined such terms as *availabism* (making use of materials at hand, which she describes as an "anti-classist, socialist tool") and *anti-naturalism,* and she was a manifesto maker and scion channeling the likes of Butthole Surfers, GG Allin, Lydia Lunch, and Exene Cervenka, though not in a copycat style but by venerating the path less traveled. Whether sewing her vagina shut in the Richard Kern film *The Sewing Circle* or cracking eggs on it, her body became an unhindered art zone indebted to teenage years spent watching bands like the Screamers, Suicide, the Swans, and, even more importantly, female punks. "The punk rockers in Los Angeles were very advanced in their gender politics. Women were treated very differently than we see today," she told *Punk Globe*. "There were androgynous women, saucy women, big girls, small girls, and the concept of beauty was not cliché at all. I feel like the women who were involved in those bands integrated with the boys. It wasn't as sexist" (Fen n.d.).

In her work, the body is polluted and deconstructed—bloodied, mutant, and flux ridden, imminently weird and foreign. She employs a warped, sci-fi kind of Kabuki stylization. The body is a site of procreativity—of remaking the self—not unlike the queering and destabilization of binaries enacted and employed by transsexuals, whom Pfahler has called "far more courageous than an academic art movement" (Fen n.d.). Instead of exploring mere gender, though, Pfahler—sometimes adorned with massive wig, painted red skin, and full leg boots—blurs corporality and otherness. She transcends junk culture materialism, for her body acts as a conduit for enigmatic pop-culture explosivity, earning its place in alternative art galleries, the Whitney Biennial, and Monet's Giverny gardens (in collaboration with E. V. Day), whose lush, fertile greenery was transposed and replicated in 2012 for an installation at The Hole in New York City, funded by Playboy.com (Pfahler's iconic look in the art environment was inspired by *Playboy*'s illustration known as Femlin by LeRoy Neiman). "With a bewigged look that is more sculpture than costuming, she presents an interesting alien injection into the almost Disneyland-esque, iconic landscape of Giverny," according to The Hole's press release. "Kembra mixes sex and power, beauty and horror, the works hint at the possibility of a bizarre and titillating new sexuality. Perhaps like a water lily itself: solitary, bisexual and radial" ("Giverny: by E. V. Day and Kembra Pfahler" 2012).

From punk hierarchy, low to high, sex and music have commingled, sometimes uneasily, sometimes cocooned in conjoined "sin," or, better yet, resistance, shock, and subversion during a time of an overtly sexist press. Even in well-intentioned alternative media like *Spin*, which describes Williams as the "first female to fellate the doors off generally accepted conventions of what women in rock should do or shouldn't do," cannot help adding, "she is one *bad babe*" who just released an album full of "*tits up*, slab-happy manipulation" of heavy metal clichés (I-Rankin' 1986). This same woman later volunteered at Quiet Corner Wildlife Refuge tending to squirrels, worked at the arcade Health Shoppe, and maintained a longtime partnership with a man who managed the band's theatrical feats with logistical precision and who is currently a resident fellow at the University of Connecticut's Center for the Ecological Study of Perception and Action. In some ways, it was full circle for Williams, who once camped outside Boulder, Colorado, working odd jobs and exploring LSD and Eastern religions, and then traveled Europe, where the law took her in at least twice, for counterfeit money and shoplifting, before becoming "The American Dream Girl Gone Nightmare" at CBGB in 1978 (Wallace 1983). Her rural post-Plasmatics life, in some ways, seemed like a purge and a return to a life of solitude.

Williams never shunted her stint as a dominatrix in Times Square skits; remained defiant in the face of sexism; boldy denounced brainwashed hyper-consumerism and environmental degradation on albums like *Maggots*; and even inspired pyrotechnician Bob Farina, one of her entourage, to open a health food store. The rest of the world saw a woman, a quickly used-up avatar of punk, exploiting her body in the glare of cameras for gyrating fans. In the end, she left Swenson a hyacinth with small, unopened buds and a few sundries, too, and walked into the woods and exercised her right in a free society: suicide (Williams 2006, 138). Hence, she never renounced the control over her own body. As one fan, a prison arts facilitator, remarked in feedback after a *Vice* interview with Swenson, the band acted "as a force of entropy in pop culture" (Scarborough 2013), not just a "bold, brash, and braless bad girl" touted by *People* magazine (Wallace 1983). Williams—a fan of the equally self-made Joan Rivers—exorcised "brass-knuckle iconoclasm" lasting well beyond her death (Wallace 1983).

One of the sharpest, most unhesitating, and cogent defenders of Wendy O. Williams in the current punk scene is Mariam Bastani, a Loyola University graduate with a degree in religious and women's studies, longtime Chicago punk organizer, and former editorial coordinator of *Maximum Rocknroll*. She also performs in the punk bands Permanent Ruin and Multiple Truth. She does not look back and laugh as if Williams were a rock 'n' roll sideshow. "Several years ago I made a mini-zine called *No Heroes*, which was started as a series of zines about people in the punk scene who ended up making contributions to the worldwide punk scene just by being who they were and doing what was natural to them," tells Bastani. "The first issue was about Wendy O. Williams. Earlier than this zine, I had been making punk mix tapes for trade using Wendy O. William's lyrics as the titles. I was still in high school when Williams stopped playing out, so all I was left with were

VHS videos of her film appearances, fuzzy and crackling tapes recorded off of MTV, and a few interviews. Eventually the Internet opened up a new world of more material [where] I could glean more pieces of information about her" (2014).

For Bastani, Williams was an ally on the front lines of a dirty gender war who used punk as a sensible vehicle of expression. "As opposed to completely romanticizing her, building a mythology of god-like status, or pretending that she was at the pinnacle of metal or punk 'good ole days,' I see her as a punk peer. She did what she wanted because she realized that she had no other choice. Williams' raw and menacing sexuality was no more than wearing little to no clothes, wearing bondage gear, pumping her fist and busting shit up . . . or was it? Critics would say she was purposely acting like a 'man' in rock, which doesn't seem so alien considering the options; however, this assessment is not quite accurate," Bastani argues (Bastani 2014).

"At the time, men could do these same things and be sex symbols; meanwhile, the confusion that Williams induced led a straight, white, male-dominated world, in and out of rock 'n' roll, to be utterly confused. This binary approach to rock 'n' roll is still as strong as it was before, but people like Williams actively built new models in the psyche of popular culture that opened doors to new expressions within rock and punk and eventually helped to usher in a new understanding of empowerment. Williams knew what she was doing, but she never presented herself as an *act*, nor did she allow people to undermine her regardless of her approach to sexuality" (Bastani 2014). She, in a sense, seemed to act like a Trojan horse, embedding her explosive ideas in a working-class fan orbit typically infatuated with the likes of Ratt, Dio, Kiss, and Motley Crue.

Just as impressive offstage, Williams remained steadfastly committed to waging the good fight and using the media to her advantage. "If someone made a misogynist comment, in her direct but never rude manner, it was not overlooked. If someone suggested that her approach to women created convoluted examples of all-too-present oppression, she was quick to fire and defend. Even when on inane daytime talk shows, Wendy did not yield. During her appearance on the *Sally Jesse Raphael Show*, she commented, 'I don't like people who sexually don't mature,' which pretty much encompasses how she was viewing the world. On another appearance with fellow guest Debbie Fields of Mrs.

Fields' cookies, after all the guests are eating these cookies, Williams politely begins a conversation about health, eventually asking Debbie Fields, 'Do you lie awake at night and think that you are making money by poisoning people?' It may not be as shocking as when Kanye West interrupted appeals for aid during Hurricane Katrina by saying 'George Bush doesn't care about black people,' but it's a true indictment nonetheless. Always polite, Wendy did not hold back nor was her vision the musings of an uninformed, unrealistic dreamer.

"Today, punks try to capture the 'shock value' like the swastika held for early U.K. punks and Japanese bands like G.I.S.M. using rape and racism. In particular, the trend is to piggyback on the allure, history, and controversy of fascist imagery all under the guise of reclaiming, redefining, and/or shocking people's normal and conventional sensibilities," Bastani argues. "Williams was a testament: that is total bullshit. While her expression of punk and metal is now considered campy or less shocking than at the time, one must contextualize this" (Bastani 2014).

For Bastani, the work of Williams fluidly segues into the continuum of punk politics, especially pertinent since punk has become segmented, polarized, and balkanized. "As a reaction and rejection to surroundings, early punk was originally political in nature. Yet, much of the current punk scene is defined by supporting stereotypes as opposed to breaking them. The idea of caring about anything is seen as a generational flaw that was forced on society. While in the '90s there was a shift into identity politics and a sweeping trend in punk to become more aware, much of this yielded results that were, to say the least, embarrassing in forms of co-opting and eventually colonizing ethnicity and sexuality, particularly here in the United States.

"The very same pitfalls of treating 'issues' as if they are mutually exclusive is again mimicked today in punk by the 'anti-PC' punks using 'scatological' or intentionally controversial symbolism and language. It is not approached to 'shock' into awareness or in to questioning society or measure of taste, but more in the realm of 'if it's bad, then it is good,'" she adds. "Armed with this polarity and singular thinking, slapping a death's head skull on an album cover is regarded as edgy and anti-punk policing, but when bands are questioned about such symbolism, the excuses usually come up dry. Under the guise of art, these same punks create nothing new and rely on socially established images and ideas of what is shocking instead of questioning them or creating anything new. 'The brainwashed do not know they are brainwashed.' During a TV interview with Dweezil Zappa, in reference to listeners' reactions to her album *Kommander of Kaos*, they hypothetically discuss what sort of film Williams would direct. When she is questioned about what sort of wild content would be in this movie, she says, 'Action and violence is a very fine line with me. I don't just like letting eyeballs drop out just for the sake of letting eyeballs drop out. You gotta draw a line somewhere. That is just dumb.' Williams was not violent, she was destructive, but she never left a wake of harm in her path for others to clean up requiring cheap, hollow excuses. Big difference.

"Many punks of her time criticized her move into the metal realm while simultaneously shunning her as a sellout for being too public. This sentiment has carried over into current thoughts about Williams. In essence, it is as if she is viewed as a parody of herself, of punk, and metal. To many modern punks, she is a caricature or relic, yet male punks of the same era are revered as symbols of what punks must aspire to. Instead of seeing this as a negative, this is a true measure that Wendy O. Williams did whatever the fuck she wanted and had her own ideology that did not sway regardless of the change in time or style. 'I was never the kind of person that fit in. I was always the kind of person who was a survivor,' she would say, and it was true.

"She had overcome some big personal hurtles in life by earning and working for what she built while simultaneously addressing larger problems within society, including blind consumerism, health, the treatment of animals, factory farming, political violence, war, sexual oppression, rampant misogyny. . . . For example, Williams often pursued multiple conversations about the priorities of the U.S. government, at a time when complicated relationships between public awareness and social intervention surrounded nuclear arms, by positing statements like, 'I'm glad that people in religion are trying to get involved in what is going on instead of staying out of what is going on.' She was educated and armed with her knowledge; she lived her vision and had foresight into how the world could change" (Bastani 2014).

WORKS CITED

Adams, Ruth. "The Englishness of English Punk: Sex Pistols, Subcultures, and Nostalgia." *Popular Music and Society* 31, no. 4 (2008): 469–88.

Al and Peter. "Minutemen." *Flipside* 32 (1982).

———. "Interview with Vic Bondi." *Maximum Rocknroll* 14 (November 1992).

———. Interview with the author. 2014.

Albanese, Catherine L. *A Republic of Mind and Spirit: A Cultural History of American Metaphysical Religion*. New Haven, CT: Yale University Press, 2007.

Albiez, Sean. "Know History! John Lydon, the Cultural Capital and the Prog/Punk Dialectic." *Popular Music* 22, no. 3 (2003): 357–74.

Alvarado, Jimmy, and Todd Taylor. "Aztlan Underground, Part I." *Razorcake* 83 (2014).

Anderson, Mark. "Positive Force: New World Order: War #1 . . . D.C. Punk Percussion Protests." *Maximum Rocknroll* 97 (June 1991).

———. "Clash's 'Revolt' a Powerful Mix of Fury, Folly." *Washington Times*. 15 March 2003.

———. Interview with the author. Phone. January 2014.

"Angelic Upstarts." *Redstar73fanzine*. 23 June 2006. Accessed December 2013.

Anger, Alan. "The Joy of X Ray Spex." *Zigzag* 86 (August 1978).

Anger, Ricardo, and Osvaldo Thrills. "Ghosts of Princes." *Zigzag* 86 (August 1978).

Anti-Flag. *The Bright Lights of America*. Insert cards. RCA. 2005.

"The Art and Politics of Netporn." Institute of Network Cultures (networkcultures.org). 2 October 2008. Accessed 14 August 2014.

Atoe, Osa. Facebook message to the author. July 2014.

Auster, Paul. *Collected Prose*. London: Faber and Faber, 2003.

Bailie, Stuart. "Popular Music: A Troubles Archive Essay." Troubles Archive. Arts Council of Northern Ireland. No date. Accessed 3 March 2016.

Bakhtin, Mikhail Mikhailovich. *Rabelais and His World*. Bloomington: Indiana University Press, 1985.

Bale, Jeff. *Loud 3D*. Edited by Gary Robert, Rob Kulakofsky, and Mike Arredondo. San Francisco: IN3D, 1984.

———. "Rock n Roll Burnout: Rockin Jeff Bale." *Maximum Rocknroll* 118 (March 1993).

———. "Read between the Lines." *Hit List* 2, no. 2 (2000).

———. "The MRR Archives Unleashed: MRR #1—30 Years Ago Today." *Maximum Rocknroll*. 3 July 2012.

"Bam-Bee and Shredder." *Hustler*. February 1985.

Barnett, Ronnie. Facebook message to the author. May 2015.

Bastani, Mariam. E-mails to the author. August 2014.

Bauman, H-Dirksen L., ed. *Open Your Eyes: Deaf Studies Talking*. Minneapolis: University of Minnesota Press, 2008.
Baumann, Paul. "Rockin' & Rollin': 'Cry Baby' and 'Mystery Train.'" *Commonweal*. 18 May 1990.
Bazzichelli, Tatiana. "On Hacktivist Pornography and Networked Porn." Tatianabazzichelli.com. 2006. Accessed 16 June 2014.
Bedford, Mark. "'This Is Joe Public Speaking': Why Joe Strummer's Passion Is Still in Fashion." *Journal of Social Sciences*. 19 June 2012.
Berger, George. *The Story of Crass*. San Francisco: PM Press, 2009.
Biafra, Jello. Interview with the author. 23 October 2014.
"The Big Boys." *Kill from the Heart*. No date. Accessed 18 April 2013.
Bilbrey, John. Letter to the editor. *Rolling Stone*. August 1980.
Bishow, Paul, and James Schneider. Joint interview with the author. 30 May 2014.
Blauner, Peter. "Hardcore Kids: Rebellion in the Age of Reagan." *New York*. 26 May 1986.
Blocher, Karen Funk. "The Clash, Bonds, NYC." *Relix* 8 (August 1981).
Blowdryer, Jennifer. *Loud 3D*. Edited by Gary Robert, Rob Kulakofsky, and Mike Arredondo. San Francisco: IN3D, 1984.
———. E-mails to the author. July 2014.
Board, Mykel. "You're Wrong." Column. *Maximum Rocknroll*. August 1996.
Bondi, Vic. Interview with the author. Portions published in "Sound and Fury Still Cometh: Brazen Vic Bondi." *Popmatters*. August 2012.
Bondi, Vic, Dave Dictor, and Ian MacKaye. "On 'Guilty of Being White,' in *Maximum Rocknroll*." In *White Riot: Punk Rock and the Politics of Race*. Edited by Stephan Duncombe and Maxwell Tremblay. London: Verso, 2011.
Boulware, Jack, and Silke Tudor. *Gimme Something Better*. New York: Penguin, 2009.
Bowles, Murray. Interview with M.D.C. *Ripper* 8 (1983).
Braden, Jeffrey P. *Deafness, Deprivation, and IQ*. New York: Plenum Press, 1994.
Bragg, Bernard, and Eugene Bergman. *Tales from a Clubroom*. Washington, DC: Gallaudet University Press, 1981.
Brewington, Jim. *Let There Be Light Please!* West Conshohocken, PA: Infinity, 2003.
Brian. "Fugazi: The Word Is Change." *Maximum Rocknroll* 66 (November 1988).
"Britain's 1981 Urban Riots." *Searchlight*. September 1981.
Brucato, Ben. "Devil's Advocate: Matt Outpunk." *Interbang* 4. No date.
Burris, Peter H. "MLK Benefit." *WDC Period* 14 (1986).
Bushell, Gary. "Angelic Upstarts." *Punk's Not Dead* 1 (1981). Accessed 10 April 2015.
———. "Carry on Oi!" *Punk's Not Dead* 1 (1981). Accessed 10 April 2015.
Cadeaux, Yvette. "Frightwig's Ferocious Feminism." *Band Age*. No date.
Calvert, Dave. "Loaded Pistols: The Interplay of Social Intervention and Anti-Aesthetic Tradition in Learning Disabled Performance." *Research in Drama Education: The Journal of Applied Theatre and Performance* 15, no. 4 (November 2010): 513–28.
Carnes, Kevin. Interview with the author. E-mail. 23–26 May 2015.
Case, Peter. E-mails to the author. July 2014.
Cervenka, Exene. Interview with the author. E-mail. 4 April 2015.
Chappe, Eric. "Stiff Little Fingers, Go for It." Review. *Relix* 8 (August 1981).
Chick. "Interview with Winston Smith." Big Bang Fanzine 1. 1996.
Ciaffardini, David. "Rockin' Roll Model: An Interview with Ian MacKaye of Fugazi." *Sound Choice* 15 (Summer 1990).
Cibula, Matt. "The Most Effective Weapon." *Popmatters*. 26 December 2002.
Civan, David. "Gang of Four, the Ritz, NYC." *Relix* 8 (August 1981).
"Clash City Rockers." *Uncut*. December 2003.
"The Clash—Know Your Rights/Should I Stay or Should I Go—28 May 83." YouTube. 1983. Accessed 13 June 2014.
"The Clash Live 1982." YouTube. 1982. Accessed 13 June 2014.
Cohen, Debra Rae. "Punk's Dream." *Penthouse*. February 1980.
———. "Madness. Irving Plaza. New York City. February 25th, 1980." *Rolling Stone*. April 1980.

Cohen, Ted. Letter to Bob Piner and Paul Sheffield. 30 December 1977. Warner Brothers.
Colegrave, Stephen, and Chris Sullivan. *Punk*. London: Bounty Books, 2013.
Cometbus, Aaron. "Interview with Fugazi." *No Idea* 7 (1989).
Cram, Christa. "The Class War Kids: Political Band Releases EP to Help Haiti." *Rebeltimeproductions*. 10 February 2010.
Cramer, Florian. "Sodom Blogging: Alternative Porn and Aesthetic Sensibility." In *C'Lickme: A Netporn Studies Reader*. Edited by Katrien Jacobs, Marije Janssen, and Matteo Pasquinelli. Amsterdam: Institute of Network Cultures, 2005.
Crass, Chris. "Building Movement, Building Power." *HeartattaCk* 49 (2006).
Creep, Mickey. Column. *Maximum Rocknroll*. April 1986.
Cripps, Charlotte, Ben Naylor, Chris Mugan, and Colin Brown. "Rock against Racism: Remembering the Gig That Started It All." *The Independent*. 25 April 2008.
Cuatt, David. *Loud 3D*. Edited by Gary Robert, Rob Kulakofsky, and Mike Arredondo. San Francisco: IN3D, 1984.
Cunliffe, Robert. "Charmed Snakes and Little Oedipuses: The Architectonics of Carnival and Drama in Bakhtin, Artaud, and Brecht." *Critical Studies* 3, no. 2 (1993): 48–70.
D'Ambrosio, Antonino. "Punk Rock." *Brecht Forum Archive*. No date. Accessed March 2016.
———. *Let Fury Have the Hour: Joe Strummer, Punk, and the Movement That Shook the World*. Philadelphia: Nation Books, 2012.
Davet, Stephane. "Sex Pistols' Johnny Rotten on the Real Meaning of Punk." *Worldcrunch*. 18 October 2013. Accessed 23 February 2015.
David, Michael. Interview with the author. E-mail. 30 May–11 June 2015.
Davis, Michael. "The Jam *Setting Sons*." *Creem*. June 1980.
"Dead Kennedys—Live Olympic Auditorium 1984." YouTube. 19 May 2011. Accessed 3 March 2016.
Dearmore, Kelly. "Ken Casey of the Dropkick Murphys Feels Responsibility to Sing about Union." *Dallas Observer*. 26 February 2013. Accessed 15 June 2014.
DeGenevieve, Barbara. "Ssspread.com: The Hot Bods of Queer Porn." In *C'Lick Me: A Netporn Studies Reader*. Edited by Katrien Jacobs, Marije Janssen, and Matteo Pasquinelli. Amsterdam: Institute of Network Cultures, 2005.
Demolition Doll Rods. Interview with the author. *Left of the Dial*. Summer 2003.
"The Dicks Interview." *Overthrow*. December 1984/January 1985.
Dictor, Dave. Interview with the author. July 2012.
Diehl, Matt. *My So-Called Punk: Green Day, Fall Out Boy, the Distillers, Bad Religion—How Punk Stage-Dived into the Mainstream*. New York: St. Martin's, 2007.
Di Perna, Alan. "Sexual Healing." *Guitar World*. August 1996.
Doe, John. Interview with the author. November 2013.
Dominique. "Canada Scene Report." *Maximum Rocknroll* 89 (October 1990).
"Don't Judge a Book by It's Cover." Red and Anarchist Skin Heads (RASH) NYC flyer. No date.
Dunn, Kevin C. "Nevermind the Bollocks: The Punk Rock Politics of Global Communications." *Review of International Studies* 34 (2008): 193–210.
Durchholz, Daniel. "Billy Bragg Channels Social Justice Pioneers for Impromptu Ferguson Concert." *Rolling Stone*. 20 August 2014.
Dussutour, Laurent. Interview with Kolaborancji. *Maximum Rocknroll* 88 (September 1990).
Ebert, Roger. "Russ Meyer Busts Sleazy Stereotype." Rogerebert.com. 15 November 1985. Accessed 10 June 2014.
Eddy, Chuck. "Goodnight, Democracy." *Spin*. September 1986.
Eileraas, Karina. "Witches Bitches and Fluids: Girl Bands Performing Ugliness as Resistance." *The Drama Review* 41, no 3 (Autumn 1997): 122–39.
Ellingsworth, Conrad. "XTC Black Sea." Review. *Upbeat*. January 1981.
Ellis, Jim. *Derek Jarman's Angelic Conversations*. Minneapolis: University of Minnesota Press, 2009.
Ellis, Ray. "The Clash 'The Call Up' b/w 'Stop the World.'" Review. *Upbeat*. January 1981.
Ely, Lydia. "Interview with Vinny of A.P.P.L.E." *Maximum Rocknroll* 44 (January 1986).

Eloquence, Daniel. Column. *Profane Existence*. Summer 2000.
"The Empire Strikes Back." *Penthouse*. April 1983.
England, Sabina. Interview with the author. 2010.
English, T. J. *Whitey's Payback and Other True Stories: Gangsterism, Murder, Corruption, and Revenge*. New York: Open Road, 2013.
Ensminger, David. "An Interview with Scott 'Wino' Weinrich of the Obsessed." *Left of the Dial*. 2002.
———. Interview with the International Noise Conspiracy. *Left of the Dial* 2 (2002).
———. Interview with Captain Sensible of the Damned. *Left of the Dial* 2 (2002).
———. "Deep South Punk Legends from Ozone City: U-Ron Bondage from Really Red." *Left of the Dial* 6 (2005).
———. "Interview with James Stevenson." *Left of the Dial*. 17 April 2007.
———. "It's Not Just Entertainment: The Legacy of Really Red." *Maximum Rocknroll* 323 (April 2010).
———. "Interview with Fred 'Freak' Smith." *Left of the Dial*. 2013.
———. "Oral History of the Deaf Club." *Left of the Dial*. 2013.
———. "Interview with Eugene Robinson." In Mavericks *of Sound: Conversations with the Artists Who Shaped Indie and Roots Music*. Lanham, MD: Rowman & Littlefield, 2014.
———. " *Punk the Capital!* Chronicling the History of D.C. Punk! An Interview with Filmmakers Paul Bishow and James Schneider." *Left of the Dial*. 30 May 2014.
———. "7 Seconds' Kevin Seconds": "Some Days I Just Want to Scream." *Houston Press*. 7 August 2014.
———. "Interview with Mia dBruzzi of Frightwig." *Maximum Rocknroll* 377 (October 2014).
———. "CBGB Survivor Cheetah Chrome's Creed: 'Honesty and Quality.'" *Houston Press*. 16 October 2014.
———. "Still Screaming from the Gutter: An Interview with Raw Power." *Maximum Rocknroll* 380 (January 2015).
Fancher, Lisa. "Interview with Demolition Doll Rods." *Left of the Dial*. 2003.
———. "A Conversation from the Past about Post-Punk: Simon Reynolds Redux." *Popmatters*. 27 November 2011.
———. E-mail to the author. April 2013.
Farber, Jim. "The Ramones: Too Punk to Pop." *Hard Rock Video*. April 1986.
Farrell, Jason. E-mail to the author. 13 August 2014.
Fatal, Rob. "Lezbophobia and Blame the Victim: Deciphering the Narratives of Lesbian Punk Rock." *Women's Studies* 41 (2012): 158–74.
Fen, De. "De Fen Chats with Kembra Pfahler." Punkglobe.com. No date. Accessed 21 July 2014.
Ferrarese, Marco. E-mail to the author. 21 May 2015.
Fine, Greta. Interview with the author. E-mail. April 2009.
Finnegan, Stephanie. "The Plasmatics, beyond the Valley of 1984." Review. *Relix* 8 (August 1981).
Flanagan, Bill, Charles M. Young, and Grant Alden. "20 Years of Punk Rock." *Musician*. June 1995.
Flippo, Chet. "Nothing Lasts Forever." *Rolling Stone*. August 1980.
Floyd, Gary. *Please Bee Nice: My Life up 'til Now*. Cowritten with David Ensminger. Houston: Left of the Dial, 2014.
Frame, Pete. *Pete Frame's Rockin' around Britain: Rock'n'Roll Landmarks of the U.K. and Ireland*. London: Omnibus, 1999.
Fritz, Steve. "Interview with Black Flag." *Terminal* 16, no. 17. No date.
Furious, Danny. E-mails to the author. January–February 2014.
Fury, Pam. Letter to the editor. *Trouser Press*. February 1984.
Gary, John P., III. "Review of the Vandals at KPFK Studios." *Flipside* 38 (1983).
Gibbons, Layla. Column. *Maximum Rocknroll*. November 2006.
Gibson, Andre, and John Springer. "The Gang of Four's Rhythm Manifesto" *Upbeat*. January 1981.

Gilfoyle, Timothy J. *City of Eros: New York City, Prostitution, and the Commercialization of Sex, 1790–1920.* New York: Norton, 1992.
Gilmore, Mikal. "Public Image, Ltd." *Rolling Stone*. May 1980.
Gimarc, George. *Punk Diary: The Ultimate Trainspotter's Guide to Underground Rock, 1970–1979.* Milwaukee, WI: Backbeat Books, 2005.
"Giverny: by E. V. Day and Kembra Pfahler." Hole NYC (theholenyc.com). 23 March 2012. Accessed 21 July 2014.
Goldthorpe, Jeff. "The Hotel Owners Laundry Company (HOLVC) Squat: 1984." Found SF (www.foundsf.org). 1988. Accessed 1 March 2015.
Good Riddance. *Symptoms of a Leveling Spirit*. San Francisco: Fat Wreck Chords, 2001.
Goodman, Steve. *Sonic Warfare: Sound, Affect and the Ecology of Fear*. Cambridge: MIT Press, 2009.
Goshert, John Charles. "'Punk' after the Pistols: American Music, Economics, and Politics in the 1980s and 1990s." *Popular Music and Society* 1 (March 2000): 85–106.
Grant, Edmond. "Cry Baby." Review. *Films in Review*. June/July 1990.
"Graue Zellen." Interview. *Profane Existence* 24 (January–March 1995).
Gray, Marcus. *Route 19 Revisited: The Clash and London Calling*. New York: Soft Skull Press, 2010.
Greene, Elizabeth. "Scream: Banging the Drum." *Maximum Rocknroll* 60 (May 1988).
Grisham, Jack. Interview with the author. June 2012.
Gross, Michael. "Pagan's Progress." *New York*. 12 September 1988.
Grossberg, Lawrence. "The Politics of Youth Culture: Some Observations on Rock and Roll in American Culture." *Social Text* 8 (Winter 1983–1984): 104–26.
———. "Is There Rock after Punk?" In *Methods of Rhetorical Criticism, a 20th Century Perspective*. Edited by Bernard Brock and Robert Lee Scott. Detroit, MI: Wayne State University Press, 1989.
Hahn, Dave. *Physical Resistance: A Hundred Years of Anti-Fascism*. Hants, UK: Zero Books, 2013.
Hahn, Lance. "Punk As Fuck: The Story of Toxik Ephex." *Maximum Rocknroll* 282 (November 2006).
Hall, Stephanie. "Door unto Deaf Culture: Folklore in an American Deaf Social Club." *Sign Language Studies* 73 (1991): 421–29.
Hannah, Gerry. "Peace! They Cried." *Maximum Rocknroll* 16 (August 1984).
Hannan-Barrett, Pat. Letter to the editor. *Rolling Stone*. May 1980.
Hanrahan, Robert. E-mails to the author. August 2014.
Hansen, Ann. *Direct Action: Memories of an Urban Guerrilla*. Ontario: Between the Lines, 2002.
———. "Armed Struggle, Guerrilla Warfare, and the Social Movement Influences on Direct Action." *War on Patriarchy, War on the Death Technology: The Collected Statements, Essays, and Communiques of Direct Action and the Wimmin's Fire Brigade*. Bloomington, IN: Untorelli Press, 2014.
Hatch, Kristen. "The Sweeter the Kitten the Sharper the Claws." In *Bad: Infamy, Darkness, Evil, and Slime on the Screen*." Edited by Murray Pomerance. Albany: State University of New York Press, 2004.
Helen. "Review of Blades, Bad Religion, Social Distortion, and Angelic Upstarts, June 28, Florentine Gardens." *Flipside* 32 (1982).
Henke, James. "There'll Be Dancing in the Streets: The Clash." *Rolling Stone*. April 1980.
Hernandez, Eric. Interview with the author. In person and e-mail. 21–22 February 2012.
Hewitt, Kim. *Mutilating the Body: Identity in Blood and Ink*. Madison: University of Wisconsin Press, 1997.
Heylin, Clinton. *From the Velvets to the Voidoids: A Pre-Punk History for a Post-Punk World.* New York: Penguin, 1993.
Hilburn, Robert. "A Positive Perspective on Punk." *Los Angeles Times*. 28 February 1978. Accessed 24 June 2014.
Hodgkinson, Will. "Dirty Freaky Things." *The Guardian*. 26 March 2004.
Hogan, Richard. "Looking Flash Means Hard Work for the Clash." *Circus*. 31 May 1981.

Holdship, Bill. "The Clash: They Want to Spoil the Party So They'll Stay." *Creem*. October 1984.
Home, Stewart. "We Mean It Man: Punk Rock and Anti-Racism or, Death in June Not Mysterious." *Stewart Home Society*. No date. Accessed 10 April 2015.
"I Am the Tempest: Chris Thomson." Interview with the author. *Left of the Dial* 6 (2004).
"Interview with Fermin Muguruzza of An'so and Ju." *Radio Change*. May 2003.
Interview with John Waters. *The Colbert Report*. 10 June 2014.
"Interview with the Big Boys." *Zone V* 2 (1983).
"An Introduction and Short History of Positive Force D.C." *WDC Period* 12 (1985).
"Investigation into the Death of Blair Peach." MPS Publication Scheme. Metropolitan Police. Mayor's Office for Policing and Crime. 2014. Accessed April 2015.
I-Rankin', Judge. "Wendy O. Williams: Kommander of Kaos." *Spin*. July 1986.
Jacobs, Greg. E-mail to the author. July 2014.
Jacobs, Katrien. "Porn Arousal and Gender Morphing in the Twilight Zone." In *C'Lick Me: A Netporn Studies Reader*. Edited by Katrien Jacobs, Marije Janssen, and Matteo Pasquinelli. Amsterdam: Institute of Network Cultures, 2005.
James, David. "Hardcore: Cultural Resistance in the Postmodern." *Film Quarterly* 42, no. 2 (Winter 1988): 31–39.
Jamieson, Lee. *Antonin Artaud: From Theory to Practice*. London: Greenwich Exchange, 2007.
Jensen, Christine. Interview with the author. E-mail. 2010.
Jes'ca. "Propagandhi." *Stance* fanzine. Reprinted in *House Broken Fanzine*. 1979.
"Joe Strummer." Obituary. *The Scotsman*. 24 December 2002.
Johnston, Jack. *20aMPC*. Gig review. March 1979.
———. Facebook message to the author. 15 June 2015.
Jolly. "Clash: Don't Give 'Em Enough Rope!" *Punk* 17 (May/June 1979).
Jones, Peter. "Anarchy in the UK: '70s British Punk As Bakhtinian Carnival." Popular Culture Association/American Culture Association in the South (pcasacas.org). 2002. Accessed February 2013.
"Joy Division: Altrincham Inn." *Joy Division/New Order: A History in Cuttings (1977–1983)*. No city or publisher listed.
"Joy Division: Manchester." *Joy Division/New Order: A History in Cuttings (1977–1983)*. No city or publisher listed.
Keithley, Joe. *Talk – Action = O*. Vancouver, BC: Arsenal Pulp Press, 2011.
Keyes, Tad. E-mail to the author. 1 July 2015.
Kim, Taehee. "Major Threat: Fugazi Flips Off the Mainstream." *Option*. November/December 1991, 79–83.
Kolb, Terry. "First Impressions of a Scene." In *Despite Everything: A Cometbus Reader*. Edited by Aaron Cometbus. San Francisco: Last Gasp, 2002.
Kowalski, Eva. "Interview with the Redskins." nodo50.org. 2014. Accessed 17 June 2014.
Kozielski, Wojtek. "Interview about Soulside Shows in Poland and East Berlin in 1989." Facebook post. 15 November 2011.
Kramer, Richard. *HeartattaCk* 20 (1998).
"Krist Novoselic: Of Grunge and Government." Washington Secretary of State Legacy Project. No date. Accessed March 2015.
KS2. Post to gogonotes.blogspot.com. 24 April 2010. Accessed 24 June 2014.
LaBruce, Bruce. "Porn Piece." In *Working Sex: Sex Workers Write about a Changing Industry*. Edited by Annie Oakley. Berkeley, CA: Seal Press, 2007.
Ladd, Paddy. *Understanding Deaf Culture: In Search of Selfhood*. Bristol, UK: Multilingual Matters, 2003.
Laing, Dave. "Interpreting Punk Rock." *Marxism Today*. April 1978.
———. *One Chord Wonders: Power and Meaning in Punk Rock*. Buckingham: Open University Press, 1985.
Lakoff, Aaron. "Anarchist and Sex Work." Originally published by *Fifth Estate*. Reprinted by *Coop Media de Montreal*. 15 April 2014. Accessed 15 July 2014.

Landstreet, Lynna. "Songs of Subversion: An Interview with Poison Girls." *Kick It Over* 14 (Winter 1985/1986).
Langman, Lauren. "Punk, Porn, and Resistance: Carnivalization and Body in Popular Culture." *Current Sociology* 56, no. 4 (2008): 657–77.
Lapin, Brad. "Can You Hear Me? (Live at the Deaf Club)." Review. *Damage* 7 (1980).
Lawson, Anita. Letter the editor. *HeartattaCk* 22 (May 1999).
Leland, John. "X: Stand by Your Band." *Trouser Press* 10, no. 13 (February 1984).
Lester, Ken. Untitled DOA tour diary overview. *Maximum Rocknroll* 24 (August 1984).
———. "Rock&Roll Resistance." *Open Road*. Winter 1990.
Levine, H., and S. Stumpf. "Statements of Fear through Cultural Symbols: Punk Rock As a Reflective Subculture. *Youth and Society* 14 (1983): 417–35.
Levitin, Daniel J. *The World in Six Songs: How the Musical Brain Created Human Nature*. New York: Dutton, 2008.
Lewis, Bob. Letter to the editor. *Rolling Stone*. August 1980.
Liles, Jeffrey. "Echoes and Reverberations: Dead Kennedys 'Rock against Politics.'" *Dallas Observer*. 30 October 2008. Accessed 31 December 2013.
———. "Echoes and Reverberations: The Ghosts of the Longhorn Ballroom." *Dallas Observer*. 6 November 2008. Accessed 9 June 2014.
Luu, Helen. Column. *HeartattaCk* 29 (February 2000).
MacKaye, Alec. Interview with the author. E-mail. 10 September 2011.
MacKinnon, Catharine. *Are Women Human?* Cambridge, MA: Harvard University Press, 2007.
Magrann, Mike. Interview with the author. E-mail. November 2013.
Manzoor, Sarfraz. "The Year Rock Found the Power to Unite." *The Guardian*. 20 April 2008. Accessed April 2015.
Marcus, Greil. "Teds, Mods, Skins, Punks, Rudies Rule." *Rolling Stone*. May 1980.
———. "After Punk: Wake Up!" *Rolling Stone*. July 1980.
Marczynski, Arek. Poland Scene Report. *Maximum Rocknroll*. No date.
Marko, Paul. *The Roxy London WC2: A Punk History*. London: Punk 77 Books, 2008. Accessed 9 February 2013.
Marsh, Dave. "Rock & Rhetoric: Power in the Darkness, Tom Robinson Band." *Rolling Stone*. August 1978.
Martin, Gavin. "Anarchy in the UK." *Uncut*. June 2000.
Maskell, Shayna. "Performing Punk: Bad Brains and the Construction of Identity. *Journal of Popular Music Studies* 21, no. 4 (December 2009): 411–26.
Matlock, Glen. *I Was a Teenage Sex Pistol*. New York: Omnibus Press, 1990.
McClard, Kent. "Interview with Econochrist." *No Answers* 8 (1989).
———. "Positive Force D.C.: The Action behind the Words." *No Answers* 8 (1989).
McRobbie, Angela. "Settling Accounts with Subcultures: A Feminist Critique." In *On Record: Rock, Pop, and the Written Word*. Edited by Simon Frith and Andrew Goodwin. New York: Routledge, 1990.
McWhorter, Greg. E-mails to the author. May 2015.
"M.D.C." *Flipside* 38 (1983).
M.D.C. Letter to the editor. *Maximum Rocknroll* 6 (May/June 1983).
Medina, Robert. E-mails to the author. July 2015.
"Memos from the Mouse Trap." *Maximum Rocknroll* 36 (May 1986).
Mercer, Torry. E-mails to the author. September 2014.
Middlehurst, Mick. "A History of Joy Division." *The Face*. *Joy Division/New Order: A History in Cuttings (1977–1983)*. No city or publisher listed.
Miller-Young, Mireille. "Sexy and Black: Black Women and the Politics of Self-Authorship in Netporn." In *C'Lick Me: A Netporn Studies Reader*. Edited by Katrien Jacobs, Marije Janssen, and Matteo Pasquinelli. Amsterdam: Institute of Network Cultures, 2005.
Mirkz, Karl. "Paul Weller: The Jam." *Flipside* 32 (1982).
Mitchell, Deanna. Facebook message to the author. 29 June 2015.
Moines, Des. "Joy Division: Leeds." *Joy Division/New Order: A History in Cuttings (1977–1983)*. No city or publisher listed.

Moore, Stephen. "Proposition 13 Then, Now and Forever." CATO Institute. 30 July 1998.

Mora, Anthony. "Who's the Ugliest Sex Symbol in Rock'n'Roll: Stiv Bators!" *Swank*. February 1982.

Morgan, Jeffrey. "Inside William Burroughs." *Creem*. March 1979.

Morris, Chris. "The Minutemen: Hard & Fast Combat." SST Records press packet. 1984.

Moser, Margaret. "Holiday in San Antonio: The Night the Sex Pistols Went Off at Randy's Rodeo." *Austin Chronicle*. 10 January 2003. Accessed 9 June 2014.

Mullen, Brendan. "Live at the Masque." *Willamette Week*. 28 May 2008. Accessed 4 July 2014.

Myers, Ben. "Fly Hangs It Out with Seth Tobocman." *Maximum Rocknroll* 211 (December 2000).

Myers, Emma. "Profiles in Criticism: B. Ruby Rich." *Indiewire*. 7 February 2014.

"Nardwuar the Human Serviette vs. Ian MacKaye." *Razorcake* 4 (October/November 2001).

"NBC News Report of Sex Pistols Tour in USA." YouTube. 25 April 2007. Accessed 9 June 2014.

Nehring, Neil. *Popular Music, Gender, and Postmodernism: Anger Is an Energy*. Thousand Oaks, CA: Sage, 1997.

Nelson, Jeff. "The Art of Jeff Nelson." Interview with the author. *Artcore* 25 (2010).

———. E-mail to the author. 15 July 2014.

"Never Mind the Bollocks, Here's . . . John Lydon in a Butter Commercial?" *Open Culture*. 13 July 2013. Accessed 2 December 2013.

Nguyen, Mimi Thi. "Punk Planet? (Jan/Feb 2005, Maybe)." *Thread & Circuits*. 28 March 2010. Accessed 3 March 2016.

Night Network. "Interview with Joe Strummer." Channel 4. YouTube. 1988. Accessed 13 June 2014.

No More Censorship. Fact Sheet No. 3. Summer 1989.

Odam, Jes, and Terry Glavin. "Jailed Couple Traded Punk Rock for Terror." *The Sun*. 24 May 1984.

Odell, Katy. "Guest Opinion." *Maximum Rocknroll* 98 (July 1991).

"The Only Good Kennedy Is a Dead Kennedy." *Kick It Over* 5 (1982).

"The Oppressed." *Barricata* 13 (March 2005).

Padden, Carol, and Tom Humphries. *Voices from a Culture*. Cambridge, MA: Harvard University Press, 1988.

Parker, James. *Turned On: A Biography of Henry Rollins*. New York: Cooper Square Press, 2000.

Parsons, Tony. "Go Johnny Go." *NME* 2 (October 1976): 29.

Phillipov, Michelle. "Haunted by the Spirit of '77: Punk Studies and the Persistence of Politics." *Journal of Media and Cultural Studies* 20, no. 3 (September 2006): 383–93.

Pifer, Lisa. Taped message to the author. August 2014.

"Police Group Files Libel Suit, Says Record Holds Officers Up to Contempt." *Houston Chronicle*. 4 April 1981.

Pollock, Bruce. "Middle of the Dirt Road." *Guitar Extra!* Spring 1992.

———. *Death Metal and Music Criticism: Analysis at the Limits*. Lanham, MD: Lexington Books, 2012.

Poor, Jerod. "Punk 1st Aid." *Maximum Rocknroll* 2 (1982).

Posner, Ron. E-mails to author. January 2014.

Pratt, Greg. "Propagandhi Reveal Details behind Upcoming Haiti Charity EP." *Exclaim!* 4 (February 2010). Accessed 5 January 2014.

Proctor, Jeff. "Wayne Kramer." *Razorcake* 82 (2014).

"Punks Not So Violent, Study Says." United Press International. Reprinted in *Maximum Rocknroll* 19 (November 1984).

Queen, Carol. "Sex Radical Politics, Sex-Positive Feminist Thought, and Whore Stigma." In *Whores and Other Feminists*. Edited by Jill Nagle. New York: Routledge, 1998.

Quint, Al. "Interview with MDC." *Suburban Punk*. Issue 6, 1983.

Quint, Al. "Interview with Verbal Assault." Reprint. *Suburban Voice* 33–34. 1993.

Ramone, Dee Dee, with Veronica Kofman. *Lobotomy: Surviving the Ramones*. Boston: Da Capo, 2016.
"Random Notes." *Rolling Stone*. December 1980.
"RASH Skins in Action." *R.A.S.H. Update* 3, no. 4 (May–August 1993).
Revolting, Colin. "'See Them Ah Come, but We Nah Run'—A View from the Ground of Campaigning against the National Front." Revolutionary Socialism in the 21st Century (http://rs21.org.uk). 5 June 2014. Accessed 3 April 2015.
Ridgeway, James, and Jean Casella. "'Complete Lawlessness' at Orleans Parish Prison." *Mother Jones*. 6 April 2012. Accessed 3 July 2014.
Riegel, Richard. "Future Shock Now (If You Want It): The Clash Give 'Em Enough Rope." *Creem*. March 1978.
———. "Devo: Actual Size." *Creem*. March 1979.
Rimbaud, Penny. *Shibboleth: My Revolting Life*. San Francisco: AK Press, 1998.
Robb, John. Interview with the author. E-mail. March 2007.
Robert, Gary, Rob Kulakofsky, and Mike Arredondo, eds. *Loud 3D: Hardcore Rock'n'roll*. San Francisco: IN3D, 1984.
Rock against Bush Vol. I. Liner notes. San Francisco: Fat Wreck Chords, 2004.
"Rock against Racism." *On the Prowl* 16. No date.
"Rock against Reagan." *Maximum Rocknroll* 6 (May–June 1983).
Rogovoy, Seth. *The Essential Klezmer*. Chapel Hill, NC: Algonquin Books, 2000.
Rombes, Nicholas. "Sincerity and Irony." In *New Punk Cinema*. Edited by Nicholas Rombes. Edinburgh, UK: Edinburgh University Press, 2005.
Rooks, Daisy. "An Interview with Marc Bayard." *HeartattaCk* 29 (February 2000).
Rowan, David. "Anarchists Sell Tune to U.S. Car Giant." *The Guardian*. 27 January 2002.
Rude Times. "The Purpose of Remembering the Past Is to Anticipate the Future. . . ." *Local Anesthetic* 1, no. 5 (1982).
Ruggles, Brock. "Not So Quiet on the Western Front: Punk Politics during the Conservative Ascendancy in the United States 1980–2000." Proquest UMI Dissertation Publishing, 2011. Accessed 20 December 2013.
Ryan, Darren. "Rock against the Rich 1988: Darren Ryan Gives the Lowdown." Ian Bone—Anarchist in the UK (ianbone.wordpress.com). Accessed 17 August 2014. 6 April 2015.
Salmon, Samuel Charles. Facebook post in response to Dead Kennedys photo. The Island group. Accessed 19 January 2014.
Sane, Justin. Interview with the author. E-mail. March 2006.
Sargeant, Jack. *Deathtripping: The Cinema of Transgression*. Creation Books, 1999.
Savage, Jon. "Death of Glory." *Guitar World*. August 1996.
Say, J. J. Column. *British Columbia's Blackout* 4 (23 June–7 July 1978).
Scarborough, Alexandra. Comment on "Revolution, Evolution, and Rock'n'Roll: An Exclusive Interview with Plasmatics Founder Rod Swenson." Vice.com. 4 September 2013. Accessed 29 June 2014.
Schalit, Joel. "Word Up, Rock Down: Punk, Politics, and The History of Spoken Word." *Punk Planet* 25 (May/June 1998).
Schwartz, Ruth. "Eugene Chadbourne: Rockin' Weird." *Maximum Rocknroll* 29 (October 1985).
Scott. Interview with Really Red. *Maximum Rocknroll* 6 (May–June 1983).
Scott, Jez. "Cake with Johnny Rotten." *The Guardian*. 20 July 2007. Accessed 4 March 2016.
Seconds, Kevin. "Some Days I Just Want to Scream." Interview with the author. *Houston Press*. 7 August 2014. Accessed 1 August 2014.
Selby, W. Gardner. "Big Boys Cause Big Disturbance Saturday Night; Union to Do Background Checks on Future Gigs." *Daily Texan*. No date. Available at www.soundonsound.org/Images/flyers_zines_etc/dailytexan9-3.jpg. Accessed 18 April 2013.
"The Sex Pistols Return to the Road." *Billboard*. 2003. Accessed 2 December 2013.
Shepard, Benjamin. *Queer Political Performance and Protest*. New York: Routledge, 2010.
Shithead, Joey. Interview with the author. E-mail. December 2015.

Simon, Bradford Scott. "Entering the Mosh Pit: Slam-Dancing and Modernity." *Journal of Popular Culture* 31, no. 1 (1997): 149–76.
Slattery, Paul "Dave McCullough Gets No Joy (Information-Wise) from Joy Division." *Joy Division/New Order: A History in Cuttings (1977–1983)*. No city or publisher listed.
Snyder, Bruce. "Sheriff's Department Nips Punk Party in Bud." *Daily Press*. 5 April 1987.
Soares, Emily, and Devon Morf. "NOFX." *Maximum Rocknroll* 97 (June 1991).
Sommer, Tim. "Slits." *Trouser Press*. March 1980.
"Southern California Scene Report." *Maximum Rocknroll* 80 (January 1990).
Spence, Paul. "Chumbawamba in Northern Ireland." *Maximum Rocknroll* 60 (May 1988).
Spence, Simon. *The Stone Roses: War and Peace*. New York: Penguin, 2013.
Spitz, Marc, and Brendan Mullen. *We Got the Neutron Bomb: The Untold Story of L.A. Punk*. New York: Three Rivers Press, 2001.
Spong, John. "On Tour with the Sex Pistols." *Texas Monthly*. 29 January 2014.
Stackel, Leslie. "Wendy O. Williams: Rock Performer & Urban Gardener." *Vegetarian Times*. July 1984.
Stahl, Pete. E-mail to the author. 25 June 2012.
Stratton, Jon. "Jews, Punk and the Holocaust: From the Velvet Underground to the Ramones—the Jewish-American Story." *Popular Music* 24, no. 1 (January 2005): 79–105.
Sylvan, Robin. *The Religious Dimensions of Popular Music*. New York: New York University Press, 2002.
Taylor, Phillip. "Flag-Amendment Proposal Inflames Passions of Notorious Flag-Burner." *First Amendment*. 26 February 1999. Accessed 3 January 2014.
Taylor, Steve. "It's Fun to Play at the Y.M.C.A. Thursday: Joy Division." Reprinted in *Joy Division/New Order: A History in Cuttings*. No date.
Taylor, Todd. Liner notes to *Protect: A Benefit for the National Association to Protect Children*." San Francisco: Fat Wreck Chords, 2005.
———. E-mail to the author. 21 May 2015.
Thibault, Simon. "Bruce LaBruce: Reluctant Pornographer or Cinematic Idiot Savant?" *Oasis Journals*. April 2000. Accessed 17 July 2014.
Thompson, Stacy. *Punk Productions: Unfinished Business*. Albany: SUNY Press, 2004.
Thomson. Chris. Interview with the author. *Left of the Dial* 7 (Winter 2004).
Traber, Daniel. "L.A.'s 'White Minority.' Punk and the Contradictions of Self-Marginalization." *Cultural Critique* 48, no. 1 (2001): 30–64.
Transom, Albert (Joe Strummer). Liner notes. *The Story of THE CLASH: Volume I*. Epic. 1988.
Turner, Victor. "In and Out of Time: Festivals, Liminality, and Communitas." Buffalo State College. No date. Accessed 9 February 2013.
Ullman, Ellen. "The Museum of Me." *Harper's*. May 2000.
"Union Dispute Delays Blondie Videocassette." *Rolling Stone*. April 1980.
Useless, Jason. "When I Am Dictator." *Maximum Rocknroll* 159 (August 1996).
Valentine, Penny. "Sandinista Now!" *Creem*, April 1981.
Vick, Hank. Letter to the *Austin American-Statesman*. Sound on Sound (soundonsound.org). No date. Accessed 18 April 2013.
Virus X. Letter to the editor. *Flipside* 38 (1983).
"Voices from Rock against Racism." *Socialist Worker*. 10 July 2007. Accessed 3 April 2015.
von Slut, Miss Eva. Interview with the author. E-mail. 25 May–11 June 2015.
Wadlow, Justin S. "'I Am So Bored with the USA': Joe Strummer and the Promised Land." In *Punk Rock Warlord: The Life and Work of Joe Strummer*. Edited by Barry J. Faulk and Brady Harrison. Farnham, Surrey, UK: Ashgate, 2014.
Wake Up 8. (No date).
Wallace, Carol. "Wendy O. Williams." *People*. 25 July 1983. Accessed 20 June 2014.
"War Is Not the Answer." Punk Percussion Protest leaflet. Positive Force. Reprinted in *No Idea* 8 (1991).
Ward, James. J. "'This Is Germany! It's 1933!' Appropriations and Constructions of 'Fascism' in New York Punk/Hardcore in the 1980s." *Journal of Popular Culture* 30, no. 3 (December 1996): 155–84.

Waters, John. *Carsick: John Waters Hitchhikes across America.* New York: Farrar, Straus, and Giroux, 2014.
Watt, Mike. Interview with the author. E-mail. November 2013.
———. E-mail to the author. 10 July 2014.
Webber, Jason. "Revolution, Evolution, and Rock'n'Roll: An Exclusive Interview with Plasmatics Founder Rod Swenson." *Vice*. 30 August 2013. Accessed 29 June 2014.
Weber, Bob. Interview with the author. E-mail. 6 August 2014.
Weller, Paul. "Welcome to the Working Week." *Flexipop*. 1981.
Wells, Seething. Self-Interview. *Maximum Rocknroll* 29 (October 1985).
———. Column. *Maximum Rocknroll* 48 (May 1987).
"Wendy O. Williams on Donahue 1990." YouTube. 1990. Accessed 21 July 2014.
Whitall, Susan. "The Clash Clamp Down on Detroit; or, Give 'Em Enough Wisniowka." *Creem*. June 1980.
Williams, Joy. *Ill Nature: Rants and Reflections on Humanity and Other Animals*. New York: Lyons Press, 2006.
Wishnia, Steve. False Prophets biography. Alternative Tentacles Records (alternativetentacles.com). 2004. Accessed 5 December 2013.
Wolk, Douglas. "Band for Sale." *Chicago Reader*. 13 Nov. 1997. Web. 30 May 2016.
Worley, Mathew. "Oi! Oi! Oi! Class, Locality, and British Punk." *Oxford Journals*. 20 March 2013. Accessed 3 March 2016.
———. "'Hey Little Rich Boy, Take a Good Look at Me': Punk, Class, and British Oi!" *Punk and Post-Punk* 3, no. 1 (2014): 5–20.
Wright, Evan. "Scenes from My Life in Porn." *LA Weekly*. 29 March 2000. Accessed 5 March 2016.
Wuelfing, Howard. Interview with the author. 20 September 2008.
XXX, Eric. "Pitching at Inclines." Column. *HeartattaCk* 32 (September 2001).
Yohannon, Tim. Untitled Overview of Rock against Reagan in San Francisco. *Maximum Rocknroll* 24 (August 1984).
———. "Dead Kennedys . . . Call It a Day—Jello Talks of Past, Present, and Future. *Maximum Rocknroll* 44 (January 1986).
Yohannon, Tim, and Martin (no last name). "Interview with Tomas Squip of Fidelity Jones." *Maximum Rocknroll* 73 (June 1989).
Young, Jon. "Outside the Bands Don't Toe the Line." *Trouser Press*. February 1981.
———. "Joe Strummer. Earthquake Weather." Review. *Spin*. December 1989.
Zicari, John. Letter to the editor. *Maximum Rocknroll* 108 (May 1992).
Zuberi, Nabeel. *Sounds English: Transnational Popular Music*. Urbana: University of Illinois Press, 2001.

INDEX

Adam and the Ants, 186, 188
Adams, Bryan, 37
Adams, Ruth, 3, 43–44
Adolescents, The, 181
Agnostic Front, 49, 79
AK-47 (band), 62–63, 71
Alley Cats, 135, 140
Allin, G. G., 163–164, 191,199
Alvin, Dave, 185
Alternative Tentacles, 17, 33, 112, 184
Amnesty International, 31, 47, 58, 84, 95, 97, 100
Angelic Upstarts, 7–8, 44–46, 60
Attila the Stockbroker, 46, 81
Anderson, Marian, 164–66
Anderson, Mark, 6, 70, 77, 91–94, 103–104, 164–65
Anti-Flag, 22, 31–32
Articles of Faith, 55
Austin (scene), 22, 29, 51, 64, 68, 71–72, 107, 127, 129–36, 159–60, 184
Austin American-Statesman, 160
Avengers, The, 15, 55, 62, 87, 108–09

Bad Brains, 4, 10–11, 70, 93, 113, 136–38
Bags, The, 108–109
Bakhtin, Mikhail, 154, 174
Bataille, George, 179, 187
Bangs, Lester, 84, 145
Barnett, Ronnie, 193
Bastani, Mariam, 202–05
Bataille, Georges, 188
Bators, Stiv, 182
Bauman, H-Dirksen L., 121
Baumann, Paul, 182
Bazzichelli, Tatiana, 179
Beatles, the, 128,
Beatless, 67
Beatnigs, the, 112–13
Beefeater, 69, 87, 105
Behind the Green Door, 186
Belmas, Julie, 169–70
Berlin Wall (site), 54
Berry, Chuck, 70
BGK, 68
Biafra, Jello, 17, 21, 26, 63–68, 71, 80, 117, 167–168, 171, 184. *See also* Dead Kennedys
Big Boys, 21–22, 130, 133–34, 138, 159–61, 184
Bikini Kill, 104, 118
Black Flag, xv, 49, 84, 110, 134–35, 140–42, 161
Blake, William, 5
Blondie, 47, 116, 130, 187, 195
Blowdryer, Jennifer, 145–151, 174–178, 195
Board, Mykel, 166–67, 180
Bomp! Records, 185
Bond, Ronnie, 38. *See also* U-Ron Bondage
Bondage, U-Ron, 62

Bondi, Vic, 92
Boomtown Rats, 17, 60,
Boon, D. (Dennis), 23–25, 154
Boston Globe, 155
Boston, MA (scene), 26
Bowie, David, 26, 116
Bozzio, Dale, 180, 187
Bragg, Bernard, 121
Bragg, Billy, 46, 51, 60, 84,
Brown, James, 134
Bow Wow Wow, 186
Bowie, Jerry, 2
Burana, Lily, 186,
Bush, President George, 30, 35, 203
Bushell, Gary, 46, 59–60
Buzzcocks, xiv, 2, 32, 57, 75, 105

Cabaret Voltaire (band), 188
Cadena, Dez, 134
Capp, Al, 183
Case, Peter, 110–12, 121, 140–42
Casey, Ken, 52
Cause for Alarm, 137
CBGB, 1, 60, 107, 159, 180, 181, 195, 198–201
Cervenka, Exene, 23, 26, 122, 199
Chantry, Art, 173
Cherry Vanilla, 187
Chrome (the band), 186–87
Chrome, Cheetah, 3, 199
Ciaffardini, David, 99
Circle Jerks, xiii, 17, 22, 47, 141, 174
City Lights (bookstore), 108, 111
Clash, The, 2, 30, 46, 72, 75, 77, 78, 80, 83–84, 100, 106, 141, 197
Cleveland, OH (scene), xv, 3, 20, 84
Cohen, Debra Rae, 116
Cohen, Ted, 82
Corrosion of Conformity, 30, 79
Costello, Elvis, 57, 130,
County, Wayne/Jayne, 192
Cramps, The, 132, 191
Crash, Darby, 21
Crass, xv, 6, 14, 18–20, 31, 68, 76–79, 103
Crass, Criss, 16
Creedence Clearwater Revival, 4
Creem, 20, 61, 145, 189
Cro-Mags, 11
Cry-Baby, 181–182
Cuatt, David, 9, 155
Cuckoo's Nest, 134, 140, 142
Curtis, Ian, 116

Dada (art movement), xiii, 13, 79, 102, 111,
Dallas (TX, scene), 38, 82 (Republican National Convention), 67–68, (television show), 83
Damage (fanzine), 125,
Damned, The, 6, 28, 60, 109, 142, 198
Davet, Stephane, 80, 82
Davis, Mike, 140
Dayglo Abortions, 186
Dead Boys, xiv, 3, 81, 182, 195, 198
De Sade, Marquis, 179, 188
Dead Kennedys, 17, 20, 26–27, 41, 66–68, 78, 112, 117, 123–24, 135, 136, 140, 142, 164, 171, 187, 195
Deaf Club (of San Francisco), 107, 114, 121–125, 148
Dearmore, Kelly, 52
Decline of Western Civilization, 141
Deep Purple, 4
DeLeon, Daniel, 165
Demolition Doll Rod, 188–89, 191–92
Detroit, MI (scene): 20, 78, 84, 188–90, 194
Detroit Cobras, 173
Devil in Miss Jones 3 and 4, The, 186
Diatribe, 143
Dicks, The, 13, 22, 66, 71, 73–74, 87, 112, 130–36, 138, 171, 184
Dictators, the, 20, 92,
Dictor, Dave, 92, 127–40. *See also* MDC
Dischord Records, 14, 94, 99, 102–03, 105
Diehl, Matt, 79
Dillinger 4 (band), 52
Dirksen, Dirk, 121
Discharge, xiv, 79, 109
D.O.A., 16, 22, 36–40, 45, 77, 135, 142, 169, 174
Doe, John, 25–26
Doors, The, 70, 116, 142
Doll Rod, Margaret, 188–189, 191
Downcast, 100
Dr. Know (band), 143, 158,

D.R.I. (Dirty Rotten Imbeciles), 35, 73, 88, 136, 139, 149, 166
Dropkick Murphys, 52
Du Plenty, Tomata, 112, 154
Duchamp, Marcel, 175,
Dunn, Kevin, 20, 32, 35
Dylan, Bob, 51, 110, 116, 128–31

Ebert, Roger, 183–84
Eileraas, Karina, 118
Electric Circus, the, 104
Ellis, Jim, 162
Ellis, Ray, 18
El Duce (singer), 163–64
Eloquence, Daniel, 35
England, Sabina, 118–120, 125
Epitaph, 79
Escovedo, Alejandro, 111
Exclaim!, 33

Faith, the (band), 89, 91
Falklands, the, 80–81, 83
Fancher, Lisa, 141
Farber, Jim, 20, 41
Farrell, Jason, 95–98
Fat Wreck Chords, 32–34, 79
Fear, 20, 135
Ferrarese, Marco, xv
Fidelity Jones, 69
Fields, Robbie, 33
Fine, Greta, 155–56
Fitzgerald, Ella, 128,
Fletcher, Gordon, 88
Flipside, 55, 135, 154, 160, 167, 192
Floyd, Gary, 72–74, 87, 127, 132. *See also* the Dicks
Food Not Bombs, 2, 16, 32, 55, 78, 99, 100, 106,
Frasier, Gordon, 139
Freeze, The, 185
Freeze the Drug War, 99
Freezer Theater, 109
Frightwig, 40, 81, 107, 163–64, 191
Front, the, 143
Fugazi, 6, 10, 14–15, 17, 30, 91–93, 97–99, 101, 103–04, 106, 113
Funkadelic, 134: Parliament-Funkadelic, 114
Furious, Danny, 108–109, 142

Gang Green, 11
Gang of Four, 17–18, 43, 77–78, 80, 185
Gavin, Ty, 131
GBH, 109
George, Boy, 149
Germs, The, 21, 124, 174, 199
Gibbons, Layla, xv
Gibson, Jim, 47
Gilfoyle, Timothy J., 179–180
Gillespie, Dizzy, 128
Gilman Street (club), 149, 164
Gilmore, Mikal, 70, 154
Gimarc, George, 181
Ginn, Greg, 141. *See also* Black Flag)
Ginsberg, Allen, 110,
Go-Go's, the, 140, 181, 187
Goldthorpe, Jeff, 88
Goshert, John, 14
Government Issue, 29, 93
Grant, Paul, 247
Gray, Marcus, 2–3, 31
Green Day, 34
Grisham, Jack, 40. *See also* T.S.O.L.
Guthrie, Woody, 24, 46, 51

Hahn, Dave, 46
Hahn, Lance, 77
Hall, Stephanie, 121
Hannah, Chris, 33
Hannah, Gerry, 29, 169–71
Hannah, Kathleen, 118
Hanrahan, Robert, 124–25
HeartattaCk, 16, 20, 55
Hebdige, Dick, xii–iv
Hermosa Beach, CA (scene), 143
Hernandez, Eric, 157
Hewitt, Kim, 118, 153
Heylin, Clinton, 195
Hilburn, Robert, 154,
Hoffman, Abbie, 70, 110
Holdship, Bill, 189–90
"Holiday in the Sun" (song), xiv
Holstrom, John, 1
Home, Stewart, 58
Houston, Penelope, 55
Houston, TX (scene), 29, 37–38, 61–64, 67, 70–71, 74, 107, 136, 159, 193
Husker Du, xiii, 139

Indiana, Gary, 147
Industrial Workers of the World (IWW), 51, 170,
Ingraham, Greg, 62
Insaints, the, 164–166
(International) Noise Conspiracy, the, 12–14
Iraq War, 27, 101–02
Iron Cross, 89–90, 93
IWW (see Industrial Workers of the World)

Jackson Five, the, 128
Jacobs, Greg, 143
Jacobs, Katrien, 178
Jail Guitar Doors (organization), 51, 84,
Jam, the, 7, 83
Jameson, Jenna, 167
James, Jesse, 167
Jamieson Lee, 161
Jefferson Airplane, 4, 70, 110
Jefferson Davis Hospital, 74
Jefferson Starship, 129
Jensen, Christine, 118–121, 161
Jensen, Ken, 36
Jett, Joan, xi, 30
John Brown Anti-Klan Committee, 16, 62, 70–71, 73–74, 127
Johnston, Jack, 122–24
Jones, Christopher, 100
Jones, Colin, 133
Jones, John Paul, 63, 66,
Jones, Mick, 19, 72
Jones, Peter, 154
Jones, Steve, 2, 181
Jonestown (band), 23
Joy Division, 116
Julien, Isaac, 164

Keithley, Joe. *See also* Shithead, Joey.
Kennedy, Bobby, 128
Kerri, Shawn, 174
Keyes, Tad, 52–53
King, Dr. Martin Luther, 40, 128
Kinman, Tony, 46
Kiss (the band), 190, 194, 202
Kleenex (the band), xv
Ku Klux Klan, xiii, 16, 62, 64, 70–74
KPFK (radio station), 154,
Kolb, Terry, 122,
Kramer, Wayne, 51, 84
Kramer, Richard, 54–55
Krishna (impact on punk), 61

Labour Party, 20, 44, 48, 58, 60, 75
L7, 30
Laing, Dave, xii, 27, 43–44
Lamy, Philip, xii
Langman, Lauren, 174, 178
Lapin, Brad, 125
Led Zeppelin, 4,
Lee, Jack, 111
Leeds, UK (scene), 19, 60, 116
Legionnaire's Disease, 62
Leland, John, 22–23
Lester, Ken, 16–17, 66, 77
Levin, Jack, xii,
Letts, Don, 58
Lifetime, 104,
London, England, xv, 3, 12, 20, 55, 57–58, 77, 103, 115, 117, 187, 195
Lords, Traci, 180–82, 185
Los Crudos, xiii, 23, 100
Lunch, Lydia, 174–76, 186, 199
Lydon, John, 154, 197. *See also* Rotten, Johnny.
Lynch, David, 123
Lyxzén, Dennis, 12–14

Mabuhay Gardens, 46, 107, 111–12, 121–22, 124, 140
MacKaye, Alec, 88–91
MacKaye, Ian, 10, 17, 92,99,167,
Madonna, 138, 185
Magrann, Mike, 40
Mahavishnu Orchestra, 128,
Manchester, England, xii, xv, 7, 77, 79, 105, 116
Manzoor, Sarfraz, 43, 57, 60
Marcus, Greil, xiv, 11,
Marko, Paul, 159
Masque, The, 107
Maximumrocknroll, 25, 33, 42, 48, 54, 60–61, 68, 87, 92, 135–36, 138, 145, 149–51, 156, 164–69, 170, 180, 201
Max's Kansas City, 124, 181
MC5, 4, 17, 20, 51, 70, 92, 110
McClard, Kent, 25, 105–06

McDonnell, Allen, 149, 175
McLaren, Malcolm, 2, 17, 43, 184, 186, 197
McNeil, Legs, 188
McRobbie, Angela, 15
McWhorter, Greg, 143–144
M.D.C. (Millions of Dead Cops), 13, 23, 26, 87, 127–140
Medina, Robert, 98–99
Meese, Attorney General Ed, 102–03, 185
Meltzer, Richard, 69
Meyer, Russ, 183–84, 199
Ministry of Truth, 143
Minor Threat, xiv, 17, 102, 136
Minutemen, The, 23, 25, 30, 69, 141, 142, 154
Miss Eva Von Slut, 164–66
Mitchell Brothers, 186
Mitchell, Deanna, 163–64
Moore, Michael, 29
Moore, Stephen, 140
Morello, Tom, 84
Morf, Devon, 28
Morris, Chris, 23, 30
Morris, Keith, 22, 141
Morrison, Jim, 116
Moser, Margaret, 82
Muir, Mike, 195. *See also* Suicidal Tendencies.
Mullen, Brendan, 21, 141, 184
Mydolls, 29, 38, 70, 159
Mystic Records, 143

Nelson, Jeff, 102–103
Nelson, Willie, 129
New Wave Hookers, 178, 185
New York City, 1, 12, 20, 57, 60, 67, 70, 107, 124, 128, 129, 136–38, 148–50, 159, 174, 180, 188, 190, 200
New York Dolls, 3, 129, 146, 186, 190
Newport Beach, CA (scene), 143
National Front, the, 43–45, 48, 57–60, 80
Nicaragua (country), 6, 24–25, 27, 91: Solidarity Campaign, 46
Nirvana, 30, 49,
NOFX, 28–29, 34–35, 106
North Beach, San Francisco, CA (scene), 111–12, 123
North, Oliver, 102
Novoselic, Krist, 30, 49, 51
Nuns, The, 108

Obsessed, The, 92
Ochs, Phil, 4, 24, 110
Offs, the, 122, 124
Offspring, the, 34, 49, 164
Oi (genre and movement), 44–45, 56, 59–60
Oi Polloi, 19
Olympic Auditorium, 11, 26–27, 138
Orange County, CA (scene), 142–43
Orange County Foodbank, 40
Orangewood Foundation, 40
Outpunk, xiii
Oxbow, 68

Pagans, the, 20
Pansy Division, 184
Parker, James, 155
Pearl Harbor and the Explosions, 124
Penthouse, 116, 174–75, 187
Penalty, Jeff, 192
Pere Ubu, xiv, 20, 88
Perez, Louis, 216
Perkins, Carl, 51
Pfahler, Adam, 141, 199
Pfahler, Kembra, 199–200
Pink Floyd, 129
Plasmatics, 115, 192–205
Playboy, 183, 185, 187, 195, 200
Plugz, The, 140, 185
Poison Girls, 57, 76
Pop, Iggy, 116, 153, 182, 194
Positive Force, 6, 53, 61, 77, 87–107, 185
Profane Existence, 23, 35, 52, 78
Propagandhi, 32–33
Proposition 13, 140
Punk and Post-Punk, xii
Punk Percussion Protests, 97, 101

Queen (the band), 4, 60
Queen, Carol, 168, 176
Queen Mab, 196
Queercore, 171, 184

Rabelais, Francois, 179
Raji's (club), 185
Rain Like the Sound of Trains, 6, 97, 99

Ramones, the, xiv, 20, 41, 59, 88, 126, 130, 132, 141–42, 145, 181, 190, 196
Raw Power, 5
Raw Power (album by the Stooges), 92
Ray, Dianna, 29, 159
Raul's (club), 107, 130–31, 134, 136, 184
Reagan, Ronald, 40, 56–57, 63–67, 73, 80, 102–03, 113, 140, 171
Reagan Youth, 88, 136–37, 174
Really Red, xiii, 38–39, 62–63, 70–71
Red Hot Chili Peppers, 181
Red Hot Video stores, 169–70
Red London, 45
Redskins, the, 45–46, 48
Redding, Otis, 128
Reed, Lou, 116, 129
Reynolds, Simon, 187–89
Rezillos, the, 105
Rhodes, Bernie, 3, 197
Rich, B. Ruby, 183
Rich Kids, 3
Riot Grrrl (genre and movement), 106, 118, 166
Ripper, 20, 132, 136, 139
Robb, John, 56, 75
Robbins, J., 29
Robinson, Eugene, 68–69
Robinson, Tom, 57
Rock against Racism, 8, 16, 57–60, 66, 70, 74, 77, 80, 91, 116, 136, 138
Rock against Reagan, 60, 66–67, 69–70, 74, 135–36
Rocket from the Tomb, 20
Roessler, Kira, 24
Roessler, Paul, 168
Rolling Stone, xiii, 19, 47, 57
Rolling Stones, 45, 82, 129, 145, 192
Rollins, Henry, 84, 149
Rotten, Johnny. *See also* Johnny Lydon.
Roxy, The (U.K.), 159
Roxy Music, 129

Sacred Order, 4
San Diego, CA (scene), 143
Savage, Jon, 80
Schalit, Joe, 19
Scott, Jez, 81
Scream, 87, 94–96, 101, 105
Screamers, the, 112, 154, 200
Search and Destroy, 111
Sensible, Captain, 28, 60, 198–99
Septic Death, 79
7 Seconds, 27, 36, 104, 159
Sex Pistols, xiii, xiv, 2, 7, 10, 44, 53, 70, 79, 81–32, 102, 106, 108–09, 130, 153–54, 181, 184, 186, 197
Shithead, Joey, 22, 36–39
Silverstein, 30
Simone, Nina, 4
Siouxsie and the Banshees, 3, 15, 153, 187
Sizemore, Ben, 25
Slits, the, 57, 105, 159
Smith, Fred "Freak," 105
Smith, Patti, xvi, 1, 47, 82, 129–130
Smith, Winston, 122, 187
Socialist Workers Party, 43, 48, 57–58, 70
Soul Side, 53–54, 161, 185
Sniffin'Glue, 19,
Sommer, Tim, 159
Spitz, Marc, 21, 141, 184
SST Records, 141, 143
Stabb, John, 29, 93
Stein Wilderness, 37
Stevenson, James, 72
Stiff Little Fingers, 57, 115
Stop the City (organization), 67, 77, 103
Street Dogs, 51,
Subhumans, the, 29, 62, 67, 169, 171
Suicidal Tendencies, 137, 195
Sumrall, Jon, 25
Surrealism, xiii,
Swiz, 95–97

Talking Heads, 1, 198
Ted Leo and the Pharmacists, 53, 104
Teen Idles, 102, 137,
Texas Chainsaw Massacre, 166, 198–99
Thompson, Hunter, 186
Thompson, Stacy, 20–21, 159
Throbbing Gristle, 39, 186, 188
Tool and Die (club), 148
Torrance, CA (scene), 141, 143
Toxik Ephex, 77
Traber, Daniel, 42
Tragic Mulatto, 88
T.S.O.L. (True Sounds of Liberty), 26–27, 39–40, 66, 112, 135

Turner, Randy "Biscuit," 21–22, 71, 133, 138, 160
Tuxedo Moon, 124

Udo, Vince, 143
U.K. Subs, 53

Vale, V, 111. *See also Search and Destroy.*
Vancouver, British Columbia, 36, 38, 49, 62,170
Vancouver Five, 29, 36–37, 67, 127,169
Vandals, the, 154,
Verbal Abuse, 139
Verbal Assault, 99–100

Walker, George, 165
Walker, Jerry Jeff, 129
Walker, Johnnie, 124
Waters, John, 181–83
Watt, James D., 65
Watt, Mike, 24, 30, 69, 141–43
Weil, Simone, 147
Weissborn, Henry, 61–62
Weller, Paul, 7, 60,
Whitall, Susan, 78
Whitman, Walt, 161
Who, the, 129, 132, 198
Wilcox, Thomas, 143
Williams, John Paul, 63, 66
Williams, Joe, 23–24
Williams, Robert, 175
Williams, Shane, 167
Williams, Wendy O. 115, 165, 192–205
Winters, Edgar, 128
Winters, Johnny, 128
Wobensmith, Matt, xiii
Wojcik, Daniel, xvi
Worral, Peter, 124
Wuelfing, Howard, 88–90

X-Ray Spex, 15, 57

Yohannon, Tim, 60–61, 66, 68–70, 149–151, 165
Youth Brigade, 135, 158
Youth International Party (Yippies), xiii, 60–62, 67, 70, 73, 136, 138

Zappa, Dweezil, 204
Zappa, Frank, 110
Zeros, the, 140, 148, 124

ABOUT THE AUTHOR

David Ensminger is a college instructor and the author of five books covering both American roots music and punk rock history: *Visual Vitriol: The Street Art and Subcultures of the Punk and Hardcore Generation* (2011), *Mojo Hand: The Life and Music of Lightnin' Hopkins* (2013), *Left of the Dial: Conversations with Punk Icons* (2013), *Mavericks of Sound: Conversations with the Artists Who Shaped Indie and Roots Music* (Rowman & Littlefield, 2014), and *Out of the Basement: Punk in Rockford, IL, 1973–2005* (2016).

Both the *Boston Globe* and the *Economist* have highlighted his research; meanwhile, he has written for *Houston Press*, *Popmatters*, *East of the Web*, *Adirondack Review*, *Postmodern Culture*, *Art in Print*, *The Journal of Popular Music Studies*, *Razorcake*, *Trust* (Germany), *Artcore* (Britain), *Magyar Taraj* (Hungary), and *Maximum Rocknroll*.